# WHERE EVIL LURKS

By Joseph Squatrito
c 2006

Copyright © 2013 Joseph Squatrito
All rights reserved.

ISBN: 0615933319
ISBN 13: 9780615933313

# TABLE OF CONTEXT

THE PROLOGUE · · · · · · · · · · · · · · · · · · · · · · · · · · · · · v
CHAPTER (1)   THE BEST OF TIMES · · · · · · · · · · · · · · · 1
CHAPTER (2)   THE WORST OF TIMES · · · · · · · · · · · · 27
CHAPTER (3)   THE TRIAL · · · · · · · · · · · · · · · · · · · · · 43
CHAPTER (4)   LENORE'S NIGHTMARE · · · · · · · · · · 105
CHAPTER (5)   THE CONFRONTATION · · · · · · · · · · 139
CHAPTER (6)   FOURTEEN YEARS OF HELL · · · · · · 253
EPILOG. · · · · · · · · · · · · · · · · · · · · · · · · · · · · · · · · · · 285

# THE PROLOGUE

Joey's wake and funeral were delayed because of the police investigation. The ballistics reports, and the fact that his parents had to come back from Idaho to Brooklyn. They had moved to the suburbs of Boise where the air, was clean and easy to breathe. Joey's father suffered from emphysema. After years of smoking what was known in the old neighborhood as, Guinea Stinkers. Those cigars were so strong that smoking them for any length of time, were considered lethal. Even the secondary smoke would bring tears to your eyes and cause pain in your lungs. A family member flew out to help them back to Brooklyn to attend the funeral. The trip was hard on them not only because of their grief and pain from their loss, but also because of their age and poor health. In their younger years the idea of accepting help would be unheard of, but now they welcomed it. Even the noblest and toughest Italians had to give way to the devastation of emphysema.

The funeral home was overflowing with flowers and people. It looked as if everyone in Brooklyn had come to pay their respects to the young man had lost his life in the line of duty. His family was there, along with every family who had been on his watch. Grief-stricken mourners represented every business he had protected. Uniformed police were everywhere. Everyone stood in line and waited, just to walk past the casket and pay their respects. Joey was laid out in full uniform, bearing all the medals of honor he had received. Police honor guards on either side of the casket and stood at attention for hours until the next watch relieved them. Police Emergency Medical Services, was available around the clock, both at Theresa's home and at the funeral parlor.

Mary, my wife and I paid our respects, but our presence was received with mixed emotions. The family all knew that I was like a brother to Joey, but they were very upset because I was going to defend his killer.

Many of the police officers in attendance whispered, "There's the son of a bitch who's defending Joey's killer." That rat bastard has one hell of a nerve showing up here.

They didn't understand my position, I loved Joey. So where did that put me? I couldn't bring Joey back, but maybe, just maybe I could save an innocent man and find the real killer and set things straight. As Mary and I prayed at Joey's casket. I cried uncontrollably. I bent over to kiss both parents and said," I'm very sorry for your loss, Joey was like a brother."

Joseph Tamborelli Sr said, "I know you've been his friend since you were children. Thank you for coming. He and his wife were unaware that I was defending their son's killer. As Mary and I embraced Theresa, I could see she was in a euphoric state. I couldn't determine whether, she was stoned on tranquilizers or was still in profound shock.

# THE PROLOGUE

I was very uncomfortable, even some of the distant family was making it very evident that they didn't want me there. I could understand there feelings. Mary and I stayed in the back of the room with the casual acquaintances, instead of up front with the lifelong friends. The agonizing cries of anguish could be heard for miles. Friends, relatives strangers and cops by the hundreds cried openly and unashamed as they passed by the fallen police officer, Joseph Tamborelli, in review.

"Who could have possibly wanted to gun down Joey." I wondered as I sat with Mary in the back of the funeral home. Suffocating from the press of bodies all around us, and the sweet overwhelming smell of flowers that seemed to drain every bit of air from the room. I tried to remain calm, but I felt I would panic if I didn't get out into the air immediately.

As I stood outside gasping the air, my panic began to ease up a bit. After the wake was over, Mary came out and we walked to the car. Mary could see that I was very upset, so it was no surprise to her when I asked if she wouldn't mind driving home. As Mary started the car, I shut off the radio and tried to collect my thoughts, but memories of Joey kept flashing through my mind. Happy memories of our childhood together came crashing back, like waves in a storm hitting the shore. They hurt like hell, Right from the time we first met, Joey and I were like brothers. It was very hard and painful to think of those good times. When you forge a bond of friendship or love at a young age it stays with you forever. When you lose it, it's like a piece of your heart is being ripped out of your chest.

# THE BEST OF TIMES

"It was the best of times, it was the worst of times" Now where the hell did that come from? For me a Brooklyn-born Italian guy from Bensonhurst, literary quotes are not apt to pop into my mind. But there it is, I'm more surprised than you would be if you knew me. It burst into my thoughts as I thought about a group of my best friends and me as we grew up in Brooklyn. It was simply the best of times, at the time I am thinking of. We were still unaware of the nature of the real world so, for the most part reality had not affected our lives. It was the best of times. Pretty much all the time when we were young.

I was part of the 18th Avenue Gang from Dom's Candy Store. To us in the gang, there was no better place on earth than Bensonhurst. Bensonhurst had it all, anything our hearts desired was at our fingertips. We referred to ourselves as "Our Gang" but we were not a street gang. We were just a group of best friends that lived in the same neighborhood.

We did everything together and went everyplace together. It was "All for one and one for all." That was our slogan when we were in grade school and probably the only thing we got out of our English class.

## JOSEPH SQUATRITO

My name is Salvatore Brancato Esquire." I'm an attorney. This story is about me and my best friends, Chaz Batista and Joey Tamborelli. Chaz and Joey grew up with me in Bensonhurst Brooklyn, where the only thing we had to worry about was getting to the school yard before the older boys did, so we could hold the field until the rest of our team showed up. No matter how early or sneaky we were, Joey's sister Theresa would always be there first and she would want to play. What made it worst she could hit the ball as well as the best guy in our gang.

Stick ball was the game of choice. The way it worked was that you drew a box four feet by three feet on a wall behind where the batter would stand. The pitcher would throw a fly ball towards the batter. Unless the batter hit it, any fly that landed inside the box was called a strike. Of course there were many differences of opinion to put it mildly. Actually, who's kidding who? There were knockdown, drag-out fights about what was a ball or what was a strike and right in the middle of these discussions was you guessed it Theresa Tamborelli, a tomboy, ready to turn her baseball cap around and slug it out with the best of them.

Stick ball was also played where a batter would stand at home plate and the pitcher would throw the ball on one bounce, trying to get the batter to swing. No ball or strikes were called but three swings and you were out. Consequently there were no arguments, but the best pitcher in this game of course was Theresa Tamborelli.

Dom's candy store was near the schoolyard and after the games or after church on Sundays the gang would stand around drinking Manhattan Special Coffee Soda and listen to the jukebox. Everybody knew everybody so Dom never

# THE BEST OF TIMES

had any trouble in the candy store. Also he really liked us kids and we like him. Dom had a nickname for everybody, sometimes he would shorten your last name as in the case of Charlie Batista. Dom called him "Charlie Bats" Joey Tamborelli was "Joey T." and me "Sally Bra". He even had nicknames for the girls, only he didn't shorten their last names he just made up names. Skinny Rose was "Ro Ro Bones" One of the girls had a high pitched voice so he called her "Squeaky" Mary was "Contrary" and that's what stuck. There also was "Bobby Moo, Doughnuts, Peanuts," but Theresa he called "Angel Eyes" he'd say you guys are a group of Moe-Moes wait till she grows up, boy was he ever right. If he didn't like you he would never honor you with a nickname, so it was with the new kid Michael Cavanaugh. Whenever he came into the store Dom would just say what will it be or what will you have or what do you want. He couldn't care less if Michael never came into his store.

Michael Cavanaugh insisted on being called Michael, not Mike or Mickey oh no he'd correct you if you didn't call him Michael, he was extremely arrogant and looked down at virtually everybody and it wasn't because of his six foot three inch height. He was downright obnoxious. The girls would melt when they looked into his remarkably blue eyes. In the summer his hair would turn blonde and it made him even more irresistibly handsome. We were all Italians and looked it olive skin, dark hair and eyes except for Chaz who had light eyes and skin and his hair got lighter in the summer. In our neighborhood if you were six foot you were a giant, Michael could be selective with any girl, the guys all hated him because he was so good looking. We'd say things like," He give me a toothache he so sweet", if you were that tall you'd get a nose bleed. or he never wears black he don't know how to dress, can't trust him he's not Italian what's a Cavanaugh anyway." Just young guys talking trash.

Although he was what we thought of as an outsider and it was an unwritten rule that no Bensonhurst girl should go crazy over an outsider. Still Michael had a way about him, even when he was just being "MICHAEL" The young girls all hung around him and were will to do anything, just to be accepted. He was never fully accepted into the crowd, but never really rejected either.

During our junior year in Lafayette High School we lost the city Football Championship to Staten Island's New Dorp High School. It was a close game that was lost in overtime. All the boys in our gang were on the Lafayette team, so we took the lost very personal. We couldn't believe that we lost to a team from Staten Island, God damn bunch of hicks. After all we were the Italian Stallions from Bensonhurst. We thought we were unbeatable, but we lost. So when we found out Michael could play quarterback, we had to have him on our team. As it turned out Michael was a damn good athlete, we felt he could be the missing piece that could turn next years Lafayette Football Team into a winner. If you needed a first down, you just needed to hand the ball off to Charlie Bats, he was a bull running into the line, fearless he ran straight into any situation. Sometimes his team mates called him "Charlie uh Bots" the Italian way of saying, "Crazy Charlie." It was a badge of honor.

Joey on the other hand could run like the wind and make impossible catches. He was built to play wide receiver. Even though he was under six feet he was all legs and could turn on the speed in a flash. When he leaped up for the ball, he could get higher off the ground than any other defender.

Sometimes he looked like he could fly through the air, he always maintained his balance when he hit the ground. He could have been an acrobat or a high wire walker. The way he could thread his way through the defenders was pure magic and he was tough too. He could take a hit with the best of them.

Michael as quarterback, could read the defenses just like he could read people. He was always manipulating things to find the other team's weaknesses, and always conniving to put something over on them. He had a quick, sneaky and cunning mind which was necessary if you wanted to win on the football field. We admired those abilities in Michael our quarterback, but not when he used them off the field in his social relationships. In addition, he used his success on the football field and the power it gave him to manipulate and control his admirers. With Michael at quarterback we were convinced that our senior year would be our year to win the City Championship, and just as we hoped when the time came. We were playing against New Dorp High School. It was billed as a rematch of the previous year's best two teams. The New Dorp team was defending their championship so the game was played on their home field. For three of the four quarters, good defense on both sides kept the game close. At the beginning of the fourth quarter Charlie Bats finally started to wear down New Dorp's defense. He keep bulling into the line, so when the linebacker cheated up to help the defensive lineman, that's when Michael took over the game. He started hitting Joey with sensational passes and Joey caught every pass thrown at him. Their defense couldn't stop our team. Even I made a good third down catch to keep a drive alive from the tight-end position. We scored three unanswered touchdowns! The final score was Lafayette 35, New Dorp 14. Finally we were the City Champions and the hero's of Bensonhurst, Brooklyn. The Italian Stallions walk proud and tall the rest of the school year. Even at Graduation the team was the focal point, we were all call up to the stage and received a standing ovation as City Champions. After Michael was swarmed by the girls, but not Theresa.

Theresa Tamborelli was never impressed with Michael the way the other girls were. To her he was okay, but it was Chaz (Charlie) who claimed her heart. It was well known that Theresa was Chaz's girl. She had grown up to be a real beauty just as Dom had predicted. That made Michael all the more determined to have her. He didn't really want her in a sexual sense but what he wanted, He Wanted! It was all ego with him. If you examined Michael's motives, they went deeper than the desire to control. He wanted to own you, to possess you, to have you in his power with you as his slave and him as your master. He was like a smiling serpent, enticing his victim to take a bite of his forbidden apple.

As a child, Michael was extremely shy and aloof. He was always the loner and usually out of sorts. At birthday party's he would stand alone in the background pouting because all the attention was focused on the birthday child. Sometimes he would act out his feeling and would find a sneaky way to crush a present under his foot or mess up the birthday cake before it was served. Once at the outdoor playground, Michael was at the top of the monkey bars he dared a little girl to climb to the top as she got close he pushed her legs off the rung sending her to the ground. He appeared to be so innocent that no one suspected that he was responsible. He experienced a strange new sensation when he saw the girl lying on the ground hurt, and crying. A short time later he had the same sensation when he pushed his friend Tommy Burns off a shed roof playing king of the Mountain. Tommy lost his balance and fell breaking his leg, that little bit of evil started to rear it's ugly head. As Michael got older he started peeping into the windows of girl's bedrooms and even taking lingerie from clotheslines and then going home to masturbate.

Michael Cavanaugh came from a family of police officers, his father Michael Sr. had recently retired from the police department. there were rumors that his retirement had been hastened by allegation against his son Michael Jr. for corrupting the morals of a young teenager. The chargers were never proven nor prosecuted because Michael Sr. had pulled strings and called in some favors so his boy was exonerated.

"This is the last time I go to bat for you, Michael. I'm tired of bailing you out and looking the other way. You stood by laughing while Eddie Brown was drowning, your an excellent swimmer. What were you both doing in that row boat any how. A stolen boat, a boy drowns to get you out of that one almost cost me my pension, not to mention all your sexual escapades with little girls. No more, I've had it from now on your on your own."

As time passed all the allegation dwindled away, and even the whispers disappeared. Like they say time heals all wounds so when Michael decided on a career with the police department his father was happy he was following in his foot steps. Only Michael's decision was not due to admiration or undying love for his father. He always caught on quickly and realized that a police officer's badge carried a lot of weight and could be used to pull strings. It could work to his advantage to become a police officer, he enjoyed the idea of having power and being above the average working stiff. If he attained gold shield status, his cunning and shrewd mind could freely wreak havoc with almost certain immunity from punishment. Even walking the beat had it's appeal. Being on the street would put him close to teenage girls that found street life exciting and enticing. These rebellious runaways would be easy prey for a young handsome uniformed cop. He would have his choice among a large variety of young teens, from hookers and drug addicts to innocent plums. All his for the picking, his appetite for young girls was growing stronger.

Joey T. and Chaz didn't stay close to Michael after high school, it seemed he had his own agenda and it did not include any of the old gang from 18th avenue. Michael could see the old gang had strong family values.

Everyone knew everyone. Most friends were distant relatives to each other. That's the way it was no one left the neighborhood. You grew up there,'married' there, raised a family and died there. Very few moved away. Michael felt more at home in the anonymity of New York City, he could blend in with all the perverts, weirdos and tramps. Michael moved in the world of the night crawlers, where nobody cared if you preferred kiddy porn or young girls. Your sexual preferences were your own doing. A cop working the midnight to eight shift was Michael's cup of tea, first he had to get through the Police Academy and graduate. That was not easy for him. Joey T. and Chaz were encouraged by police officer Mazza to apply to the Police Academy. He had taken them under his wing and explained all the benefits to the job and that's how they found themselves in the same rookie class with Michael Cavanaugh.

Joey T. was born to do police work. He was observant, analytical and cynical all the traits that make a good cop. Joey's motto was never trust anyone, look past the obvious. Facts, not emotion ruled the life of officer Tamborelli.

Chaz was a good police officer, but his reason for joining the force was quite different. He saw the job as a good way to provide for a family. It had a good salary, health benefits, a dental plan, vacation with pay and a good pension. He wanted to marry Theresa and raise a family, that came first. He sort of grew into the job.

The first couple of weeks at the Academy were rough. The boys were not as fit as they though they were. The physical requirements were more than tough. They had to run, jump, do push-ups, climb ropes, scale walls, and lift weights. The training made every muscle in your body hurt. Academic classes were mentally fatiguing, and homework was an unbearable load after a strenuous day. About halfway through the Academy, Michael was ready to quit.

"Who needs this torture, Chaz? Fuck the Academy and the job. I'm done man, I can't do it anymore". But Chaz talked him into staying.

"Come on Michael your better than that, you can do it. I'll help you we'll study together and work out together."

Joey overheard the conversation and when he got Chaz alone he said, "Chaz what's wrong with you? Let that piece of shit flop out, he doesn't deserve to be a cop. He doesn't want to help people, he only wants to use the job for his own personal agenda."

"I have ears and I hear things. The trouble with you is you're always with Theresa, so your oblivious to what's going on outside of Bensonhurst. Michael is no good."

"Come on Joey, give the guy a break. We're all going to be part of the greatest brotherhood in New York City. Cops stick together like brothers."

"Michael is nobody's brother."

Chaz paid no attention to Joeys's warning. He even helped Michael qualify on the firing range. He showed Michael how to lock his wrist, squeeze the trigger and anticipate the recoil of the pistol.

Before they knew it, all three of them had graduated. They were given their choice of precincts. Joey and Chaz wanted to work in Bensonhurst, Michael got to work in the First precinct in Manhattan, a dream come true for him. The graduation party was in Chaz's backyard and in full swing when Michael showed up. Michael immediately homed in on Joey's sister Theresa. She had matured and was more beautiful than Michael remembered. He wasted no time in turning on the charm.

"My God, Theresa you've grown into a gorgeous woman."

He couldn't take his eyes off of her. Although Theresa's hair was deep brunette, the sunlight brought out the fire red highlights as she stood talking to friends. Her hair set off her peaches and cream complexion and when she got excited or embarrassed, her checks turned a rosy red. Her eyes were amazing, they were hazel and seem to change

## THE BEST OF TIMES

color depending on what she was wearing. If she wore blue, her eyes were blue. If she wore green they looked green. Even the color purple effected them, she had the face of an angel and a body that inspired devilish thought in men. She had a tiny waist and a voluptuous bust, and when she wore a bathing suit especially a two piece all the guys ran for a cold shower. She was the best looking girl in our gang or any other gang for that matter, and she and Chaz made the most attractive couple on eighteenth avenue.

Michael came over to her again and said, "You should be a model. I can help you I'm a very good amateur photographer. Let me take some pictures of you sometime. I have some connection with an agent friend of mine. Maybe if he likes my pictures we can get you on a real photo shoot."

Joey's instincts told him that Michael was up to no good. I don't know if he knew about Michael's past transgressions or not, but I do know that Joey didn't trust or like Michael. Chaz on the other hand was oblivious to Michael's intentions and never gave him a second thought. Chaz knew that

Theresa loved him, and he trusted her unconditionally. After a short time on the job Theresa and Chaz were married. A church wedding and a small reception just family and a few very close friends and a very short honeymoon was all they could afford. When your young and in love all you need is each other, the passion of love will take you where ever you dream of being.

Michael was stationed in New York City, while Joey and Chaz were stationed in Bensonhurst. Having Joey and Chaz in the neighborhood made all the merchants on 18th avenue feel like they had special protection. After all they grew up there and they knew everyone by name it was like a family. Two young police officers watching out for the children making sure no one tried to sell them dope or crack in the schoolyard. At night even after their shift was over they would check doors to see if they were properly locked. They would check the dark alleys to make sure no one was lurking in the shadows. While my old friends were protecting New York and Brooklyn I was away at college working on my law degree. When I came home we would alway get together and renew our friendship.

One afternoon, Chaz and Joey were patrolling 18th avenue working a four-to-twelve shift. It was an ordinary day, with business going on as usual on the avenue. People were shopping and the restaurants were getting ready for the after work crowd. Teenagers, both boys and girls were hanging at Dom's candy store. Dom was no longer there, he had retired a while ago and sold the store to his cousin Paul. Nevertheless it was still the same as when we were kids, stopping in for a soda, an ice cream or just to play the jukebox. The small forty-five record had given way to a much better sound through advances in technology. The sound level of mono was now stereo an increase of about a thousand percent! It sounded like a concert was being held in the store.

About 5:45pm Chaz and Joey decided to stop at Tony's Pizza, best in Bensonhurst.

"Come on Joey, lets get a slice or two before we leave the avenue."

"Its early Chaz."

"What do you want to do stop at eight o' clock? We'll be forty blocks from here by then. Besides all I had to eat today was a cup of coffee and a jelly donut and that was ten this morning."

"Okay, you'll only haunt me until I say yes. So let's go."

"I'll double park out front, and you can run in. Get four slices."

"Hey Chaz why me? You're the one that wants pizza!"

"Come Joey be a pal."

"I don't see why I have to go."

"I'm driving the squad car."

"You Chaz, your a real pain in my ass."

"Joey lend me three dollars, and get a coke too."

"Son of a bitch, I gotta pay too! Chaz you're lucky your my brother-in-law, or I'd give you a shot in the head. You really know how to piss me off."

While Chaz was waiting for Joey to come out of Tony's a teenage boy from the neighborhood ran over to the squad car.

"Officer Batista, two guys are holding up the convenience store around the corner"!

"Are you sure?'

"Yes, I was walking by and I saw one of them taking money out of the register. He had a gun in his hand."

Chaz hit the siren and signaled for Joey, who understood immediately and ran back to the car. Chaz burnt rubber as they sped around the corner and screeched to a halt. They jumped out of the car with guns drawn and identified themselves.

"Police! Drop your weapons."

The two armed robbers, looked for a quick exit. They ran to the back of the store, but the steel door was locked from the inside with three large padlocks. They were trapped inside. Joey positioned himself just outside in front where he could peek through the glass door. He could see the gunman scurrying around, looking for a place to hide. The owner of the store Mr. Russo, lay motionless on the floor. There was blood coming from his head. At first glance, Joey said

"Chaz, call for back up and EMS. Mr. Russo has been pistol whipped."

Chaz called for backup.

"Robbery in progress, backup and Ambulance or EMS needed. Convenience store at 18th and Broad, owner has a head wound."

He turned to Joey.

"Can you see who these guys are?"

Joey took a another look and quickly pulled his head back.

"Shit. They have a little girl. She looks about ten or twelve.

A voice came out from the store.

"We got a little girl here! Let us go and we won't hurt her."

Chaz asked again.

"Joey can you see who these guys are, take another look."

"Oh shit, it looks like Julio Rodriquez and Felix Mendez! Two psychos."

These two creeps were not only bad guys, but dope users. They used mainly Angel Dust which made them unpredictable. If they were robbing the store because they needed a fix, things can get ugly real fast. Fifteen minutes which seemed like hours went by.

"Give up Felix. You've nowhere to go."

"Fuck you cop, I'll shoot the kid unless you let us go."

"Can't do that. Put your guns down and come out with your hands over your heads.

"Hey Batista is that you? Come out where I can see you so I can cap your ass."

"Let the girl go before back up arrives and I'll look the other way."

"I don't believe you cop."

Joey peeked in for a better look and then ran around the back of the squad.

"Joey why the hell did you give up your position?"

"Chaz they have Rocko Mastori's daughter in there!"

"The Mafia boss?"

"You got it."

"We are really screwed."

"Kill us now, kill us later. Chaz if those psychos kill that little girl, Mastori will nail us to the wall! What do we do? Where the hell is backup?"

In the far distance they could hear sirens approaching.

"If we're going to do something it better be quick. Joey look the front steel cellar doors are unlocked. If you go through the basement and come up behind them. I'll create a diversion and you can nail them. Five minutes is all we got, go."

Chaz waited five minutes and then threw a wire wastebasket from the street through the front window. Glass flew everywhere as he rushed the front door. The sound and commotion covered Joey's entrance from the basement and he got the drop on the robbers.

"Drop it boys, before I cap your asses."

Julio and Felix dropped their guns and Joey and Chaz read them their rights and cuffed them.

# JOSEPH SQUATRITO

The Emergency Medical Services was first to arrive and attended the two victims. The little Mastori girl was unharmed and Mr. Russo needed a few stitches. As Joey and Chaz walked out of the store, police cars arrived from every direction.

Chaz asked, "What took you guys so long? Go back and have a cup of coffee, we already saved the day."

A very angry Sergeant Lopez responded." Hey big shot you weren't supposed to do anything but maintain the situation until we arrived."

"We had a hostage situation with a wounded man and a little girl being held by two psycho fucks on Angel Dust or Crack. How long do you think it would have taken until they were so strung out that they started shooting? Waiting for a negotiator, would have probably cost the victims their lives."

Joey said. "We know these guys. We busted them before but they keep getting out!"

"Don't give me your bullshit Tamborelli. You two just wanted to be heroes."

"We did our job, it's over end of story."

"Next time do your job by the rules."

"We've got to go now and take these guys in and book them for armed robbery. Take it easy Sarge."

Joey and Chaz received a commendation for bravery from the mayor of New York and a medal of bravery from the New York Police Department. They risked their lives even knowing that the little girl's father was a Mafia boss from Bensonhurst. Three months later Joey and Chaz were subpoenaed to appear in court to testify against Mendez and Rodriquez. District Attorney Monroe handled the

# THE BEST OF TIMES

case himself and announced "This time they won't get off because of a legal technicality."

The trial was held before Judge Shirley Basehart. Both sides agreed that a jury was unnecessary. A Public Defender represented Julio Rodriquez and Felix Mendez. It was an open and shut case, which nailed two three-time losers who should have been put away a long time ago.

Maria Rose Mastori was under age, so her mother and their family lawyer accompanied her. She was first to testify.

D.A. Monroe stood by the judge's bench and after the little girl was sworn in he gently asked her.

"Maria Rose Mastori, is that your full name?"

"Yes."

"Your twelve years old?"

"I'm almost thirteen, My birthday is next week."

"Okay, your almost thirteen. Do you understand what it means to be sworn in."

"Yes, it means I have to tell the truth."

"That's right. Can you tell us what happened on the day of the holdup in Mr. Russo's store"?

"I was in the store near the back, I was getting milk out of the refrigerator case when those two men came in."

She pointed to the two defendants."

"Let the record show Miss Mastori has pointed out Julio Rodriquez and Felix Mendez your honor.

"They pushed Mr. Russo to the floor and went behind counter and opened the cash register. The tall man said, where's the rest of the money old man. Mr. Russo said, that's it we had a slow day. The man started hitting Mr. Russo. I couldn't move I was so scared. Then the man took out a gun and said. I kill you if you don't tell me where the rest of the money is. The other man saw me and he walked back towards me, he said don't scream and you won't get hurt. Then he grabbed me and put his hand over my mouth. Mr. Russo said, don't hurt the little girl I'll tell you where the money is. There's a false drawer under the cabinet, push it up and back and it will open. Then he hit Mr. Russo on the head with his gun, I could tell he was really hurt bad because he was bleeding even before he fell on the floor. Then the Cops showed up and everything happened so fast. The man who was holding me used me as a shield. The other man hid behind the counter and yelled, we'll shoot the little girl if you don't let us go! I was so scared, I'm not sure what happened next but there was a loud crash of glass and that police officer."

She pointed to Officer Joseph Tamborelli.

"Came up from the back cellar and got behind them and they surrendered."

"Your witness Counselor."

"No question, your Honor."

D.A. Monroe called John Russo the store owner to the stand and he gave his testimony as best as he could remember. He was unconscious, most of the time.

So he could not tell about the police showing up at the scene.

Officer Joseph Tamborelli and Office Charles Battisa gave their testimony exactly as it occurred from the time they arrived on the scene to the cuffing and reading the defendants their rights. It was a cut and dry 'verdict-guilty' as charged. The two hoodlums were sentenced to ten to twenty years, to be served at Attica State Penitentiary for armed robbery, assault with a deadly weapon and assault of a minor.

Judge Basehart crashed the gavel down and said.

"Bailiff, escort these prisoners away. Case closed."

Joey and Chaz left the courthouse. As they walked down the outside steps they were approached by the man himself,-Mafia Boss, street lord Rocko Mastori.

"I want to thank you both for saving my little girl's life."

"We were only doing our job, Maria's life was our main concern."

"The super duper cops of 18th avenue! I won't forget this. If you ever need a favor or if there's anything I can do for you, don't hesitate to call me."

"No thanks, it's not likely. Watch out we may come calling on you someday."

"If you guys came to arrest me, I'd take it like a man."

"Come on Joey lets go."

As they turned and walked away, Chaz said to Joey.

"What balls on that guy"!

"Hey Chaz, you never know."

Time passed and Theresa gave birth to her first daughter, Lenore. I came home for the Baptism. My fiancee Mary was Godmother to Lenore and Joey was Godfather. We all met at two o'clock in front of Our Lady of Guadeloupe Church. After the Baptism, they had photos taken on 86th street by professional photographers. At 5 o'clock a party was held at the Knights of Columbus Hall on 86th street and 12th avenue. Almost everyone from the old gang attended. Chaz invited a few fellow police officers from his precinct, but no one was more surprised than I was when Michael showed up. About an hour into the party in he walks with a very young, very sexy attractive blonde named Susan. I take that back Joey was the most surprised and outraged.

"Sal, what the fuck is that piece of shit doing here? Who the hell, invited Michael?"

I had all that I could do to calm him down.

"Joey, you've had a few to many, I'm sure Chaz must have invited him. He wouldn't just show up on his own uninvited, even he don't have that much nerve.

"I guess your right, Sal. I just hate that guy he's just a sneaky bastard. I hear things on the street about him that would curl your hair, if you only knew what I know."

"Joey this is not the place or the time. Lets enjoy the party, come on look Bobby Moo just walked in. Lets go say hello."

Michael went over to Chaz and Theresa to congratulate them.

"Your baby is beautiful, she's going to look just like Theresa when she grows up. I can see it but I just want to thank you for inviting me, oh this is my good friend Susan."

"Thanks for coming, all the old gang is here. Sal, Mary, RoRo, Joey, Bobby Moo even fat Doughnuts only now he's skinny. Eat, drink dance it's a party man go mingle and say hello. Come on Theresa lets dance, maybe tonight we'll make another beautiful baby."

"You're getting a little drunk Chaz, one dance and then I have to see to the baby."

The party was great, the food was unbelievable. As a special thanks to Chaz for giving more of himself than just the time on his beat, most of the merchants on 18th avenue had sent over free food.

Michael kept a close eye on Theresa, he followed her around the room looking for an opportunity to talk to her alone.

"Theresa got a minute"?

"Sure, what's on your mind Michael?"

"I just want to say that you still look great, even after giving birth. Most women get fat and sloppy, but not you. I still think you've got a great shape, motherhood agrees with you. I'd still love to photograph you, with the baby of course.

"Michael your little friend is looking for you. What is she eighteen, nineteen maybe?"

"I'm not really sure, I never asked. She just photographs great in the nude. Outstanding body and she knows how to work it."

"Watch that you don't go to jail for robbing the cradle. Michael!"

As Theresa went back to her guests, Michael returned to his so-called friend and escorted her to the dance floor. Susan put on quite a show for all the men in the room and Joey became even more irate. The music stopped while photos were taken of the Batistas and baby Lenore with the beautifully decorated Baptism Cake. Coffee was served, it was a welcome break but for some it was more needed than preferred.

"Joey have some black coffee, you need it my friend."

"I'm not as drunk as you think, Sal."

"Okay have some coffee and cake and then you and I will have a drink together. What do you say?"

"Maybe you're right, I could use some black coffee. Who has the Sambucca?"

## JOSEPH SQUATRITO

When Michael left, the party was still in full swing. Joey had calmed down even though he was still having a nip or two. I went over to Chaz and asked.

"Who's driving Joey home? I don't think he should drive."

"Don't worry Sal, we'll take care of him."

"Well, then Mary and I are going to leave now, it was a great party."

We said our good-byes and I took Mary home. As we drove back to Mary's house we were both very quite. Then Mary broke the silence by saying.

"Michael's girl friend is very attractive, but she looks a little young for him don't you think?"

"Yeah maybe just a little."

"Well, it didn't seem to brother all you guys, judging from the way you were all staring at her. I thought your eyes were going fall out of their sockets as she put on her little dancing exhibition."

"Are you a little jealous Mary?"

"No why should I be?"

"Come on I know you had a thing for Michael in High School."

"Michael was a pig in school, he treated girls like dirt."

"Seeing him after all these years didn't bring back old memories?"

"Absolutely not."

"Okay lets just drop it, the past is the past."

I parked in front of Mary's house and kissed her goodnight, but for some strange reason she was miles away in an other place.

# THE BEST OF TIMES

"Mary I have to leave early to get back to school, I'll see you next weekend. Maybe we could spend some us time together, seems like every time I come home were lucky if were alone long enough for a goodnight kiss. I love you Mary"!

"I love you too, Sal."

I walked her to her door and we kissed again. Then I headed home for a few hours sleep before the long ride back to school.

Chaz and Joey had already received a Mayor's Commendation for bravery because they saved a little girl's life during a holdup. They knew her father was a Mafia Capo from Bensonhurst, but that didn't matter to them and they risked their lives to save her. It was an act of bravery above and beyond the call of duty. In the two years that followed it, Joey and Chaz became the two most decorated officers on the police force.

A month before my graduation from law school, Theresa delivered her second daughter Ashley. Again I was able to get home for the Baptism, this time there was no big party no hullabaloo and no drunkenness just a quite ceremony. Just a few close friends and family. Mary and I were invited back to the house for a sandwich, cake and coffee. Chaz had a spouse and two children, a small house with a big mortgage so money was tight. The celebration was modest, but it didn't matter because it was great seeing everyone again.

I chose Criminal Law as my specialty and after graduation I got an opportunity to join a very successful law firm in Brooklyn. The job was everything I wanted. I would be working at what I dreamed of and what I studied for,

## JOSEPH SQUATRITO

Criminal Law. The best part was that I'd be working close to home, so I often could see my best friends and family.

Mary and I were married at City Hall. Chaz was there as my best man and Mary's sister Helen was Maid of Honor.' We didn't have much money so all we could afford was a weekend in New York for our honeymoon. We promised each other that we'd take a real honeymoon in Las Vegas, but we figured it wouldn't happen for a long time. It was a common goal we had, a dream something to shoot for and something to work for. At that point in our lives, everyone in our old gang was doing well. All of us had found careers, some of us married our high school sweethearts and started families. All were in good health and even as adults we stayed close and enjoyed each other's company. I guess the strong family bonds we came from stayed with us. They say you're lucky if you have one true friend you can rely on. I considered myself to be a very fortunate and rich man because I had two best friends in Joey and Chaz.

Before I knew it four years had passed and I had become a junior partner in the firm. Chaz and Joey were still well known and loved by the people in the neighborhood. Joey had been honored twice more and had started doing undercover work. Because of his youthful appearance, Joey was sometimes called to infiltrate high schools to uncover drug use and drug sales. Occasionally he asked to sit on stakeouts with vice officers. Eventually he asked to be transferred to vice. He had a passion for justice and hated the criminals he had to deal with. Most of all he despised pedophiles. He felt the system didn't go far enough to punish them. To him, justice called for a child molester to be turned over to his victim's family. To say he was obsessed with these perverts was an understatement. He had heard the rumors about Michael, before Michael became a cop, and found it hard to be around him. Joey was smart enough to realize that if the rumors were true, a pedophile doesn't quit his perversion just because he becomes a cop. He became increasingly suspicious of Michael. Most on the job would not have given Michael a second thought but the hate Joey had for him ran long and deep.

# THE WORST OF TIMES

One summer, Chaz and Theresa Batista were holding their annual fourth of July barbecue. It was in full swing when Joey got there. After greeting his old friends, he looked for Chaz who was busy cooking on the grill and trying not to burn the food or himself. When Joey found him, Chaz was losing the battle.

"Have a drink Joey, and bring me a Scotch' whiskey with ice."

"Chaz, I have some business to discuss with you."

"Not here, not now, said Chaz. Go have a good time, we'll talk later."

Suddenly Michael appeared behind them from out of the crowd.

"Congratulation Joey, I hear your doing a fine job in vice!"

"The job makes me look under every rock for slime balls, because you might step on a rock and hurt yourself." Joey responded.

Joey stalked away, leaving Chaz alone with Michael. Chaz apologized to him saying, "Joey had had a bad day and then he quickly changed the subject.

"What can I get you from the grill, Michael?"

"Nothing Chaz, I'm really not hungry but I will grab a cold one."

He walked in the opposite direction from Joey and they didn't talk to each other the rest of the day. Michael did talk with some of the other guys on the job from Joey's precinct, always keeping a close eye on Theresa. I'm sure he was thinking what every guy thinks when they see Theresa, wow how can she keep getting more beautiful with age. The mother of two small children and she still turns heads no matter where she is or where she goes. One afternoon a few weeks later, Theresa was shopping in the neighborhood on 86th street Michael spotted her coming out of French Secrets, a fancy lingerie store. He pulled over his car, rolled down the window and called her over. Theresa walked over to the car and Michael said.

"I never got to thank you for inviting me to the barbecue. I'd like to show you my appreciation, how about a quick lunch?"

Theresa agreed and they went to a near by restaurant. After ordering a couple of cocktails, Michael started to make a pass at her.

"I couldn't take my eyes off of you Theresa. You were the perfect hostess, attending to everyone it seemed except me.

"Don't you know that I've always admired you and fantasized about you?"

"Please Michael, lets just enjoy our lunch as two old friends."

Michael realized he moved too quickly. Theresa was a real beauty, worth his time with her. A picture of her as a kid playing stickball flashed before him, not only was she a good athlete, but she had an assertive no nonsense attitude. Conquering her would take some doing. He'd have to bide his time and wait for the right opportunity. He immediately switched gears and turned the conversation to general neighborhood news and gossip about old friends A mutual friend from the avenue came over to say hello. They had a delicious lunch and got ready to leave, walking out on the sidewalk Michael said.

"If there ever comes a time when you need me, I'll be there for you."

"What are you talking about"?

"Theresa you know I love you!"

"Michael please."

As Theresa started walking away she turned and there was Michael throwing kisses and laughing. She though to her self what foolishness is that all about. People in the neighborhood were close, it didn't take long for the news to travel of what they saw and as each person told their story it grew a little more than it was. When Joey heard about his sister's encounter with Michael, he went straight to her house. Joey burst into Theresa's home and started yelling at the top of his voice.

"Are you stupid or something are you that naive? How could you go to lunch with Michael? Theresa all he wants to do is get in your pants, and you like it don't you?"

"It's none of your business Joey! Who the hell do you think you are coming into my house screaming at me like this. I'll do what I damn please! It was just two old friends having an innocent lunch, what the hell is wrong with that"?

"I'll tell you what's wrong, now you need to know the truth about Michael."

## JOSEPH SQUATRITO

Theresa enraged by his insinuations refused to listen. She struck her brother and tried to shove him out the front door. Joey surprised at the strength of his sister, lost his balance and fell to the floor. As he started to get up a barrage of slaps and kicks came at him and although there is no question that she was no match for him, Joey had to defend himself.

As he just tried to cover up from being hurt, he accidentally caught Theresa's eye with his elbow. She fell to the floor holding her already swelling eye. Joey was horrified at what he had done, he tried to help her off the floor.

"Get away from me you son of a bitch, get out of my house"! Just wait till I tell Chaz what you've done he'll fix your ass.

"I didn't mean to hurt you, it was an accident. Theresa please, please forgive me!"

"Get out of here you bastard, and don't come back. I can't believe you treated me like those bimbos you're always arresting, working vice is really screwing with your brain. Now get the hell out of here".

Theresa slammed the door on Joey's back almost sending him sprawling down the front steps. She was still furious with Joey, but she had no intention of telling Chaz so he would go after Joey. She ran to the nearest mirror and examined her face, as she looked back at herself she thought, "Damn it my eye is starting to get black and blue already. I better get some ice on it, Chaz will go crazy when he see this. I can't call him because he'll come home like a lunatic. Anyway he's on duty until midnight. Hopefully the ice will help and I'll be asleep by the time he get home. Tomorrow I'll explain how it was all my fault."

## THE WORST OF TIMES

Joey drove around while he tried to cool off. He was still upset and thought to himself, "Chaz is going to beat the shit out of me when sees what I did to Theresa. I better call him and explain, I don't want any confrontation in the precinct locker room. Captain Nolan was really pissed the last time we got into a fight there. He warned us that if anything ever happened like this again, we'd both be put on suspension for a month or longer without pay. I better straighten this out, it's all my own fault."

He called dispatch and asked to be patched through to Chaz's location. Chaz's new partner officer Dan Fields, answered and explained that Chaz had left the patrol car just for a few minutes to deliver some food to a sick old woman in the neighborhood. Dan said, "What can I do for you Joey"?

Reluctantly Joey explained his confrontation with Theresa.

"Dan you know how crazy Chaz can get where Theresa is concerned. Please tell him that I didn't mean it and that I'll see him at his house tomorrow morning right after my shift is over."

Dan Fields may have been Chaz's partner, but he was no friend. As Dan hung up the phone he let out a strange and ominous whisper.

"We got you now, you asshole."

When Chaz returned to the patrol car, Dan acted as if nothing had occurred. Dan stopped at a pay phone, the first opportunity he had explaining to Chaz. "I got a hot broad I want to talk some shit to. I'll only be a minute Chaz." He dialed without hesitation, it was a familiar number. Turning his back to the near by patrol car he spoke softly.

## JOSEPH SQUATRITO

"We got the rat bastard!"

He explained briefly the circumstances that led up to the call from Joey and related the message Joey had asked him to give to Chaz. Then he listened for orders concerning the wheels of motion he was about to put into play.

"How long do you want me to keep him in the bar tonight?"

After receiving his instructions, Dan said, "No problem, I'll bring Bob Bradley with us. Those two assholes love talking police shit. I wish I were going to be there with you when the spicks throw him a beating, tell them to kick him in the ass for me. Good luck!"

The devious smile on Dan's face vanished as he got back into the patrol car. Chaz said. "How'd it go? Are we still on for tonight?"

"Sure, I'm going to need a few good drinks before I meet this hot tomato. She says she wants to hurt me real good, tonight I'm going to get the fuck of my life."

They looked at each other and started to laugh, as they continued with what was left of their shift. Hugo's Bar was the usual stop for most of the cops that worked the eight to twelve shift, a few good boiler makers always took the edge off a brutal night shift. Chaz continued from beer to boilermakers trying unsuccessfully to get rid of the taste of the nights carnage. He tried several times to leave but Dan did his job well saying

"The next round is on me, what's the rush we finally got Bob to come out with us and the banana head isn't even drunk yet."

"Okay one round on you, one round on me and then I'm out of here."

# THE WORST OF TIMES

He got home an hour later and quietly stumbled up the stairs to check on his little girls as usual before going to his own bed. After he stripped off his clothes and lay down, he lustfully reached for Theresa. There was no response.

"I love you, I need you honey."

Theresa laid silent not moving in hopes he would roll over and fall asleep, she could smell the liquor on his breath but he began to rub her breast getting her nipple hard. Then he moved his hand down between her legs gently rubbing her until she began to roll over. As Theresa slowly turned to face him, the moonlight revealed her secret. The sight of his wife's swollen face appalled him.

"What the hell happened to you? Your eye is all swollen and back and blue!"

"Now don't blow a fuse, it's not what you're going to think Chaz. Joey stopped over before his shift and we got into an argument. You know me and my Italian temper! I started it, it was an accident he didn't mean it. His elbow just, Chaz calm down I can see your getting crazy, he didn't mean it".

She turn to explain, she didn't realize that she was talking to herself until she heard the car start. Chaz tore out of the driveway. The bumper hit concrete as he backed into the street sending a shower of sparks flying into the night. Chaz was drunk and he was furious.

"Joey, you son of a bitch nobody touches my Theresa." He shouted to himself.

His mind was racing a hundred miles an hour, and so was his car. He sped through red lights and passed cars, without regard for oncoming traffic or safety of others.

## JOSEPH SQUATRITO

At the same time, Joey lay face down on the concrete. The bullet had ripped a hole through his body and his life's blood was spilling out of him.

Chaz had no idea the evil some men will go to, to get what they desire most. He tried to remember what Joey had told him the night before. He told him something about an undercover assignment he was on. All Chaz could remember was the location Joey had talked about. It was the warehouse district in Gramercy, which was a very dangerous place especially at night.

It was known for its drug deals, burglaries, gang murders and rapes. Chaz realized that an unarmed cop wandering around could be in grave danger. He remembered that he was unarmed, so he made a U-turn and headed to the precinct to get his service revolver.

At the same time, a man was sneaking up the back stairs of the precinct leading to the locker room. The man very quietly entered the locker room, opened a locker returned a holstered gun and quickly left without being seen.

Chaz drove straight to the station house. It took all of his strength to hide his condition as he entered the precinct and was confronted by the desk sergeant.

"Forgot something in my locker, Sarge. I'll only be a minute."

"Something wrong Chaz?"

Chaz quickly brushed him off, "It's a family matter, Sarge" and headed directly to the locker room. It took less than a minute for him to get what he had come for. On his way out, he checked the assignment roster and then he quickly exited the precinct. He returned to his car, which he had left running and sped away into the darkness.

# THE WORST OF TIMES

An hour or so before, Officer Joseph Tamborelli had quickly entered a dimly lit parking lot. His undercover squad car silently eased to a stop. With gun drawn, he cautiously responded to a burglary in progress at the Acme Warehouse. He was startled and then relieved to see his backup coming out of the shadows of a loading dock. For a split second, he was puzzled at how quickly his support had arrived on the scene, but nothing prepared him for the force of the blow that hit his gut. There was no one near enough to punch him with such a tremendous force. He immediately felt the air rush out of his lungs and he shook his head totally confused, then he realized.

"I've been shot! Jesus, Mary and Joseph," he cried out," I'm dying" and he crumpled to the ground.

The last thing he saw right in front of his nose, were shoes with a mirror finish, the kind you could shave with. The shoes belonged to the person standing there watching him. Joey lay on the concrete pavement, he was bleeding profusely. He couldn't move and he knew his life was about to end.

"Take this gun, replace the bullet and return it to Chaz's locker. Try not to be seen, wipe the gun and the replacement bullet clean. I want to see this asshole die. I may even wait for Chaz to show up."

"Don't worry, I'll go through the back door that leads up to the locker room. I have the code number to get in. There's never anybody around at that hour of the night."

"When you tell me not to worry, that's when I worry. Wipe the gun and everything to touch clean!"

A final thought rushed through Joey's brain, "I should have known that bastard would kill me."

## JOSEPH SQUATRITO

After repeated attempts to reach Officer Tamborelli, dispatch sent backup to Joey's last known location. Chaz had already gotten there, he could see Joey's car as he entered the parking lot. He approached the car only to find it empty. As Chaz got out of his car, he saw Joey lying on the ground.

Chaz rushed over, "Joey, oh my God."

He bent down and cradled Joey's head. He fought back the slowly emerging realization that Joey was dead.

"God damn it Joey, don't you die!"

Lights from an approaching squad car caught his attention and at that very moment, Chaz heard someone or something moving in the dark shadows.

As he stared, almost mesmerized into the darkness he drew his gun. Although he could not see anyone he was sure he must be staring at Joey's killer. He was jolted out of his trance by the voice of a police officer screaming out," Drop your weapon, drop your weapon or I'll shoot"!

Chaz recognized the voice." Mike it's me Chaz"!

"Chaz drop your weapon."

Mike's partner, Jim whispered, "Mike it's Chaz what do we do?"

"I don't know, let just do it by the book" and he called again to Chaz.

"Chaz drop your weapon, lay face down, hands behind your head!"

Chaz covered in Joey's blood, reluctantly did as he was ordered. Mike said

"Jim, call for backup while I read Chaz his rights and cuff him."

## THE WORST OF TIMES

In a matter of minutes, ten squad cars replied to the "Officer down" call and Chaz was brought to his own precinct. Hours passed like minutes in all the confusion. Somehow the newspapers already knew what happened. Captain Nolan remembered Michael Cavanaugh as a family friend.

"O'Malley, Sergeant O'Malley!"

"Yes, Captain, I'm here."

"Quick, see if Cavanaugh is on duty. He's stationed at the first precinct in Manhattan. We have to get someone over to the Batista home to tell Theresa the terrible news."

O'Malley finally found Michael at home and handed the phone to Captain Nolan. The Captain briefed Michael about what had happened.

"Michael your a friend of the family. Get over there first before the newspaper boys beat you to the house. How in hell did they get a hold of this so fast"?

The morning edition' headlines read." Three-Time Decorated Police Officer Killed by Fellow Cop"! I couldn't believe my eyes as I read the story. One of my best friends was dead and another was being blamed for it. I knew there was no way Chaz could have killed Joey, so I immediately went to his defense. I entered the holding cell. Chaz looked up with tears in his eyes and said." Sally, I knew you'd come, I didn't kill Joey. You believe me don't you?"

"Chaz if I though for a second you did it, I wouldn't be here for you!"

"Thank God your here to help me".

"Chaz tell me what happened, tell me what you know".

## JOSEPH SQUATRITO

So Chaz told me his side of the story. I knew Chaz all my life I looked into his eyes and I knew he was telling me the truth as well as he could remember it. I said, "Chaz don't worry it's all circumstantial evidence. I'll get you out of this."

"Sally, please go see Theresa. Tell her I didn't kill Joey."

"I'm sure she knows that. I'll go see her right after we're through here."

After my meeting with Chaz was over, I went straight to Theresa. When I got there, she was in a state of shock. She didn't fully understand what had happened. Only that Joey was dead and that Chaz was being held for his murder. I was surprised to see Michael there. He was being very comforting and understanding. Theresa seemed to lean on him, no one not me or Theresa or anyone knew Michael's real motive. With Theresa in a state of shock because her brother was dead and her husband was being held for his murder-all because of her. Michael only seemed caring, his real purpose was to slip her mind-controlling drugs so that he could poison her mind against Chaz. She was stoned on valium prescribed by the doctor, so Michael found it easy to add his drugs and get her into a complete state of confusion. He fed her all sorts of false information and told her over and over that Chaz was guilty. He brainwashed her so he could gain full control of her. He did it without anyone being aware of what he was doing. Michael was a master of control and once he had his hooks into someone it was all over. Theresa was his puppet, and he manipulated her with great skill. For the next few days, the newspapers had a field day with the story.

# THE WORST OF TIMES

Then the ballistics tests proved that Chaz's gun was the murder weapon and the Brooklyn District Attorney's office moved to indict Chaz for the murder of Officer Joseph Tamborelli. It was now my job to get Chaz off the hook and I knew it wasn't going to be easy. I brought the bad news to Chaz and told him about the ballistics test results.

"Sally it's impossible, I didn't shoot my gun. How could it be the murder weapon? I'm being set up."

The more Chaz let the news sink in the more upset he got.

Soon he was screaming and yelling and not making much sense. I realized that he needed time to settle down, so I left. I tried to put the pieces together in my mind as I drove back to my office. I couldn't make any sense of it. I think I needed Chaz's help more than he needed my help. He was the only one who could fill in the missing pieces of the puzzle. I now had a month to prepare, but I had very little ammunition to fight with. I wished I had more to go on because I believed in Chaz, and I knew in my heart and mind that he was innocent. And that was not going to win this case and get him free, all the cards were stacked against him. The idea of circumstantial evidence was out the window, the ballistic test saw to that. My only angle for a defense was he was being set up but even that was skating on thin ice. The two days of Joey's wake were filled with confusion, emotion and despair. Totally draining the human spirit. The words, "How could this have happened?" rang out all over Bensonhurst.

On the day of the funeral, there was a one hour viewing. It took almost two and a half hours because of the large number of people who showed up. The funeral procession was composed of two flower cars, five limousines and fifty cars. A full police escort took Joey from the funeral home to Our Lady of Guadeloupe. The church held over four hundred people. As the procession reached the church, hundreds of uniformed officers lined the street in front of the church. A bagpipe brigade followed the casket into the church, as the honor guards at each side marched in perfect precision. Captain Nolan eulogized Joseph Tamboreli's career, describing him as a brave and outstanding officer. He listed all the honors and medals Joey had received.

"Today we not only bury a fine police officer, but a decent upstanding human being. A role model for young and old alike, I was honored to know him and to serve with him. As his precinct commanding officer there was no assignment to dangerous that he would not undertake. He was an asset to the job as well as the community and he will be so missed."

When the mass was over, the police escorted the funeral cars to Fair Lawn Cemetery, on the border of Queens and Long Island. A piper and honor guard followed the casket to it's final resting place. The police guard honored their fallen brother with a twenty-one gun salute. The rife fire cracked the air. It was a sound that was unfamiliar to most of the people in attendance. For some, each round of fire represented great honor being paid to a deserving man.

For others, the shots reminded them repeatedly of how Joey died.

The mourners were invited to go back to a catering hall on 86th street in Brooklyn for a brunch. Mary and I did not attend. I knew I had a much more important job to do. I had paper work to prepare to hopefully save Chaz, not only from an unjust verdict but from himself. A week later with no more evidence to help our cause, I went back to talk with Chaz.

"Chaz you're the only one who can help me fully understand what happened on that night. Try to remember everything you can."

"Sally, I only want to know how Theresa and my girls are. Does she know that I didn't kill Joey? How did the funeral go?"

"Chaz, everything is okay at home. You have to concentrate on helping me so I can help you."

"Sally, don't talk to me like a lawyer. Tell me about my family!"

"Your life is on the line here Chaz. Do you understand?"

"Yes."

"Okay then, tell me how your gun could have killed Joey if it never left you?"

"My gun was in my locker. I left it there after my shift because I was going drinking that night with the boys."

"So how did you have your gun at the scene of the crime?"

"I went back for it after I saw Theresa and she told me Joey hit her."

"Lets see if I've got this straight. Joey and Theresa had a fight earlier that day, Theresa got a black eye. You didn't find out about it until you got home after your shift and having a few drinks. You then went back to the precinct and got your gun and went looking for Joey. Who was already dead when you found him. Is that right so far?"

"Yes, that's right."

"When you went to your locker to get your gun, had the locker been tampered with?"

"No, I don't think so. At least, not that I noticed."

"Then the question is, how did the bullet that killed Joey come from your gun?"

"I don't know."

"Who was able to get into the locker room at the precinct?"

"Nobody, only a fellow cop."

"So you were set up."

"That's what I've been telling you all along!"

Later, back at my office as I was tapping my pen on my note pad. I tried to prepare Chaz's defense. The tapping didn't help to either calm me or to bring my mind a brilliant defense. From what I knew then, the only hope we had was for me to put enough doubt into the minds of the jury that they wouldn't find him guilty. I had to start thinking of other cop involvement as to a set up, the timing of Joey's death as to the time, Chaz was on the scene. The window of opportunity as to the time he left Hugo's bar. The most important time of all was the exact time he left the precinct, as to the time Joey died. All this had to be placed in the right order of my defense if Chaz was to have any chance at all. If I could place enough doubt in the mind of at least one juror, by casting a large shadow of doubt in the courtroom. Then maybe I could get a hung jury, and have the case dismissed. Was I hoping for to much? Was I reaching for straws? In my mind did I think that I was that good an Attorney to pull the preverbal white rabbit out of my hat and save my best friend from a life of misery.

# THE TRIAL

"All rise, The Honorable Judge Martin Lowenstein presiding. The judge entered the court room and crashed his gavel down to start the proceeding. Brooklyn District Attorney Robert Monroe addressed the jury.

"Ladies and Gentlemen, you will hear convincing evidence that Officer Charles Batista used his own Service Revolver killed fellow officer Joseph Tamborelli. Mr. Batista engaged in excessive drinking and went into a rage losing total control of himself. He left his house in a rage and hunted down Office Tamborelli and killed him at point-blank range."

Chaz screamed out, "I didn't do it! I loved Joey!"

I tried to calm Chaz down best I could. The judge's gavel crashed down.

"Order in my courtroom! Mr. Brancato, I'll have your client removed or restrained if there's one more outburst like that! This not a circus, this is a court of law!"

Before I knew it, it was my turn to address the jury with my opening statement.

"Ladies and Gentlemen, you heard the prosecuting attorney's opening statement. He omitted some facts. For example, no one witnessed the killing. Also there was no way Charles Batista could have been at the scene of the crime at the exact time of the shooting. My client is innocent and I will prove it."

As the questioning began, the district attorney called Robert Bradley to the witness stand. Mr. Bradley was sworn in.

"Is it true that you were on the same shift and working in the same precinct as Charles Batista on the night in question?"

"Yes, that's right."

"Did you go to Hugo's bar and grill after work with Charles Batista on that night?"

"Yes!"

"Were you and Mr. Batista drinking heavily?"

"We put away a few good ones."

"How was his temperament"?

I objected the question, but my objection was over ruled so the district attorney continued.

"As a trained police officer, would say Mr. Batista was out of control?"

"No, not that I was aware of."

"No more question, your honor. Your witness counselor."

I responded," I don't wish to question this witness at this time, but I reserve the right to question this witness at a later time."

The judge responded with "Request granted."

Captain Nolan was the next witness called by the district attorney. After he was sworn in, he was asked.

"Captain Nolan you had both officers, Joseph Tamborelli and Charles Batista in your command did you not?"

# THE TRIAL

"Yes that's correct."

"Did you ever have reason to expect a physical confrontation between them?"

I cut in saying, "Objection! He's asking for an opinion, not for facts."

The district attorney said, "I'll reword my question. Captain Nolan have you ever seen a physical confrontation between the two men in question?"

"Yes I have, several times. Only days before the killing of officer Joseph Tamborelli. A fight broke out in the locker room, I called both men into my office and told them it had better be the last time or I would have them transferred out of my precinct."

"No further questions, your honor."

"Your witness, Mr. Brancato."

"Your honor, I reserve the right to cross examine at a later time."

"Granted."

As the testimony continued, things came out that were not in Chaz's favor. For example, it seems that as far back as their childhood together although they were the best of friends. Chaz and Joey always got in each others face and would duke out their problems. These confrontations were always resolved and forgotten, but the district attorney was hell bent on repeating instances of this type of behavior, repeatedly for the jury's benefit.

District Attorney Monroe then called desk Sergeant O' Malley to the stand.

O'Malley was sworn in, and the district attorney began his questioning.

"You are Sergeant Patrick O'Malley?"

"Yes!"

"Were you the Desk Sergeant on the night of the murder of Officer Joseph Tamborelli?"

"Yes, I was."

"Can you tell the jury what a desk sergeant does?"

"Sure, they receive anyone who comes into the station house. They refer most visitors to the proper departments, fill out any complaints and do any other job requested of them."

"Have you worked as a desk police officer all your career?"

"No."

"Is it true that you were a street police officer at the beginning of your career? That you walked a beat, then rode in a squad car and really experienced all phases of police work?"

"Yes, that's right."

"How long have you been a police officer?"

"Nineteen years."

"Will you tell the court what happened on the night Officer Tamborelli was murdered?"

"Officer Batista came into the precinct after his shift was over. He then returned later, rushing in and said he forgot something in his locker."

"Did he say what that was?"

"No, only that it was a family matter."

"Was he drunk?"

"Well, you could see he had a few. He still had those bunny rabbit eyes."

"What does that mean, exactly?"

"His eyes were red, glassy and open like slits."

# THE TRIAL

"Was he cognizant of his actions?"

"He seemed to me to be aware of what he was doing."

"What was his temperament?"

"He was upset. I guess he got what he wanted because, after going into the locker room he came out and left in a hurry."

"No further question, your Honor."

"Your witness, Mr. Brancato."

"No questions at this time your Honor. I reserve the right to bring this witness back at a later time."

"Request granted."

The clincher was the ballistics report, showing that the bullet that killed Joey came from Chaz's service revolver. After a week of questioning, the district attorney wrapped up his case. It was now my turn to mount my defense and get Chaz freed from the charge of second degree murder. I called Officer Michael Riley as my first witness for the defense.

"Officer Riley, you and your partner Officer James Smith were the first to arrive at the scene of Officer Tamborelli's murder?"

"Yes that's right."

"Can you remember what happened when you got out of your squad car?"

"Yes I can."

Then Officer Riley told the court exactly what happened, right up to the handcuffing of Chaz and the reading of his rights.

"Did you reach for Officer Batista's service revolver?"

"Yes."

"How did you pick up the gun?"

## JOSEPH SQUATRITO

"By the barrel."

"Was it hot?"

"No

"Was it cold?"

After a long pause, he answered. "Yes, it was."

"Do you know the exact time you arrived at the murder scene?"

"Well we got a dispatch to get to Officer Tamborelli's last location, at 3am. It took about seven minutes to get there."

"So is it reasonable to say that 3:07A.M. is the actual time or close to the actual time you arrived?"

"Yes."

"The pathologist's report states that Joseph Tamborelli died at approximately 2:30A.M. If the report is correct and Charles Batista is guilty, don't you think it's odd that Mr. Batista waited by Officer Tamborelli's body for you to arrive and arrest him approximately 37 minutes later?"

The district attorney objected on the grounds that, I was leading my witness.

The judge ordered the last part of my question, struck from the record and said. "Mr. Brancato, please rephrase your question."

"In your experience on the police force, have you ever come across or heard of a murderer remaining at the scene of the crime for more than a half hour until the police arrive?"

"Not that I can recall or heard of."

I felt I had scored some points and I was going to hammer this fact home by asking several other related questions, but the judge interrupted me before I could continue and the momentum was lost. He said, "We will recess until one o'clock."

# THE TRIAL

During the break, I pleaded with Chaz to let me put Theresa on the stand.

He replied with an absolute, "NO WAY!"

"Chaz we may have to. She's the only one who can make the jury believe you're not a violent man and that even though you and Joey got physical when you argued, it was more like horseplay. She could tell the jury that you and Joey always made up and were truly the best of friends with each other."

"I said, No Way. If she can't face me, she doesn't believe in me. She's not here to support me, is she? It's obvious she thinks I killed her brother. I guess, in her case blood is thicker than water!"

"Chaz, you're just not thinking straight. You're not letting me help you."

"I said no, and I mean it. Don't push it or I'll get another lawyer!"

As I left the holding cell to go back to the court room, I started to think this might be a lost cause.

At 1o'clock the trial was resumed and I call Officer James Smith, my first witness of the afternoon. After he was sworn in I continued with my questions.

"Officer Smith you are Michael Riley's partner are you not?"

"Yes, that's right."

"When you arrived at the crime scene, did you recognize Officer Batista right away?"

"No, not until he spoke."

"You've been a trained police officer for fifteen years, haven't you?"

"Yes, I have."

## JOSEPH SQUATRITO

"In all your fifteen years of experience on the force, have you ever been at a crime scene before?"

"Yes, many times."

"Do you think Officer Batista was acting like a man who had just committed murder?"

"I don't think so. He was calm even though he was crying, I mean."

District Attorney Monroe objected, "This is not fact he is leading the witness for an opinion."

The judge overruled saying, "Please continue Officer Smith."

"I mean he wasn't in a state of panic. It seemed he was ready to defend himself, but not against us. He stated our names and acknowledged himself to us, even though he stared into a very dark area as if he expected someone to show them self."

"No further question your honor."

I was so busy concentrating on what Officer Smith said that I almost jumped when the judge smashed down his gavel, saying.

"Court will resume tomorrow at 10A.M.

I came face to face with District Attorney Monroe as I was leaving the court house, he said.

"Your boy is going down and you know it!"

"Is that why you only went for Murder Two? You made it easy on yourself."

"That's where your wrong. The newspapers are having a field day with this Good Cop, Bad Cop bullshit. The City needs to have this over and done with."

"Bob, I'm going to give you the fight of your life. You can count on it!"

# THE TRIAL

"I wouldn't want it any other way."

The next day my first thoughts were to address the physical confrontations between Chaz and Joey. The district attorney had brought up a good point by establishing the previous physical fights between the two men. It was up to me to explain this type of behavior, to put enough doubt in the jurors' minds. Understanding these skirmishes were not a major issue.

"Your Honor, I call Captain Nolan to the stand."

He was reminded that he had been previously sworn in and that he was still under oath. I said.

"Captain Nolan, earlier you told the jury that you had reprimanded both Charles Batista and Joseph Tamborelli for fighting?"

"Yes that's correct."

"Did you do that immediately after the fight?"

"Yes."

"Did you witness the actual fight?"

"Well, sort of. I was walking past the locker room when I heard the commotion. I entered and yelled, Break it up you two."

"What happened next?"

"They were pulled apart and I called them into my office where I reprimanded them, by telling them this was the last time I wanted to see this ever again!"

"Was there blood?"

"What do you mean?"

"Blood, was either of them bleeding?"

"No."

"You mean two big strong men went at each other and one was bleeding?"

"It was more like wrestling."

"What exactly did you see before you yelled. Break it up?"

"Batista had Tamborelli in a headlock."

"So, would it be safe to say that when they got physical it was more of a pushing and shoving match. Rather than a punching, kicking, 'biting' type of fight?"

"I can't really say."

"I can. I've sen it all my life."

"Objection your Honor!"

Judge Lowenstein interjected, "Mr. Brancato approach the bench."

He covered his microphone with his hand and said.

"Another stunt like that and I'll hold you in contempt." Then he turned to the jury and said.

"Jurors, please disregard Mr. Brancato's last statement. It will be stricken from the record. Now Mr. Brancato you may continue."

"No more questions, Your Honor."

"Call your next witness."

"I recall Officer Smith."

As Officer Smith entered the witness stand, he was reminded that he was still under oath.

"Officer Smith, I have just a few questions that I didn't get to yesterday. Have you ever heard of a murder suspect waiting thirty minutes or more, for the police to arrive?"

"No sir, never. I mean the murderer is long gone by the time we arrive on the crime scene."

"Objection. That's opinion, Your Honor."

"Please Your Honor, I said. As a professional police officer, Officer Smith's opinion is most certainly valid."

# THE TRIAL

The judge said, "I'll let it stand. Objection overruled."

I turned back to Officer Smith and took a few a moments to collect my thoughts.

"Officer Smith did you handle Officer Batista's service revolver?"

"No, but my partner picked it up from the barrel. It wasn't hot so we bagged it as evidence."

"Did you know that the gun was fully loaded and that five of the bullets had Officer Batista's fingerprints on them, but the sixth bullet was wiped clean. No prints what so ever, clean!"

"Not at the time, but I know it now."

"As a professional Police Officer, don't you find this odd? I mean how many times have you heard of a murderer reloading his gun with a bullet he wiped clean after he shot someone to death?"

"Never, not to my knowledge as a professional police officer."

"That's all Officer Smith, you can step down now."

After weeks of back and forth testimony, the day came for the District Attorney to call Chaz to the stand. Chaz was totally dejected. The fact that Theresa had not come to the trial caused him to fall into a deep depression. It was as if he hadn't heard a word that was spoken, pro or con during the trial. As he walked to the witness stand, the strain was etched on his face. His attention focused on the rear doors as he was sworn in. Now with this new vantage point, he could watch for the miracle he hoped for. All he wanted was for Theresa to walk though those doors and be at his side.

"Do you swear to tell the truth the whole truth and nothing but the truth, so help you God!"

"I do."

"State your name, for the court."

"Charles Batista.

The district attorney stated his first question, but Chaz didn't answer he just keep looking towards the rear doors. The district attorney repeated his question.

"Were you drinking on the night in question?"

"Yes I was drinking."

"Did you in a rage, go looking for Joseph Tamborelli?"

"Yes, I went looking for my brother-in-law."

"Did you find him alive?"

"No, I never located him. Alive!"

"Didn't you go from your home to the precinct to get the service revolver you earlier left in your locker because you knew you'd be drinking that night?"

"Yes I went to the precinct and got my weapon."

"Did you fire your service revolver that day?"

"Yes, I qualified on the range that morning."

"You admit that you fired your gun on the day of the murder?"

"Well yes, I did fire my weapon but only on the firing range that morning and at no other time that day or night. I didn't kill Joey."

"No further question, Your Honor."

It was now my turn to question Chaz. I could see it was taking ever ounce of his strength to stay focused. As I walked towards the witness stand, I decided to approach the bench and ask for a side bar.

# THE TRIAL

"What's the problem, Counselor?" The Judge asked and motioned for the district attorney to join us.

"Your Honor, I just want you to be aware of my client's state of mind. Under the circumstances, I would appreciate the court's gracious understanding if I take a little more time with the questions."

"I'll allow you some leeway on this, but don't get carried away and abuse our understanding."

"Thank you, your Honor."

I turned to Chaz and slowly began my questions." Mr.Batista, did you always leave your service weapon in your locker?"

"No."

"Why now?"

"Paranoia."

"Can you be more explicit?"

"My oldest daughter, Lenore began to take an interest in my revolver.

"Will you explain to the court what you mean by, an interest?"

"She would ask why I wore a gun and she would ask if she could touch it. She ask if she could have one of her own to play with. I learned at the Academy that good habits and prevention techniques are worth their weight in gold. So as a preventive measure, I started to make a habit of leaving my gun in my locker after my shift was over. I was afraid of getting careless or lazy when coming home after a few drinks and maybe leaving my gun on the nightstand. I use to do that before the girls were born, my wife Theresa and I decided that there should be no guns in the house. Loaded or unloaded."

"You said you fired your gun that morning, on the firing range?"

"Yes."

"And you didn't fire it afterwards at any time of day?"

"That's right."

"You loaded your gun yourself after qualifying?"

"Yes."

"Did you load five bullets with your bare hands and one bullet with glove on? I ask this because the lab report states five bullets were found to have your fingerprints on them, but the one bullet left in your gun was completely clean and had no fingerprints on it."

"I loaded all six bullets with my bare hands. I used no gloves!"

"Mr. Batista, did you go looking for Office Tamborelli to kill him?"

"No, never!"

"Then can you explain why you went back to the station house locker room to get your service revolver?"

"I remember Joey, Officer Tamborelli was on assignment down in Gramercy, in the warehouse section of the docks. It's a very bad place at night. It's well known as a hangout for gangs and drug dealers. There are many burglaries, rapes and even murders there."

"So you feared for your life?"

"Yes, an unarmed cop looking for an undercover cop that might not want to be found could be inviting trouble. Big time trouble, being down in that area at night without fire power is like playing Russian Roulette."

"What were you going to do, if you found Officer Tamborelli that night?"

# THE TRIAL

"Have one of our usual face to face screaming matches like we'd always had ever since we were kids. Joey and I knocked each other around occasionally to make a point stick. It was our way of saying that whatever it was should never happen again. It wasn't what it looked like to other people. We never hurt each other physically. It was more like making a statement and getting it off our chest and when it was over it was over. There's never any hard feelings. It was just one to one, man to man."

"Then you, didn't go there to kill him?"

"No, killing Joey never entered my mind."

"No further questions, Your Honor."

I walked back to my table and hoped I had put enough doubt in the minds of the jurors to prevent a guilty verdict. The trial ended with the summations. District Attorney Monroe spoke first.

"Ladies and Gentlemen of the jury, I know we have shown without question that Charles Batista is guilty. You have heard sworn testimony from each witness proving his guilt. First, you heard how Mr. Batista was drinking excessively the night of the murder, his on going rage when he left his home looking for Officer Tamborelli. Second how he went back to the station house locker room to get his service revolver. Third how he was found in a pool of blood at the scene of the crime when police apprehended him and read him his rights. Last and most important, ballistics experts conforming that the bullet that killed Officer Joseph Tamborelli came from the service revolver of Charles Batista. I ask you, do you need any more evidence? I don't think so, if you examine the evidence, the facts you will see clearly that there is no other verdict you can return but. Guilty!"

Even though I believed my client was innocent, inwardly I agreed with my distinguished opponent. On the evidence presented guilty was the only verdict the jury could possibly bring in. I hope in my heart I was wrong but my gut told me other wise. Still I was going to give the summation of my life, I would present it with as much fervor as I could muster.

Ladies and Gentlemen of the jury, you have heard District Attorney Monroe tell you that my client is guilty, beyond a shadow of a doubt. He failed to tell you all the facts. He omitted the very important fact that the window of opportunity, in which my client could have committed the murder does not coincide with the coroner's stated time of Officer Tamborelli's death. The coroner stated that the murder took place at least one half hour before Charles Batista was first found at the scene, cradling his best friend and brother-in-law's body. I ask you, what murder waits for over a half hour with his victim so he can be arrested? No, one's testimony stated they saw Charles Batista pull the trigger because no one saw the shooting. You heard a bullet in the barrel of his gun was wiped clean. Why! Because the person who replaced the bullet could not and would not leave his fingerprints. The answer to all these questions can only tell you that the verdict you must bring in is. NOT GUILTY!"

As I walked backed to my seat, I drew a heavy breath in my heart the ache was for Chaz. Did I do enough to win or were the cards stacked against us right from the beginning. It's not as if I didn't give it my all, but I was hampered

# THE TRIAL

by Chaz's refusal to have Theresa testify. For me it seemed even more terrible, Chaz was my best friend and his life was on the line.

The jury deliberated for a short time. When I was called back into the court room I knew this was not a good sign. If I had gotten to even one juror and put a doubt in their mind they would not have been able to bring in the verdict this quickly. The jury foreman gave the verdict to the court officer who handed it to the judge. He read it to himself, handed it back and said.

"Have reached a verdict?"

"The jury foreman said. "Yes, we have, we find the defendant Charles Batista. GUILTY, of second degree murder.

He was later sentenced to a prison term of fourteen to twenty-five years in Attica, New York State Penitentiary.

He was taken from the courthouse to Rykers Island to begin his life in prison. It took me months of hard work to try to find an exchange state for Chaz. This was not a federal incarceration, where I could get him sent anywhere in the continental United States. No, this was a New York State problem. There was no governor in any state who was willing to take this problem into his own prison system. So after months of trying to a void it, Chaz was shipped off to Attica, the hellhole of New York State. Housing the worst collection of killers, drug dealers, robbers and mobsters.

In all the time that had passed since the night Joey was murdered, Chaz never heard a single word from his beloved Theresa. To Chaz that was more painful than anything he was about to endure in Attica. He agonized over what his two beautiful daughters, Lenore and Ashley would think of their father. Would they forget about him? He didn't know how he would endure his life without them. He maintained the will to live so that when he was free, he could be reunited with them and explain to them what really happened.

On Sept 9th 1971 there was a riot at Attica State Prison, 2200 inmates took over the prison for four days. The riot was sparked by a guard being punched the day before. The next day a guard was hit on the head setting off a change of events and a full scale riot broke out. The prisoners took 33 staff members hostage and dozens of guards. The appalling conditions in the prison believed to be the direct negligence of Warden Vincent Mancusi. The prisoners listed as their complaints bad food, poor medical conditions, filthy cells, beatings and unwarranted solitary confinement. The prisoners wanted Mancusi fired but Governor Nelson Rockefeller stood firm against this demand, and ordered 1000 State Police to storm the prison and take it back no matter what the cost.

As a direct result of these actions 9 Hostages, 10 Guards and 28 Prisoners were killed. Mancusi was made superintendent and another warden took his place, but the fear of another riot was on the minds of the correctional department.

By the time Chaz boarded the bus to Attica things were much better for the prisoners. The bus ride from New York City to upstate New York took hours, but to Chaz it seemed like days. He knew that because he was a former police officer and a cop killer and he'd be a marked man. Staying alive there would take an angel on his shoulder or the hand of God, himself. Chaz could only image that the worst of times lay before him. It occurred to him that he might even have to commit murder just to earn the respect of the other inmates. By the time the bus arrived at Attica, the buzz among the guards was that a cop killer was coming in. Chaz had a reputation even before he got to Attica. Quite a few guards were talking about showing the cop killer a few lessons when a cop killer breaks the rules! So Chaz had his back to the wall even before he was put in general prison population. He had endured great pain at Rykers Island, thinking about Theresa and his daughters. At Attica, he was introduced to something he never could have dreamed of, even in his wildest nightmares.

He became a one man island, for an indefinite stretch of time. He figured the guards were already plotting against him before he even got off the bus, and he wondered what the cons would have in store for him.

When Chaz got to Attica, he had a private meeting with the warden and the captain of the guards. They informed him that there was a leak about his arrival and that he was already known as a former N.Y.P.D. cop as well as a cop killer. The warden decided that, under the circumstances Chaz should be put in a private cell in an area away from the general population. He told Chaz that it would be the best way and maybe the only way to ensure his survival. So Chaz was put in a solitary situation until some time in the future when the warden felt the issue was defused. Chaz responded," I only want to do my time and stay out of trouble. If I have to be alone, that's fine with me. Anyway, I've got my own private hell raging in my head. You won't get any trouble from me."

So he was led away to begin his time in solitary. The warden at Attica was fearful after the riot that having an ex-police officer, cop' killer in his penitentiary would ignite a new situation and possibly a new riot. His number one concern was to keep Charles Batista under wraps.

He instructed all his guards to keep Batista under wraps far away from all other inmates even if it meant giving him preferential treatment. He said, "I don't care if you don't like it, just do it! I will not have another riot like the one we had in 1971. Not while I'm the warden here!" So Chaz began his undeserved sentence. The first night in his cell, he dreamed of Joey. He hadn't dreamed of Joey since the trial began then it was only Theresa that had his thoughts day and night. In his dream Joey said to him, "Don't worry I'll look after you, I know you didn't do it. I'll protect you while your here."

As he woke from his dream, Chaz would have sworn that Joey was right there in his cell. Even though he was still in a sleep daze he could see Joey, he even reached out to touch him.

"My God, I must be losing my mind."

As time wore on, Chaz learned to look forward to his dreams. They were his only companions. His bitterness melted and his love for Theresa and his daughters Lenore and Ashley grew in his heart as each day passed. His love and his dreams got him through each day. He was able to get a tape of the Roy Orbison song, "In Dreams." He played it repeatedly until he knew every word and phrasing so he could sing it to himself anytime or anywhere. In the afternoon, each day he ran in a private courtyard to exercise and keep fit. The guards would hear him sing, "In dreams I walk with you

In dreams I talk to you

# THE TRIAL

In dreams your mine
All of the time. I'm with you
Ever in dreams, in dreams
And just before the dawn
I awake to find you gone

It seemed that Joey had given Chaz back the one thing that would get him through his time, and that was his love for Theresa, Lenore and Ashley.

Almost a year had passed since Chaz first step foot in Attica. I made the drive up to see him with maybe some good news but certainly some bad news. The guards brought me to an old area and told me that's where Chaz was kept for his own safety. I was brought to and empty room with a door at each side and a table with two chairs in the center with an over head light.

I waited for Chaz to enter, when he did he was very glad to see me. Little did I realize I was the only person other than the guards he had seen in almost a year." Sal I can't tell you how good it is to see you, tell me about my girls."

"Chaz I've requested an appeal to a higher court for a new trial." "Sally, you tried your best, you were right I didn't help my own cause by not letting you putting Theresa on the stand. I just can't go through that again so just let it be, leave it alone.

"Chaz I didn't come hear just to tell you about the appeal. I have some bad news."

"Is everything okay with my girls?"

"Yes, the girls are fine, but Theresa wants a divorce. She says she wants to go on with her life, not only for herself but for the sake of the girls."

"Does she still think I killed Joey?"

"I don't think so, but it's hard to know because she doesn't talk about it. All she said was that the past is the past and that she has to get on with her life."

The look on his face told me that he understood. I felt he and Theresa had put away the anger and hurt towards each other and were simply resigned to look to the future. So Chaz signed the papers I had brought with me, freeing Theresa from their marriage. Then he said, "Sal, deliver one message for me. Just tell her I still love her and my girls, someday I'll get out of here and right the wrong we've all had to endure."

I turned to Chaz as I started to leave. "Remember, I'll always be on your side no matter what, no matter where."

With a half smile on his face he said. "I know. All for one and one for all you, me and Joey forever."

I walk away without letting him see the tears in my eyes, but on the drive back to New York City I had to pull over to the side of the road. I was emotionally drained after being the one to bring the bad news of the divorce. Leaving him there brought tears from my eyes, he was my best friend and I was helpless, frustrated and scared for him. Here I was free, I couldn't even imagine what he must be going through. He had lost his freedom for a crime I know he didn't commit, lost his best friend and brother-in-law and now his wife and two daughters. I only hoped that this divorce would not throw him into a deep depression. Could there be, or would, there be light at the end of the tunnel for Chaz only time would tell.

As the weeks and months passed, I learned that Michael Cavanaugh had moved in with Theresa and her daughters. I knew that Michael was a rat, but to stoop so low

# THE TRIAL

against one of his supposed best friends was way beyond me. If Chaz found out about this, it might push him over the edge. I knew that Michael was a charmer and that he was giving Theresa the comfort and strength she needed, I knew she was vulnerable. I wanted to warn her but she was an adult and capable of making her own decisions. My only concern was for Chaz, so I didn't pay much attention to what went on with her life with Michael. They were not the kind of people I wanted to be friends with anymore. I had lost all my respect for Theresa after what she had done to Chaz and especially after her choice to live with Michael.

As far as Michael was concerned he could drop dead, the rat fuck! I was beginning to see him for what he was, I remembered some of the bad things that had been said about him. Maybe they were all true. Joey had always warned us that Michael was a slime ball. I began to think that maybe I should have looked into Michael's closet for some evidence that might have helped to get Chaz a verdict of not guilty. I had no idea what I would have found, but I was having strong feelings something was there. Maybe I was barking up the wrong tree, but if you looked for who would benefit the most from Joey's death and from Chaz's prison sentence, things pointed to Michael.

It had always been rumored that Michael had the hots for Theresa, and that he had them big time! The gang all knew that what Michael wanted, he wanted no matter who got hurt. Was he really capable of murder? I began to wonder if I was going off the deep end. Was my mind running away with it's self? Was I beginning to lose it, or had the light bulb finally gone off in my head? Chaz was going to be in Attica for who knows how many years,

## JOSEPH SQUATRITO

I decided to go on a quest. If Michael even spit in the wrong direction, I wanted to know about it. I was going to keep both eyes on him for as long as it would take. A year later, when all the paperwork was final, Theresa and Michael were married. The memory of Chaz had faded from the minds of his two daughters and they soon started to refer to Michael as "Daddy." Theresa began to think her life was again back on track. Her children had stability and someone to look up to. She had a man who loved her and made her feel alive, the sex was great again and they had no money problems. Theresa started a new career in nursing.

Although she could never forget her brother Joey or her ex-husband Chaz, she no longer dwelt on her memories of them. The pain was behind her and God had given her a second chance for happiness. She was determined to make the best of it for herself and for her girls.

After more than a year of solitary confinement after his divorce, Chaz started to signs of cracking up. Even his songs weren't working anymore. His singing turned to babbling. He wasn't sleeping or exercising and he stopped his normal daily routine. The prison guards talked to each other about his behavior. At the end of his shift the captain of the prison guards stopped in at the warden's office. Captain Sam Jenkins had worked at Attica for over twenty years and was well liked by the inmates as well as the guards under his command. He was known as a fair and honest man who always gave you help if needed. He was not one of the Guards taken hostage during the riots and he was the only one the inmates would talk to during the negotiations. That's how well respected he is and the new warden did not have much experience behind him. The receptionist informed the warden.

"Captain Jenkins needs to talk with you, he says all he needs is five minutes of your time."

"All right send him in."

Captain Jenkins stood at attention after entering the wardens inner office. Warden Stankowitz was seated behind his desk attending to piles of paperwork. He looked up and said," What's so urgent Captain? I'm very busy here."

"Sorry to bother you sir, but it's about inmate Batista."

"Yes, what about him?"

"Sir I've been here for over twenty years, as you well know. In all that time no one has ever been in solitary confinement as long as he has. He's losing it big time."

"Well, what do you want me to do? If I send him into the general population, how long do you think he'll last before they kill him? Remember he's an ex-police officer from New York City. How many of those inmates are here because he personally arrested them. Every gang will be fighting to get their hands on him, do you want another riot on your hands, I don't think so."

"Sir he won't last much longer in solitary. Maybe we can work him into a controlled environment. He's really not a bad guy, he gives us absolutely, no problems and he does what he's told to do. Cell bock A has single bed cells all the inmates are not lifers most are on a short term until they get released."

After a long pause, the warden said," Okay let's try it. You take charge of what ever you think will work, but if you screw this up. I'll have your ass in a sling!"

"Thank you sir, I'll get on it tomorrow."

## JOSEPH SQUATRITO

As Captain Jenkins left the warden's office, he hoped that he had't bitten off more than he could chew. He thought to himself, "I keep getting this feeling about Batista. Somewhere deep inside, something tells me he got a raw deal. I keep hearing this voice in my head every time I look into his eyes, saying that this guy is innocent. Maybe I'm crazy, not him but this gut feeling just won't leave me. So now it's up to me to shoulder the burden. Late at night when I'm sleeping I swear I see someone, or something is telling me to help this guy. I'm starting to think I'm possessed!"

The next morning at breakfast he told his wife, "I'm starting to have the strangest dreams. I can't really pinpoint exactly how it happens, but I keep hearing someone telling me to help one of the inmates."

"Your just working to hard Sam, you need a vacation. We all need a vacation from this town."

"Maybe your right, I have to go in early and catch up on some paperwork. I'll see you tonight."

When he got into work, he called a meeting the prison guards working the early shift in solitary. He told them that inmate Batista was going to be worked in with some of the inmates in the general population of cell block A. He wanted them to select the less violent ones with the shortest time remaining before their release. His next statement he stressed with most concern saying," We'll watch the group very closely to make sure Batista isn't SHANKED!" (the prison term for stabbed to death)

Chaz's first day with the other inmates started with breakfast. He was told to sit at the last table in the main dining room, with his back to the wall. An armed guard stood at his side. Chaz started eating his food without looking up from his plate. The other cons started asking questions, one inmate at the next table yelled out," Hey #463920, did you kill the Pope?"

Another said, "Man you must rate to have your own personal guard!"

"I never killed anyone."

"Yeah and I'm "Mary Poppins!"

It seemed that none of the other cons recognized him as a New York Cop that killed a fellow officer. He got through breakfast, the next part of the journey was mingling with the cons in the yard. He was restricted to a small area for recreation and he was allowed to shoot baskets in a well guarded isolated basketball hoop. Another wisecracking con had something to yell out to Chaz. He answered by yelling back, "I'm just trying to get through the day" and so it went. Chaz was beginning to get a new chance at life. When the siren sounded yard time was over and everyone moved inside, Chaz was last to enter cell block A. Captain Jenkins stopped him and asked, "How do you like your new surroundings, are you getting along with the other cons? Everything okay?"

"Yes Captain, it's much better."

Chaz was unaware that it was Captain Jenkins that went to bat for him.

"Captain, I only want to do my time and not give anyone any trouble."

"I know, we all want that."

With that, Chaz was locked up for the night. Captain Jenkins reported to the warden that everything was going well and that each day they would give inmate Batista a little longer leash. Always keeping a close eye and a strong watch on him day and night. Jenkins knew that the more Chaz was allowed to mingle, the greater the chance of him being recognized as a former police officer. Eventually one of the cons would make the connection. Attica was composed of an underground world filled with networks of gangs based on color, ethnic background, social levels, drugs, homosexuality, physical strength and the ability to kill to prove a point. Then one day the embodiment of 'Captain Jenkins' fear crawled out from under a rock, and it was a fellow guard who leaked out the information that Batista was a N.Y.P.D. pig. It was like a spark on dry tinder, it flared into a full flame in the prison yard." Where going to off a pig, pass the word a pig goes down." Rosco ( the snake) Ortiz went to Captain Jenkins looking for special favoritism in exchange for some very hot info. Captain Jenkins replied, "Give it up Ortiz and I'll tell you if it's worth what your asking for."

"No deal. You give me your word that I get light duty, extra smokes and some free time with my girl when she comes to visit. If my info isn't good enough to warrant what I am asking for, you can put me in the hole."

"Ortiz I can put you in the hole any time I want."

"No, because you're one of the good guys. You would do that."

"Stop fucking with me, you're starting to piss me off!"

"Okay, I'll trust you, everyone knows Bastia is an ex-cop from New York City. He's a dead man, and the word was given out by one of your own men.

"Who talked?"

"That I don't know, I swear."

# THE TRIAL

"You know everything, now tell me who talked and I'll give you a free cell to play in when your girl comes next month. You can fuck her brains out, get a blow job what ever so talk!"

"I truly don't know. Me telling you this I could be a dead man."

Captain Jenkins could not believe what he had just heard. One of his own men had just stabbed him in the back and he was determined to fine out who it was. He went to one of his own stoolie's, Carl (the ratman) Barkley to confirm the information. Ratman said, "I was just going to come and tell you myself, I swear boss, I swear."

Jenkins knew that Batista had to go back to solitary for his own protection. He immediately located inmate Batista's whereabouts and told him about this new situation and that for his own safety he would return to solitary. There was no way to keep him safe even with an armed guard the cons would figure out a way to get to him and not knowing which one of his own guards talked who could he trust. Even God above couldn't stop this from happening. Chaz was determined not to go back to solitary confinement.

"Captain, I really appreciate your help. You truly are one of the good guys, but I can't go back to solitary. I just can't, I'll take my chances and see where the chips fall."

"Where not talking about a game here, it's your life. They're out to get you, every gang wants a piece of you. The blacks, the spics and the whites. Killing you fast would be a blessing, if they get their hands on you it will be slow and painful. Give me some time to work this out, it's my ass on the line here to. I took full responsibility for you, sorry Batista back you go. It's for everybody's good."

Chaz was lead back to solitary and Captain Jenkins went to Warden Stankowitz to inform him of the extreme situation at hand. Much to Jenkins relief the warden was quite understanding and agreed that keeping Batista alive was their first concern.

"Okay, Captain Jenkins lets see how long he can last in solitary. Maybe knowing his life is on the line will give him inner strength."

"We'll see, God knows we'll see."

"Okay keep me informed."

Jenkins left breathing a sigh of relief, because as he went in, he though his ass was grass or worse. Maybe that little voice he heard was whispering to the warden too. So Chaz started his second go around in solitary confinement. About a month later while Chaz was sitting in his cell listening to some old rock and roll tunes, Captain Jenkins informed him he had a visitor he said. "Get cleaned up, your lawyer is here and waiting for you in the visitation room." Chaz was led from his cell to ensure his safety. He entered the room saw me and a big smile appeared on his face.

"Sally, I'm real glad to see you. What brings you up to this hell hole?"

"I came to tell you that our latest request for an appeal was turned down again. I didn't want you to hear it from the warden, plus the fact he told me of your situation here. The word is out that you are an ex-cop from New York City and the gangs want to make an example of you. I'm going to report this to the prison board about the danger your in. Maybe I can get you transferred to another prison.

# THE TRIAL

"What's the sense, it will only be the same there too. Eventually someone will recognize me as an ex-cop. Sally, you can't run from who you are. Tell me how are things in the neighborhood? Have you seen my girls?"

"Okay everything 's the same. Your Mother and Father moved to Florida, I help them with all the legal necessities. The pressure got to much for them. To many memories back there, plus at there age they needed to get away from the cold and the snow.

"I know they write me all the time, I'm glad there safe and warm from the elements. I still wish I could see them but I know the trip up here would be to much for them. Still.

"Chaz, they could never see you like this, it would kill them. Don't be mad at them, maybe someday they'll surprise you."

"Yeah maybe, what about my girls."

I paused for a minute not knowing how he would react, "I ran into Theresa last week on the avenue, she was shopping with the girls. There all very well the girls have grown so, my God their beautiful. Lenore is the picture of her mother. I look at her and I swear I'm back in school with the old gang. Ashley is you man she's adorable.

"Did they ask for me?"

I shook my head, NO and didn't say a word. I couldn't, the word no, would have gotten stuck in my throat.

"Sal your the only link I have to the life I use to have back in Bensonhurst. All I ask is that you stay my friend and visit me whenever you can."

"Always Chaz, you me and Joey. Remember all for one and one for all! Just like when we were kids in school."

## JOSEPH SQUATRITO

My visitation time was over and I had to leave Chaz to face the dragons from within and the threats all around him. As I drove home I prayed for him to have the mental and physical strength to endure it all. The months passed slowly and Chaz began to show the strain of his second time in solitary confinement. One night Joey came to Chaz in a dream, it had been a long time since Chaz had felt Joey's presence and had seen him in a dream. At first, it was a flash back to the time they were kids getting into mischief. Then it was when they had been decorated police officers, being honored by the city. Chaz began to sweat profusely as the dream turned into a nightmare and he saw himself holding Joey's dead body covered in blood. He was crying and screaming for Joey not to die. In his nightmare he told Joey," Don't you leave me like this I'd rather be dead with you than live in this hell." Joey's voice in the dream said," I'm here to help you, don't worry I've fixed everything. Soon you'll be out of solitary, trust me, trust me Chaz as the voice faded away."

Days turned into weeks then months and Chaz was still in solitary, hanging loosely on Joey's words not knowing if they would ever pass. He contemplated suicide. Things looked bleak and hope was fading. In his mind if the wanted him so badly let them have me, it's better than living in this hell. Life for Chaz was not worth living any longer.

Rocko Mastori, underboss of the Sanzonni family in Brooklyn had been sent to Attica on a manslaughter charge. Rocko was a hard nose street Capo who came up through the ranks the hard way. He also had the largest crew in New York and half of them were in Attica for all sorts of crimes. So to say that he had all the muscle he needed,

# THE TRIAL

was an understatement. Before long he was in solid and controlled the drugs, black market goods, Cigarettes and corrupt guards. All the gangs took orders from Rocko or they paid the price. They knew he could reach out to get anyone on the inside or anyone's family on the outside. That's how far his word could travel. His first order of business was to find Julio Rodriquez and Felix Mendez, who were doing time for armed robbery. Rocko let them know the convenience store they attempted to rob was on his home turf.

The little girl they held hostage was his daughter. Rocko gave the order and his crew made an example of Rodriquez and Mendez by cutting their throats. He was now in complete control of all inmates. There would be no gang that would go against him. His next order of business was to let every inmate know that Chaz Batista was not to be harmed in any way. When he was asked why he told them Chaz Batista and Joey Tamborelli had saved his daughter in that holdup, they risked their lives to save her. Batista was free to move about the general population with no fear for his life. Captain Jenkins understood the inner world of the Attica inmates and was willing to except the terms. One afternoon I was sitting behind my desk when my secretary buzzed my intercom, "Mr. Brancato there's a long distance phone call for you from Attica State Prison."

"Okay Beverly, I'll take it. Hello?"
"Sal Brancato, the lawyer?"
"Yes, that's right and you are?"
"Rocko Mastori."
"What can I do for you?"

"It's what I HAVE DONE for your friend, Chaz Batista. I want you to know that everything is all right with him. As his lawyer and best friend you don't need to worry anymore. Me and my crew will be his guardian angels. From now on he'll be well protected."

"I don't quite understand, why are you doing this? He can't pay you back, he has nothing."

"He saved my daughter's life when he was on the job. I may be on the wrong side of the law, but I know this guy doesn't belong in Attica! It's my turn to pay him back, everyone in Bensonhurst knows Batista is one of the good guys. He couldn't have done it, Joey Tamborelli didn't deserve to die the way he did."

"I'm glad he has someone to watch over him. If I can ever help you, don't hesitate to call."

"In fact you can. My nephew, Alfonso Grasso is in Rykers Island waiting for a hearing on a drug charge. This kid is clean. There's no way he's guilty. There's a ring of dirty cops on the job, it's a setup to get me and my crew to look the other way while those cops cash in on the sale of drugs in Brooklyn. My turf is clean. We don't deal drugs in the neighborhood, Bensonhurst is off the map as far as drugs are concern. Take the case and get my nephew off."

You will learn a lot about your old friend Cavanaugh. Take the case."

He hung up before I could ask any more questions. I wondered if I should get involved, but I was intrigued with what I might uncover about Michael and just how did he fit in with all Rocko said.

I decided to go to see the innocent Mr. Grasso. While I was driving over to Rykers, I kept mulling over all that

# THE TRIAL

had been told to me. I had always made it a rule to refuse to take any case involving the mob, but strong forces were telling me to break the rule. I was as helpless as a fly in a spider's web and the spider was coming closer and closer. I didn't know if I was going to be drawn into a disaster or led to some answers that had eluded me for a very long time. Why couldn't I turn my back on all this? I knew Chaz was safe, but Rocko Mastori's voice had put a strange hold on me. Why on earth should I believe this known Mafia Capo? He's a convicted felon and a killer for the mob. Yet for some strange reason, I do. As I entered the Rykers Island facility, I remembered my last visit when I started working on Chaz's case. At least that time I knew my client was innocent. This time there was a good chance that I was being used. I waited with my attache' case in hand. Bells started ringing and steel doors opened and then closed behind me, as I went deeper and deeper into the bowels of hell I was led to an interrogation room. Alfonso Grasso, flanked by two guards entered from the opposite side. He and I sat down on the two chairs at a bare table. At first glance, Grasso looked like a scared punk. When he opened his mouth his arrogance emerged.

"So you're the lawyer my uncle hired to get me out of this shit hole. You better be good, cause I was set up. The bulls stopped me on a routine traffic violation and searched my car. They opened my trunk and came out with a pound of coke. No fucking way, cock suckers! They knew I was Rocko's nephew.

"So you're innocent, okay why the plant?"
"Because."

"Because why? You're not telling me everything, are you?"

He paused for a long time then he said, "You're my lawyer, right? We got client-lawyer privilege or what?"

"I'm only here because your uncle is protecting my friend in Attica."

"I don't talk unless your my attorney."

"Okay, I'm your attorney. Start talking I'm all ears."

"With my uncle in the joint. I was the go-between for his crew.

Did you know his Brooklyn turf is drug free. If the cops put enough of Uncle Rocko's crew away, we won't have the strength to keep the dealers and the gangs out of Bensonhurst, Bay Ridge and Dyker Heights. Any idea the kind of money we're talking? Cavanaugh is behind it all, with his own private crew. On the streets they're known as the "Boys in Blue Crew" dope, porn, shakedowns they do it all.

"Can you prove it? Have you any evidence?"

"Of course not, but that don't mean it's not true."

"Okay, you have my full attention. I'll take your case, I'll start working on getting bail so you can get out of here. Now get me some evidence against Cavanaugh."

We shook hands and I left. I realized that the spider's web in which I was entangled, was getting tighter and more dangerous. Not only was I defending a 'mob related' character, but also now it looked like I might be up against dirty cops. The next day, I called the District Attorney's office and asked for Robert Monroe. His secretary said he was out of the office until the afternoon. She took my name and number and promised to have him return my call later when he got back. About two o'clock my phone rang and D.A. Monroe was on the other end.

"Salvatore Brancato, what's so urgent that I have to return your call?"

"I just want to let you know that I've taken the Alfonso Grasso case."

"Since when have you lowered yourself into taking wanna-be-punks for clients? I could understand Batista, but Grasso! I thought better of you."

"Everybody deserves a defense. Can we talk about it?"

"Sure, come to my office tomorrow morning about ten thirty."

"Thanks, I'll be there on time see you then.

So there I was at ten thirty in the morning, standing in front of the receptionist's desk.

"Salvatore Brancato to see Robert Monroe."

She reached for the intercom and said, "Mr. Monroe, your ten thirty appointment is here.

After a short pause, I was instructed to go right in. D.A. Monroe was all business. He looked up from behind his desk, stood up and offered me his hand.

"What can I do for you, Brancato?"

"You know Grasso was set up."

"Really?"

"You have some dirty cops involved."

"Have you got proof of this?"

"I'm working on it, believe me. I'm working on it."

"I was going to let one of my assistants handle this case, but you're making it a personal slap in the face. I think I'll handle this case myself. See you in court, counselor. This conversation is over."

## JOSEPH SQUATRITO

As I rode down in the elevator I thought that maybe I shouldn't have tipped my hand, it will certainly give him thoughts provoking. If he's as honest as everyone thinks he is, he may start his own investigation. Maybe between us we can nail Michael Cavanaugh's ass to the wall, and if he's not honest... My thoughts were interrupted when the elevator reached the lobby. The doors opened and everyone started to rush out before the new passengers pushed their way in. I walked out onto the sidewalk, looked up and stared at the sky. I started thinking the spider was spinning his web faster and faster and I was caught like a helpless fly, with no escape. I walked to the lot where my car was parked. My mind whirled with questions about what I had just done." What if Monroe is a little dirty, with a few skeletons in his closet. Would he bend the rules to protect a few high ranking police officials? Everyone has a few pay backs they must submit to. Every District Attorney makes deals, who's to say there isn't a skeleton or two he's trying to hide. The next day I was in court appearing before Judge Harvey Stone, and successfully arranging for bail for Alfonso Grasso. Getting him out of Rykers Island was the first step. The next was preparing for his defense, and that would not be so easy. On the drive back from Rykers Island Correctional Prison to Brooklyn I told him, "Let your uncle know you're out and I'm on the case. Remind him of Chaz Batista's good health and long incarceration. I want you in my office tomorrow at eleven so we can review the whole case. Don't keep me waiting." Now all I had to do was prove what was theory, is fact. That this was a setup just to get control of Rocko's turf. The next day Grasso was on time, at least he was cooperating and showing me he wasn't the punk I first took him for.

"Okay tell me what happened, where it happened and why."

"I was stopped around 76th street, as I was driving my car on 18th avenue. I don't know why I was stopped."

"Were you speeding or driving recklessly?"

"No, no way."

"You're telling me that they stopped you for no apparent reason?"

"Yes. I looked up at my mirror because the flashing red lights caught my eye. I pull over to the right and stopped. A patrol car stopped behind me, two cops got out one comes over to my side of the car. I rolled down the window and ask what's wrong? He ignores me and asks for my driver's license and looks it over. His partner says. "you've got a broken tail light."

Then I said, what the fuck are you talking about? I just washed the car by hand, myself there's no broken tail light." Then he said," Get out of the car." "I knew I was screwed, I got out of the car and he said," Open the trunk." I told him there was nothing there but a tire and a jack, he looks around and fines nothing but with the trunk opened I can't see inside the car. The cop in the back with me yells look under the seats. I tell him I'm clean, what's going on. The other cop comes out with a small white package.

"What have we got here?"

He tosses it underhand to me aiming at my face, so I catch it out of reflex. Then they bend me over the hood and read me my rights as they put their hand cuffs on me.

Before I know it more cops show up, and I end up in Rykers until you show up and got me out."

"What time of day was it?"

"Afternoon. I don't know maybe two or three o'clock."

"Were you changing lanes?"

"No. I was stopped for a red light."

"Were you high."

"At two in the afternoon."

"You weren't stoned?"

"I don't do drugs."

"Are you involved in your uncle's crew?"

"I just keep him in formed as to daily activity. Nothing heavy."

"How do you live?"

"What do you mean?"

"How do you earn a living? Where do you live

"I live with my mom and dad and I work for my uncle Joe. He owns a die-cutting factory, I'm a sales rep."

"Okay, Grasso that's enough for today. Keep your nose clean, your walking on thin ice until the trial. Don't fall through, no clubs, no booze, no crew members, nothing! Go to work and stay home. Do we have an understanding here?"

"Yes, I get the message nothing stupid."

After he left, I started to go over what he said to determine my defense. I decided to walk down 18th avenue the next day and see if anyone saw or knew what had happened. Maybe somebody would have a conflicting story. After a week of investigating and questioning I couldn't turn up any supporting help. It seemed that no one saw much of anything.

# THE TRIAL

The owner of the fruit and vegetable store on the corner was in Florida, on vacation. He wouldn't be back for about a month according to his daughter who was running the store until her parents returned. She had nothing to add, she didn't see anything because she always worked inside. Her father always worked outside, picking over the produce and stacking them as he had done for the past thirty years. She said, "he loves to talk with the customers in the neighborhood and he knew everybody." I was sure I'd have enough time to talk to him when he returned. A trial date had not yet been set, so I decided to wait until the time was right and then return to question him. My assistant brought me a copy of the arrest report, it was very interesting. The arresting officer was Dan Fields, Chaz Batista's last partner and Michael Cavanaugh's new best friend. Could Michael be behind it all? So why arrest Grasso, didn't make sense. There had to be more to it. I knew I wasn't seeing the big picture at that point. It was time to buy a few street rats for the inside scoop.

After weeks of payouts, the street rats began to paint a new picture. A group of cops and a few high-ranking detectives had made a deal with a Colombian Drug Kingpin, Carlos Mendez. He was the cousin of Felix Mendez, who had been killed by Rocko Mastori in Attica. The deal was that Carlos would get forty percent of all street action and Bensonhurst would be his. The plan was simple, the cops would take Mastori's crew off the streets because after all, Mastori's boys were the bad guys. With them off the streets, the door was open for Mendez's men to start pushing drugs while the cops would look the other way. Millions would be made, it was a sweet deal. Mastori still had enough crew members out there to put up a good fight. By arresting Grasso, they sent a message to Rocko. They were going after his whole family. They were going to get personal. My main objective was to make sure I got Grassso off. What happened on the streets was out of my control. Two days later, I received a phone call from Attica, it was Rocko, thanking me for taking the case to help his nephew. I reminded him about keeping his word to protect Chaz Batista.

A week later, Alfonso Grasso and I appeared before Judge Harvey Stone. Once again. I faced off with Brooklyn District Attorney Robert Monroe. The judge informed us that the trial date was set to begin in four weeks, with a jury selection to begin in three weeks. The judge turned to the D.A. "Mr. Monroe, having you prosecute this case is not going to turn my court into a circus, is it?"

"No Judge I hope not."

"Lets see that it doesn't. Perhaps you might like to assign an Assistant D.A. to the case."

"Yes, your Honor, if it better suits the court."

"I think it does. You're both dismissed."

As we left the courthouse, I turned to Grasso and said," We just lucked out. I think we can mount a stronger defense against an assistant D.A. who's a less experienced prosecutor."

Before I knew it, the jurors were being selected and I still didn't hve a strong defense. I decided to return to 18th avenue in Bensonhurst to interview Luigi Ponterri, the owner of the 18th avenue produce store. I hoped he had returned from his Florida vacation. Maybe he saw something on the day Grasso was arrested, that could help our defense. Since Luigi had been a merchant in Bensonhurst for over thirty years, he knew my family and he remembered me from the time I was a kid, so he was quite willing to help. We talked about the day in question and when we were finished, I told him I would have to subpoena him to appear in court to testify about what he saw.

I was worried that he might be afraid to appear, but his response was simple, "The truth is the truth." He said as he shook my hand good by.

The trial began with Assistant District Attorney Louis Johnson's address to the jury. Then I gave mine. Fortunately Johnson did not mention Grasso's family ties to the mob. He discredited his character by informing the jury of his police record which contained charges of bookmaking, drunk driving and a bar room brawl all minor offenses. He now faced a drug charge, the police said that they found enough cocaine in his possession to mark him as a dealer. The maximum sentence for this was twenty years in Attica.

Officer Dan Fields gave his testimony concerning the arrest. He explained that he had a broken tail light warranted the pull over. In his opinion he looked stoned, so they searched the car and found the cocaine. They read Grasso his rights and cuffed him.

When the Assistant D.A. Johnson was finished, I called my only witness Luigi Ponterri and he was sworn in. I started to question my star witness, "Mr.Ponterri you are an Italian-American and a nationalized American citizen, are you not.

"Yes!"

"Please speak louder Mr. Ponterri, so the court stenographer can hear your answers."

"Yes okay, sorry. I'll try to speak louder."

## JOSEPH SQUATRITO

"Didn't you serve our country in Korea and win a "SILVER STAR!"

"Yes, I did."

"Isn't it true you lost a son in Vietnam?"

D.A. Johnson interrupted," Objection you Honor, I can't see the relevance of this information to this case."

"Your Honor, I'm just trying to establish the character and creditability of my witness.

"I'll allow the question, continue Mr. Brancato."

"Thank you your Honor." I paused briefly to collect my thoughts and then I continued with my questions." Mr. Ponterri, have you ever been in trouble with the law?"

"No, never!"

I displayed a large chart representing the positions of the street, the store, Grasso's car and the squad car. I then established the position of Grasso's car and the squad car with relation to the store and the line of sight to where Mr. Ponterri was standing at work.

"Mr. Ponterri, will you please in your own words tell this court what you saw on the day in question. Please feel free to use this pointer and the chart if you think it will help you." He took the pointer and he use it as he related what he had seen.

"Well the flashing lights caught my attention, I was behind the fruit stand which is about four foot high I was getting out a roll of plastic bags. I saw the first car pointing to Grasso's car on the chart stop at the corner and the police car pulled behind the first car. Two police officers got out of their squad car and one walked over to the drivers side of the first car. The other police officer stayed behind Mr. Grasso's car, then I saw the second police officer hit the taillight with his nightstick and break the lens. The driver was ordered out of the car and asked to walk a straight line. Then they opened the trunk of the car and looked inside.

The other police officer then looked inside the car, put his hand under the front seat and pulled out a small white package. A funny thing happened before he put his hand under the seat he reached into his pocket and took something out. I can't be one hundred percent sure but I think he was trying to conceal it with his hand and body."

"What happened next?"

"They hand cuffed the driver and took him away."

"No more question your Honor."

The Judge asked Assistant District Attorney Johnson if he had any question, and if he would like to cross-examine.

"No questions, your Honor."

Judge Stone, slammed down his gavel and said, "Ladies' and Gentlemen of the jury I am declaring this a mistrial. Mr. Johnson, it sounds to me like your police officers made a false arrest. Alfonso Grasso you are free to leave, this trial is at an end. I believe that there may be new charges filed concerning the arresting officers, Officer Fields I think the District Attorney's office will want to talk to you."

I left the courtroom with my client, we were lucky my only witness was an excellent witness. As we left the building walking down the front steeps the thought came to me sometimes lucky is better than smart. Alfonso thanked me over and over, I just said, "Make sure you tell your uncle

Rocko that I held up my end of the bargain."

I turned to walk away and realized that I had opened a very dangerous can of worms with this trial. Dan Fields was in hot water, but he was just part of the corruption. I wondered if he would give up his cohorts, it would have been sweeter if we had nailed Michael Cavanaugh. Maybe next time. I was determined to get to the bottom of the relationship between Michael and Dan. I petitioned the court on behalf of my client, Alfonso Grasso and demanded a monetary settlement in a civil action suit. I hoped that it would flush out Dan Fields associates, they might come to his aid during his trial. It was a minor beef at best, but the threat of losing his pension and being unable to support his family who knows what might be stirred up. The District Attorney wouldn't care much, a perjury rap was hardly ever prosecuted and a false arrest charge wouldn't stand up in court. Not when an old man thought he saw a taillight being broken. If those sons of bitches could tangle with the mob, they wouldn't stop at intimidating the fruit peddler or worse his family.

But, I didn't care. It was my right and the right of my client to pursue this. That's when I received another call from Attica.

"Hello?"

"We work on opposite sides of the street, if you get my meaning but we have a mutual interest. I want to keep the streets clean from drugs, because I want to keep them for myself. My turf, no drugs with no interference. You want to make a name for yourself by nailing those degenerates who are corrupting our streets, our kids our people. There are some individuals who remind me of the vultures that wait for the car to run over an animal. Then they swoop down to feast on the road kill. If they get the chance, they even pick the tire so clean that it looks as if it went through a car wash. This guy is destroying our moral fiber by preying on the innocent and unsuspecting. This guy must be stopped, for my sake as well as yours. I'm in here under the protection of our penal system, but you will be tested to the limits. Call on me anytime, my resources are at your disposal."

Before I could answer, he hung up. What the hell did he mean, I'll be tested? How deep did this go? I had nothing to hide, nobody owned me. I didn't owe anybody anything. I wondered what the hell I should do. If I uncovered corruption and the higher establishment was involved, I might put my family and me in danger. If I succeeded and the corruption was purged, then the streets were fair game for thugs like Rocko. In essence I would be putting bad guys away so that other bad guys could stay in business.

When I got home my wife, Mary greeted me at the door. I walked in and sat down in the living room. I was wiped out and full of despair. Mary said, "Sal you look terrible, what's bothering you? Can you tell what's wrong?"

"I need a drink, make it a double. I'm caught in the middle of something and I can't see a way out. I would never burden you with this Mary, but I need to get good and drunk so I can tell you one hell of a story."

My wife listened patiently as I explained how I was caught in a vise to the point where I almost couldn't breathe. Making what I feel is the right decision, 'trying' to bring down a corrupt police department could hurt you and the kids. Making the wrong decision could hurt Chaz and maybe the family. She held my hand as I talked and looked at me with all the love a wife, could give. I could see in her eyes she was scared too.

Mary said," Sal your not going to cure all the ills of this world. Who cares if there's corruption in the department?

## JOSEPH SQUATRITO

You think the public cares? Everyone cheats at something, as long as it doesn't touch us here in our home who cares? If what you suspect is true, we'll move. We'll go away and leave all the corruption behind us, let somebody else be a hero. Not you Sal, not you! There'll always be a Rocko or a Sonny or a Carmine walking among us, you know it, I know it everybody in Brooklyn knows it. Let them kill themselves, not you."

"Mary, this doesn't sound like you. Why are you so afraid? Is it because its the Mafia or because it's Michael. Haven't I always provided for you and sheltered you. I thought you would be proud of me, I know Michael Cavanaugh is involved big time. He may be the major player in the corruption. He's always been a con artist even in high school, but once he got a badge to hide behind."

"Sal please let's get out of here, lets go far away. Just you, me and the kids. We can go where no one can ever find us."

"Where the hell are we going to run to, your over reacting! This is only in the talking stages. I can back off any time I want and do nothing. Didn't I always tell you that I 'd protect you and the family."

The next day I called Alfonso Grasso and relayed the conversation I had with his uncle Rocko. He already knew about the call and began to call in some marker to get more information on Dan Fields. I was getting in deeper, but my sense of justice overcame my fear and good judgement. If I backed off, Chaz would lose his protection, if I continued the mob would have me by the balls. I decided to go for the big men and end the corruption in the department, maybe even get to the bottom of Joey's murder and prove Chaz was innocent. I was elated, but cautious. Later that afternoon I received a call from Alfonso to meet him at Conte's Restaurant in New York about 9:00. When I got there I was dumbfounded to find Dan Fields and Alfonso sitting in a corner booth, sharing a bottle of red. I was even more disturbed when Alfonso slipped out of the booth and practically ordered me to slide in next to the wall. I was trapped. Dan Fields took charge of the meeting, explaining the order of business.

"There will be no civil suit, there will be no investigation into either of our businesses. (nodding toward Alfonso) You counselor will mind your own fucking business from now on."

I looked at Alfonso, as he sat with slumped shoulders and head down.

"And if you don't mind your own fucking business, we'll have your friend Chaz killed! You fucking mook."

When I heard him say that I really lost control, pointing my finger in his face and reaching for him I said, "You're a dirty cop, tell your boss that now I'm coming for him too." I turned to Alfonso, "You made a deal with this piece of shit, what now your branching out on your own? So now I'm coming after you next!"

I pushed my way out of the booth, almost knocking Alfonso to the ground and gave them both the Italian (fuck you,) Salute. Walking away I looked over my shoulder and saw Dan Fields jump out of his side of the booth. Instead of running after me in anger he just laughed and said, "Hey hero go talk to your wife and then let me know what you want to do."

## JOSEPH SQUATRITO

I broke all speed limits driving home, I don't even remember driving over the Brooklyn Bridge. I practically broke the front door down, fearing the worst. What did they do to Mary and the kids? The house was in complete darkness when I entered. I rushed up stairs and found the kids sleeping peacefully, I rushed into our bedroom but Mary was not there. What the hell was going on? I when back down stairs, it was then I saw the silhouette of my wife sitting in the dark with what looked like a gun in her hand.

"Don't come near me Sal, let me die I just want to die!"

"Mary no, please I know they threatened you but we'll fight them together. I'll never stop until I bring those bastards to justice."

"No one threatened me, it's you who are being threatened."

She let the gun slip out of her hand as she covered her face in shame. There was a plain brown letter size envelope on the sofia. I opened the envelope and a note was first to come out, it read." I've got plenty more of these that I can put on display, so back off if you don't want your wife to be known for the whore that she is."

It wasn't the note that stunned me it was the pictures that fell out of the envelope. Tears welled up in my eyes as I looked at photos of Mary, in various stages of undress. Showing off her baton-whirling expertise. There was only one man who know her in high school and could get that close to her and it was Michael. "I'll kill that bastard." As I looked at more pictures it got worst, there was Mary nude with her legs spread wide open and a line of bare ass guys waiting their turn. I new Mary wasn't a virgin when

# THE TRIAL

I married her, everyone deserves a second chance, but a gang bang.

That was to much to bare, but the next picture completely blew my mind, Mary on her knees giving a blowjob to a guy that was hung like a horse. The last picture was her and Michael, even though his head was not in the picture he was wearing his number seven football jersey. You let that asshole fuck you! I collapsed on the couch and mumbled, "How could this be, how could this happened?"

"Sal I never meant to hurt you like this, we were kids in high school. Michael invited a few of the girls over to his house for a victory party, his parents weren't home. He said the whole team and all the cheerleaders were invited. We didn't know we were being setup. We got there early and he spiked our drinks with something, it felt insane the girls were burning up we started taking off our clothes. The next thing we knew they were taking pictures and we were having sex. I had my cherry broke on a gang bang line I couldn't walk for a week. After that night, I never had sex with anybody until you, and I've never been with nobody but you. Sal you knew I wasn't a virgin the first time we had sex, it never bother you. Please forgive me!"

Mary cried uncontrollably, I held her and tried to comfort her. I knew Michael had won, there was no way I could pursue my investigation. It was time to back off, both sides got what they wanted. The streets would be divided equally. Mary was right, let them kill each other. They deserve each other! Maybe someday Michael would get his. I hoped there was an avenging angel waiting for the right time to appear and take care of that bastard!

## JOSEPH SQUATRITO

During the years that followed, I would occasionally bump into Theresa and the girls. Once I saw them at the feast on 18th avenue, we said our casual hello and I commented on how big the girls were getting. She talked to Mary as if they were still the best of friends, which led me to believe they may still be secretly in contact with each other. It was something I didn't want to know, maybe my Mary opened her closet and let out all the skeletons to Theresa way back when they were best of friends. It's true somethings are left better unsaid, and I didn't want to hash up old dragons and dead skeletons any more. A couple of years later Mary and I were with the kids walking along the boardwalk in Coney Island and we again ran into Theresa and the girls, after a quick hello I walk away with my kids to play some games leaving Mary and Theresa to talk. I couldn't look Theresa straight in the eye, I wondered if she could see the shame of disappointment I held for her and the hatred I had in my heart for Michael.

The only good thing was that each time we would meet Michael was nowhere to be found, and that was just fine with me. When I returned they were still in normal type conversation between old friends. I watched Ashley, her younger daughter running and jumping excitedly calling for Theresa to come and play this game or that. Then she dashed to the cotton candy machine and begged for some. Lenore who is older and at the age of a young teen about to turn into a young woman. She was as beautiful as Theresa was at that age but much less a tom boy. Even Theresa wasn't built like her at this age. Lenore had a knockout body. She dragged Ashley back and held on to her and wouldn't let go. At the time I thought she was just being her big sister afraid she may get lost, but her concern seemed unnatural to me. Lenore was being to over protective, too controlling. Ashley couldn't even enjoy her time at the beach, I noticed something else even though she was in that awkward stage that girls go through as they are blossoming she had a haunted look on her face. Her eyes had dark circles under her vacant eyes, eyes that had no light, no brightness, no gleam like other girls her age. What could possibly make this little girl so tormented? Maybe I was making to much of nothing more than a teenage girl of thirteen struggling to catch up to her hormones.

Theresa on the other hand looked fabulous as usual, as I stood there she brought us up to date about what was going on in her life. Something I really didn't care about. She was getting ready to take her final examine to become an administrator in charge of nursing at Montgomery Medical Center out on Long Island. We didn't ask about her husband and she didn't volunteer any information, I was glad about that. I keep my feelings to myself if she knew what I was thinking, she would have gone out and bought a black mourning dress. I just couldn't figure out what to do about Mary and Theresa's bond. Some time after seeing Theresa at Coney Island, I heard that she was living in East Hampton, Long Island. There are times we can't see the most obvious things until later, long after the moment has passed. I realized that not once during our conversation on the boardwalk, did Theresa ever mention Chaz. I mean come on, nobody is that strong or so void of curiosity that she wouldn't want to know what happened to the father of her children. It was as if he never existed! I dismissed my observation, I had enough to worry about, without wondering why Theresa hadn't asked about Chaz. I have to say after talking to her at Coney Island my lack of respect and anger did melt.

She was still that wonderful, feisty girl of our childhood who was simply trying to rebuild her life after the murder of her brother, and the conviction of her former spouse for that murder. When I looked at her I realized that she had lost a brother, lost a loving husband and had to rebuild her life. She had unknowingly married a very evil and manipulative man. Mary said to me, "Give Theresa a break, it's not her fault what Michael has done to us. I have to tell you something, I told her if she ever needs us not to hesitate to call."

"Okay, for your sake I'll agree with it."

A year or so later, I was sitting in the courtroom ready to plead for bail on a client's behalf when I got an urgent page of all 9999999's on my screen. That was the code Mary and I decided on in case of an emergency. I apologized to the judge for the disruption, and asked for a continuance. My client went nuts, he had to go back to jail until I resolved his bail situation. If he could have, he would have beaten the shit out of me and I really couldn't have blamed him. For now I had more pressing things to worry about. My first thoughts were those rat bastards are back their not going to leave us alone, then I thought something must have happened to the kids. This urgent message was freaking me out, I couldn't find a phone so I ran to my car in the municipal parking lot to use my cell phone. Of course my home phone was busy, and to add to my anxiety I couldn't find the attendant to get my car out of the lot. I returned to my car and asked the phone operator to break in on my home phone and ask my wife to call me back.

Finally a path was cleared and I was able to get out of the parking lot. Mary called me back as I was driving home. I navigated the city traffic as I attempted to make sense out of what I heard. The message was difficult to understand because of all the static and silences caused by the interferences of the tall surrounding buildings. About all I could make out was Theresa's name and something about Michael hurting Lenore, and Mary asking me to go to the Essex Diner off Sunrise Highway. My mind was whirling trying to fill in the pieces I wasn't able to hear. If Lenore was hurt how come Mary asked me to go to the diner instead of a hospital or doctor's office. It just didn't make sense to me. I approached the diner with great trepidation, what in the hell was I getting into now! As a lawyer, mixing in a domestic dispute I had no standing. As a friend, I do what I could maybe give her advice? I could see Theresa sitting with Lenore opposite her, in a booth in the back of the diner.

Theresa was facing me and Lenore's back was to me. As I approached them nothing seemed out of order. It appeared Lenore didn't have a mark on her. Again I thought what in God's name was going on? Before I had a chance to question Theresa, Mary came out of the bathroom. As I was about to say you got here before me, she shook her head signaling me to stop, she gently took Lenore out of the diner. For all the times I'd told my wife not to get involved in my business or other people's business, I thank God for her interference this time. I didn't ask Theresa where they were going. What I heard for the next hour and a half made my skin crawl. I felt like heaving, the waitress kept coming over to us offering a second cup of coffee, water whatever. I finally slipped her a twenty dollar bill and told her to leave us alone. Theresa was disoriented and frantic, to say the least. I had never seen her like that, she wore something like a housecoat a garment she would never be seen in outside the house. She had no make-up on her face, no lipstick and her hair was unwashed. She was a sad guilt ridden woman whose life and the life of her daughter had been shattered and changed forever. She painfully related the events that started the nightmare.

Theresa was the Head Nurse at Montgomery Medical Center. She coordinated her midnight and eight to four shift with her husband so there was always an adult with the girls. Michael was now the Chief of Detectives in the Borough of Brooklyn. One evening while on duty a gunshot victim was rushed to the emergency room, they could do nothing to bring him back to life and so his chart was stamped, "DOA." This incident brought back the painful memory of the night her brother was murdered. She was startled back to reality when an alarm went off sounding the alert of incoming burn and accident victims, whose estimated time of arrival was five minutes. Theresa was always self-confident and efficient under stressful conditions, she shook off the painful memory and took charge. When she arrived home after an exhausting and unusually gruesome evening. Theresa checked on her two daughters, Lenore was now fifteen and Ashley was twelve. She was satisfied by the rhythmic breathing that all was well. She prepared to go to her own bed when something in Lenore's room caught her eye. Clinging to the side of Lenore's bed was an empty film cartridge. She chuckled, "My husband, the Daryl F. Zanuck of the neighborhood, has been at it again adding to our family album. I'll check his handy work in the morning."

Theresa slept late the next morning, and was awakened by Lenore's attempted breakfast of pancakes and bacon. Although the mess in the kitchen appalled her, she bravely smiled at her daughter and hugged her in appreciation. Lenore stiffened when her mother asked to see the pictures Daddy had taken the night before. Lenore answered with," What picture are you talking about? I don't know what you're talking about."

Theresa held up the empty cartridge. "I found this in your room last night."

Horrified, Lenore broke down uncontrollably and the years of degradation at the hands of the man she called father bubbled up and out of her. She related how it all started. With Theresa's tender assurance of her love, Lenore began to paint a grisly disgusting picture of Michael.

One night Daddy, no not Daddy! I can't call him that, one night the monster came to my room. It was late at night, he got into my bed and said he was lonely for you Mommy. Then held me close and he put his hand on my leg and moved up to my thigh, he told me my skin was smooth, not like older woman who have hair on their legs. Then he started to do something to himself down there under the covers. He made such loud sounds that I thought he would wake Ashley. After he was quite again and he thanked me for being a good girl. When I heard Ashley's door open I jumped out of bed to stop him from walking in and doing what he had just done in my room. He said, "I won't wake

Ashley if you promise me that I can sleep with you again. Okay?"

"I promise." This went on for a long time until one night he put his hands under my panties and put my hand on his private. He said "This is how people who love each other show their love for one another. You do love me, don't you Lenore?"

"I love you Daddy!"

Then he began to take pictures of me in the bathtub, he gave things to play with that looked like him, down there only they were made of rubber. He kept tell me if I didn't do these things he would get Ashley to do them.

As Theresa was relating Lenore's story, I thought about the time a year ago when we met them at Coney Island. This explained why Lenore looked so haunted and why she didn't want Ashley out of her sight. I again gave her my fullest attention as she continued with her story. Lenore told her one night the monster took her into the shower with him and put soap all over her. He picked her up so her legs would wrap around his waist, he told her this was so she wouldn't fall.

Then she said, "He hurt me down there. There was even blood, I watched as the shower washed it away. I didn't know what happened, I was scared and when I put my legs down to stand, it hurt more. I thought I was going to die. He told me I was a woman now, and that I made him feel better than any other woman in the whole wide world. He always put on his video camera when he did these horrible things to me, and then he'd watch them over and over. The most horrible thing was his smell, his body reeked when he sweat, and his breath stunk of booze. He lick me and sucked my breasts. I thought his smell would never leave so I washed over and over every chance I got. I wanted to tell you, but he said if I told you he would show everybody the pictures, so I said nothing." Theresa described to me how as her abused little girl related the horrible details, Lenore began to break down and finally had to stop. Theresa was afraid Lenore would be driven over the edge if she had to continue, but Theresa knew there was more. Possibly much more.

I advised her to wait until he went to work, it would give her a full eight to ten hour head start. Go home pack what ever to can, get as much money as you can out of the bank. You can't take a plane, train or bus as a police Detective he could track you by name and find your destination. No use of a credit card he can track that too. You have a fairly new car so that will be your means of travel. My grandfather left me and old house, a little rustic, on a lake in Florida. Here's the key and address. You can hide there until we can come up with a long range plan. Theresa sprang into actin she went home and started to pack clothes for all of them without Michael's knowledge. When to the bank and withdrew most of their money, leaving enough so the bank wouldn't alert him as to the close of the account. When he started his midnight shift she waited a short while woke the girls and started out. She left Michael a letter on the kitchen table it read.

"IF YOU EVER COME NEAR ME OR MY GIRLS AGAIN, I'LL KILL YOU DO NOT ATTEMPT TO FIND US. I KNOW WHAT YOU DID!"

Theresa who was guilt-ridden and desperate to get her children as far away from her perverted husband as she could. Starting her journey at midnight was best, there was light traffic and no delays at bridges and tunnels. She could put as much mileage behind her as she could while her daughters slept in the back seat. She drove relentlessly until she was so exhausted it would be to dangerous to continue.

To reduce the chance of being found, she paid cash for a room in a near by motel just as Sal had told her. A room with a hot bath and soft bed was just what she needed to get regenerated. She picked up an out going order of food in a near by diner and they eat in the room. She thought only a couple of days and we'll be safe in Florida. She was sure Mary and Sal would not reveal their final destination. The next night, Theresa and the girls reached somewhere in Georgia. Staying off the main highways would take a little longer but she was sure Michael had put out an APB Alert to every highway patrol car from New York to California. She was having no luck in finding a motel room on this route. Eventually they settled on an out of the way motel that a gas station attendant had been kind enough to recommend to them. It turned out that he was not as kind as they thought. He saw that Theresa and the girls were alone, that is with no man. Later he watched and waited until they settled into their room and the lights were out. Picking the lock on a low rent flee bag motel was easy, the next morning Theresa's jewelry and most of her money was gone. It was a good thing she had hid some in her shoe. Thank God, she and the girls were not harmed. She didn't tell them, there was no sense in spooking them any further. They left the room as if nothing had happened or as if they were unaware of the theft they got in the car and simply drove away. A lesson to be learned don't trust anyone, Theresa let her guard down and paid the price.

As Theresa began the rest of the journey, she was filled with despair and hopelessness. She started to feel sorry for herself, until she looked into Lenore's lifeless eyes reflected in the rearview mirror. She saw Lenore sitting back there, staring at nothing and suspected that her daughter was reliving her horrors heaped upon her by that evil man she once thought was her chance for a new life. The directions I had given her brought them to the edge of the everglades. The smell of stagnant water and decaying flesh invaded their senses, it was so strong that at first they gasped for breath. They traveled along a bumpy road, it was littered with old car wrecks. A broken down tool shed, garbage that people had dumped along the way and rotting trees. At the end of the road Theresa and the girls found refuge in an abandoned ramshackle house, resting in a worn decaying orange orchard. The inside was not as bad as the appearance they saw on the outside. Theresa got some clean blankets from the trunk of the car, they covered the beds and fell asleep.

# LENORE'S NIGHTMARE

That night, Theresa was suddenly awakened by Lenore's screams.

"Mama, I'm frightened. What if he finds us?"

Theresa tried to calm her by saying, "I promise you no one is ever going to hurt you again. I won't let it happen."

As Lenore lay in the dark, she shut her eyes as tightly as she could, but she couldn't escape the images." Is this whole thing a dream? Please make it go away."

Later when she drifted into a troubled sleep, the nightmare began again.

Lenore honey come with daddy, I want to take some pictures of you taking a bath. No mommy made me take a bath before she left for work. This is a pretend bath, now take off your pajamas and keep quiet, we don't want to wake Ashley. Now do what I tell you to do, I'm going to make you a STAR!

Lenore continued to indulge her daddy's fantasies about becoming a movie star. She became frightened and confused when he made her shower and then took her into the bedroom while the video camera recorded a testimony to his lust making. This degradation continued well into her early teens but what really pushed over the edge was when he introduced her to young male costars. She was forced to have oral sex and anal love making. Again Theresa was awaken by Lenore's screams, again she tried to comfort her. "I'm here baby, don't cry. No one will ever hurt you again, she held her tighter and rocked her to sleep in her arms. In her sleep she keep saying, "I'm sorry mommy, I'm sorry I'll be a good girl, I'll be a good girl."

Theresa's heart was ripping out of her chest, she was crying uncontrollably but she won't let Lenore go. They fell asleep in each others arms. Theresa once again dreamed that she was calling for help, she could see herself and the girls wandering aimlessly looking up to the sky. It was filled with ominous dark storm clouds rolling angrily across the sky.

"God help us, give us strength. Help us Oh Lord."

A bolt of lightning, which illuminated the entire room and a clap of thunder shook the house woke Theresa. She rose from her pillow collected her thoughts and came to the realization that they had to leave. Her instincts told her that if she stayed, Michael would find them. She remembered as a little girl her mother saying a bad feeling was the angels talking to you.

Her gut feeling told her to wake the girls and leave immediately.

"Wake up Lenore, wake up Ashley we have to go."

"Mommy I'm tired, I want to sleep." Murmured Ashley.

"No, get up now we're leaving this place. Get your things lets go!"

They ran for their lives, they had very little money left and down on their luck. Theresa knew she had to use her money on gas to get out of the Florida Panhandle and into

# LENORE'S NIGHTMARE

Arkansas. She stopped at a small diner and talked to the owner. He agreed to let her wash dishes for a breakfast of flapjacks and coffee, milk for the girls. After they ate she washed a pile of dishes and scrubbed the toilet. On there way out he handed her a paper bag filled with sandwiches and sodas, it was his way of letting her know she did a fine job. She stayed off the main highway for fear of being found, they slept in the car and ate the sandwiches for next couple of days. By the time they got to a small town outside of Flagstaff Arizona she was broke, at the last gas stop she asked the garage owner if he knew any car dealers that bought used cars. He told her of a car lot called Big Jim's Auto, he said the owner was fair and always looking for good cars to put on his lot. Theresa knew she would get screwed but she needed cash and most importantly get her car off the road until she could put more miles behind her. The direction to Big Jim's was perfect, when she got there she was welcomed with a big western, "Why hello 'little lady, what can I do for y'all."

Theresa told Big Jim she wanted to sell her car, what can he offer her. He looked the car over with a fine tooth comb. A one year old Buick, fully loaded with low milage and not a body dent to be found. Well, the Kelly blue book read a price of $19,600 which meant he could sell this car for at least $22,000. Then he worked his con, you do have the registration an title for this car. I got to be sure there's no lien on her. Theresa was one step ahead of him because she knew eventually she would have to dump the car, it was just a matter of when or where. So when she took all the papers out of her hand bag Big Jim raised an eyebrow. He offered to cut her a check when his mechanic okayed the engine and transmission. Theresa let him know this was a cash deal only. Jim had a keen eye on character, a woman with two young daughters looking for a cash deal, to him it meant a woman on the run most likely from a boy friend or spouse. Jim told her "If you can wait a couple of days I could raise some more cash, but right now petty cash I can offer you 12K. Theresa barked back WHAT! I paid $25,000 for it a year ago, no deal I'll just have to fine another dealer who's not looking to screw me.

   Now hold your horses little lady, look I tell you what there's a diner across the road with some really good home cook food. Just go in and tell Florence lunch is on Big Jim and you can order any thing you like. Just give me an hour or so and I'll come up with a cash deal you'll like, an hour won't kill you and your girls look hungry. Theresa thought for a minute, we certainly could use a good meal. "Okay Jim you got an hour, lets go eat girls. An hour later with full belly's Theresa and the girls came back, Jim was all smiles like he just unlocked the vault and was ready to give Theresa a great deal. Well, 'little lady $ 13,500 now what do think of that! Theresa went into her three act play, I told you not to play me. The car doesn't even have 10,000 miles, the engine isn't broke in yet and G.M. coverage is 50,000 miles bumper to bumper what do you say Big Jim? "Final offer 15k cash right here right now!" Theresa thought for a minute, $15,000 and a ride to the nearest bus depot. You got a deal, where's the money. Theresa counted the cash in Jim's office and signed over the car, he held up his end of the deal and took them to the nearest bus depot. There Theresa bought three tickets to Henderson, Nevada. She remembered one of her female patients telling her it was a quite little town with good opportunities for a good nurse.

Half way to Henderson, the bus broke down on the highway within walking distance, was a Quality Inn. The thought of a hot bath and a clean bed was irresistible. After the girls had their bath and were watching T.V., it was Theresa turn to self indulge and relax. Being in a Quality Inn gave her a greater feeling of security with a door that had a double lock and little to no chance of a reenactment of Georgia. The next day Theresa and the girls had breakfast in a truck stop diner across the highway. They sat in a booth in the back, she was unaware she could still turn heads, especially compared to local woman. A hot bath, a good nights sleep, lipstick, eyeshadow and fresh clothes can do wonders for a classy attractive woman. She sat with her head down thinking what her next move would be, staring into her coffee she looked like a troubled woman A younger woman came over to her and said, "Hi honey, are you all right?"

Theresa looked up from her coffee and said, "Fine, I'm fine. Do I know you?"

"No, my name is Eve. I live in Henderson, where are you headed?"

"I'm really not sure, I was going to Henderson with my daughters but the damned bus broke down yesterday. I'd be glad to give you a ride, I'd love the company. What do you say?"

"Sure why not. I'm Theresa and this is Lenore and Ashley."

"I have some food at the counter, may I join you."

"Yes we have plenty of room, slide over girls let Eve sit with us."

After breakfast, Theresa and her new friend Eve along with the girls started their journey to Henderson together. As they drove along Eve said, "You are one sexy lady, your obviously well-educated I can tell by the way you talk and carry yourself. What do you do for a living?"

"I'm a nurse, I was the head of nursing in a big hospital back east."

"I knew you weren't just a mama."

Theresa didn't answer, she started to wonder what she had gotten herself into

"Are you staying with anyone in Henderson?"

"Why do you ask?"

"I know a real clean boarding house, it's real clean and they serve breakfast and dinner if you want. You and the girls could stay there until you get settled in and find your own place."

Theresa wondered if this was 'deja vu'? All over, again. Was this woman trying to set them up, just like the gas station attendant did just to rob them? She decided it wouldn't happen again, this time she'd play it smart.

"I really appreciate it, but I'd rather go to a Holiday Inn or a Hilton Inn."

"Honey, you're going to pay three times what it would cost you at Mama Mabel's. Believe me, you'll love her, she was a real saloon dancer in Las Vegas in the 1930s'. Now she just loves helping women in trouble. You know, been there-done that. She took me in when I first got there, I stayed with her till I could afford my own house. My kids just love her."

For some strange reason, Theresa believed Eve. It was something she couldn't explain, maybe it was the tone of Eve's voice that was reassuring.

Theresa decided to try it, but only if Eve took her to the bank first so she could secure her money.

"Eve, do you have a Wells Fargo Bank in Henderson?"

"Sure, it's on the way to Mabel's"

"Would you mind if we stop there first? Then we'll try Mabel's, okay."

"Great, I'll take you to the bank first. It's not far from exit to get to Mabel's."

At the bank, Theresa opened a safe deposit box so she could stash the $15,000 she had gotten for her car. If there was any funny stuff about to happen, they weren't going to get her money.

She keep a few hundred dollars for pocket money just in case things didn't work out at Mabel's. It only took a few minutes to fill out the signature card and pay for the deposit box. She informed the manger that she was new in town and planned to stay and establish herself as a new resident. She told him when she got a nursing job, she'd be back to open a checking account and a savings account. As she was ready to leave the bank she asked, "By the way do you know of a boarding house called Mama Mabel's? The reason I ask is a new friend I met on the road getting here keeps insisting to stay there. The manger smiled and said. "If your going to Mabel's, don't worry. Mabel is like a local angel, she helps with love and understanding. You'll be safe there, I guarantee it.

So Theresa walked out of the bank with a heavy weight lifted from her chest. In the relatively short time they had spent running from Michael, she had gone from a gregarious, but streetwise person to a suspicious person. Now she was reminded that not all people should be judged by the actions of a few. When she got back in the car, her conversation with Eve was quite different. Theresa was relaxed and less defensive. They soon arrived at Mama Mabel's, their first sight of their new home was a circular driveway in front of a beautifully restored Victorian Manson. The grounds were manicured to perfection. It reminded her of a topnotch bed and breakfast with a western flare. Even the old hitching posts, fitted with brass rings were still in place. Many a cowboy must have visited here. Mabel greeted them on the front porch, and Eve introduced Theresa and the girls as her new friends. Theresa extended her hand and said, "Hello, I'm Theresa and these are my daughters Lenore and Ashley."

"Welcome to Mabel's, this is my home and as long as you stay here consider it your home!"

It was obvious that Mabel had been a beautiful woman in her day. It looked as if her features had not changed, but her skin could not conceal her age. She had the high cheekbones of a model, a small nose and perfect shaped full lips. She was quite attractive, only the wrinkles in her skin and the crow's feet around her eyes hinted of an earlier time, and a long hard struggle. Her blonde hair, streaked with grey was swept up in a turn of the century hairdo called the Gibson Girl look. She was still very shapely for her age, and her warm personality won your heart in an instant. You just couldn't help loving her. There was an instant bond between them. Mabel could see that Theresa and her girls were in trouble.

She could sense they needed help, that was all she needed to know. Her arms opened like the gates of heaven. She was determined to keep them safe and secure. As they entered the house, the newcomers looked around, the interior was pure magic. The decor was western, but not overpowering. There were many old pictures scattered here and there of Mabel with famous movie stars. Mabel and Eve showed the new guests to their rooms. Mabel offered Theresa two adjoining rooms for the price of one. She told Theresa this setup will give the girls more space and provide you a little privacy. Get unpacked take bath and settle in, dinner is at 7:00. Mabel had the best kitchen around and nobody made better homemade apple pie. Mabel always said it was the apple trees out back, they were a gift from heaven, and the result was pure heaven. Mabel said, "Lets go Eve and give Theresa a chance to unwind. Don't forget dinner is seven sharp, we'll talk then. Theresa took the advice of Mabel she took a hot bath followed by a well needed nap. She didn't realize how much energy she had been spending, constantly looking over her shoulder. She reassured Lenore and Ashley that everything would be all right. At seven sharp they all went down to dinner.

The dinning room had a large table that could seat twenty people at one time. Eve was there, along with fifteen guests. Some were boarders and others were just there for a good meal. Eve was right, Mabel's kitchen prepared a wonderful dinner. The dessert Eve promised followed it was the best apple pie they had ever tasted. During dinner Mabel introduced Theresa and the girls as her new guests.

The conversation was light and not informative. Mabel made sure none of her other guess asked any off color or too personal a question, she jumped right in saying," You know better than that."

Afterwards the girls were allowed to watch T.V. in the living room. Theresa and her two new friends went outside on a porch that wrapped around the front of the house for an after dinner brandy. Theresa asked Mabel.

"Do you know of any jobs for a nurse, maybe in a local doctor's office?"

"No honey, maybe in Las Vegas at the hospital."

"No not Vegas, I want to stay local where I'm close to the girls."

"This is a small community, not many jobs available but why not look maybe you'll get lucky."

The next day, Theresa started her quest for a job. Mabel was right there wasn't much work available for skilled professionals.

The only jobs listed in the newspaper were for dancers, bartenders, strippers, waitresses and short order cooks. Day after day she went out looking she even answered and applied to a receptionist job at a doctors office but made the mistake saying she was a head nurse back east. Overqualified was the answer she got. She applied for a job as a medical records clerk but when she talked to the office manager the job paid seven dollars an hour she just couldn't see herself working for such low pay. She came back one afternoon filled with despair, sat on the bench on the front porch not wanting to tell Lenore and Ashley she still was having no luck in getting a job. Mabel came out and sat with her on the bench, she put her arm around her and said," Theresa honey, with your looks and body you could be making five hundred dollars a night as an escort to the big shot high rollers in Vegas."

"No mabel, I have to stay low-key. You don't understand."

"Theresa there's not much I don't understand. I can see your on the run, bad marriage?"

"Yes, but it's worse than that."

"You can tell me, what you say stays with only me. As they say, I been there done that. I've seen and heard it all."

Theresa let her guard down and told Mabel everything. It had been a long time since she felt she could trust anyone. She needed to vent and tell someone, she let it all out telling Mabel about every despicable thing Michael had done to Lenore.

"Honey out here we would have taken him out back and shot his balls off and hung them from a tree. How could anyone hurt a child like that? I would have shot his balls off myself."

Theresa found out later that throughout the Southwest territory Mabel had a singular reputation. In her younger days she carried a six shooter and could shoot the eyes out of a snake. It's rumored that even now she carries a two shot pearl handle derringer. You wouldn't want to cross her or hurt anyone she loved, hell has no fury like Mabel when she's pissed off. She holds hands with the most influential and powerful men in the Southwest.

"Mabel what am I going to do? I need a job. The girls have to start school in three weeks. We can't stay here forever, we need to make a new start, get a house. Why has God forsaken us?"

"Don't worry, you know the old saying. God works in mysterious ways.

He closes one door and opens another, we'll get through this."

"Theresa just pay me whatever you can afford, and when you get on your feet I'll take whatever is fair. You and the girls can stay here as long as you like."

"Why are you being so good to me? You really don't know me or my girls."

"Maybe you remind me of myself. I had it very hard when I was young, so just let Mama Mabel watch out for you. Maybe this is one of those open doors."

A few days later with no luck finding a job Theresa talked with Mabel about her suggestion of escort work. She asked straight out," How do you know so much about the work, the salary and availability?"

Mabel answered honestly, "Well honey, it's my service. I own it, Eve works for me and she does very well. Eve doesn't have your looks, figure or intelligence. You could be a real find."

"I'm not a tramp, I don't deal in sex!"

"You got it all wrong, nothing like that. This is real honest work. All you need to do is look beautiful, carry yourself with class and style and conduct some intelligent conversation. My client list is high-class business men who don't want to be alone for dinner, or a show. Sometimes a private dinner party with a politician, Governor or business associate. They need a companion for window dressing, they know up front what they're getting. No funny stuff, if they want sex they can go to the bunny ranch. My girls are strictly for show."

"Okay, I'll it a try."

"Fine, let's get you an evening dress and I'll start you tonight."

That night a limo picked up Theresa around eight o'clock. When she came out of the house the driver helped her down the stairs, opened the door and when she got inside, he closed the door behind her. Inside a fine dressed man introduced himself as "Ken Smith."

"Hello, I'm Theresa!"

They went to a really nice, Italian restaurant called "Bistro" outside of the Vegas strip. After dinner they made the Midnight show at "Caesars" they were among the last to enter before the show started yet they got a front row table.

At two in the morning the limo they went with brought them back to Mabel's, her gentleman date slipped her an envelope and said," I'd like to see you again on my next trip to Vegas. It was a pleasure to met such a classy and beautiful woman. Maybe next time you'll be less uptight."

"To be perfectly honest with you, this was my first experience at escorting. I promise that I'll do better next time. Thank you for being a gentlemen."

The door opened and Theresa got out, her evening was over and the rewards were most generous. The limo driver escorted her to the front door and waited until she was inside. Mabel was waiting up for her like a mother lion watching over her young.

"Everything okay Theresa?"

"Yes, I had a lovely time with a very nice man.

"Next time will be easier. Now go to bed. We'll talk money in the morning."

Theresa had a good long sleep and came down late to breakfast the next morning. Lenore and Ashley had already eaten and were watching television. Theresa said to them, "Girls after I eat we'll go out for the day."

She walked into the dinning room and found Mabel enjoying a cup of coffee. Mabel asked, "Hungry child?"

"Yes a little."

"What would you like?

"Whatever you have, don't go to any trouble I know I came down late."

Mabel yelled out to the kitchen cook, "Make some pancakes and bacon right away and bring out more coffee. Sit with me and have some coffee."

Theresa sat down and handed Mabel the envelope she had gotten from Ken the night before.

"What's this you're handing me?"

"Well I guess this belongs to you. I'm working for your service."

"No honey, that's yours. My clients pay me up front, go on open it and look inside.

Theresa opened the envelope and found a hundred dollar bill.

"A hundred dollar bill on your first date! You must have made some impression!"

"That's good, isn't it Mabel?"

"Very good, now eat your pancakes and enjoy your day. Tomorrow you'll be working again. He's a fine gentleman and a very good friend from California. His name is Tom Shanks, he's a regular so you don't have to worry. I have a new dress for you to wear, I want you to look extra special for Tom."

## LENORE'S NIGHTMARE

The next night was the same kind of the same deal as the first night, except she had a new look and felt more relaxed. It made her look even more beautiful, it was a cocktail party filled with socialites and celebrities. Theresa handled the conversation with class, she was able to mingle with the other women and give some advice on medical problems. She fit in like a glove and Tom picked up on it long before the night ended. Theresa was more than he expected, Mabel told him she was beautiful and would be the perfect addition to the evening. On the ride back to Mabel's Tom asked, "Are you available for the next four nights? I 'd like the pleasure of you company, if your schedule is clear."

"I think it is Tom, but I have to check to be sure. Can you call me in the morning?"

"Yes, I can do that."

The limo stopped in front of the house, the driver got out an opened the door. As he extended his hand Theresa turned to Tom and said, "Goodnight, I had a wonderful time, thank you Tom!"

"Goodnight, I hope to see you tomorrow!"

Theresa gave her hand to the limo driver, there was no envelope this time. The driver walked to the door and waited until she was inside. She thought to herself no envelope but he wants to see me again, what's that about. The next morning she came down to breakfast and Mabel told her, "Your working for the next four nights, Tom called early he had a very early Tee Off. After you eat, we have to go shopping. You can't wear the same dress twice, Tom is a very influential man."

"That's going to be very expensive, four more new dresses!"

"Don't you worry your pretty little head, over it, That's my department.

The main thing is you have to look the part, nothing less than fabulous is acceptable where Tom is concern."

The next four nights with Tom were every women's dream. She never thought that was the way the rich and famous lived. Theresa was flying like a cloud in a windstorm, but Theresa had to put it in it's proper perspective it was a job and her last nights work just ended. Tom said his goodbyes and handed her an envelope then he said, "I come to the Vegas area five nights a month. I'll ask for you and hope your available, it was so nice to meet a women with your looks and class. Someone who can hold an interesting conversation, I've enjoyed being in your company." Theresa said, "The pleasure was all mine!"

Theresa went up to her room and opened her envelope, it contained five hundred dollars! Not only did she appreciate the money, but also she had a feeling of pride and satisfaction. She now knew she would be able to earn a living for herself and her daughters. She enrolled Lenore and Ashley in school, hoping she had finally found a place to live. Ashley was in grade school within walking distance from the house, Lenore was in high school and she would have to commute by bus. For the next two weeks before school started she worked every night, they were all nice, gentlemen but they weren't Tom! During he day Theresa spent as much time with the girls as she could, they shopped for school clothes and shoes. The local mall was becoming Lenore and Ashley's favorite place on earth. Although she was invigorated by her good fortune, she was ready to collapse from fatigue. One afternoon, she had a long talk with Eve about an apartment.

"Theresa give yourself some time, you only got here two months ago. I stayed with Mabel a lot longer before I left. Mabel told me that you need a real good nest egg before you leave. Don't be so anxious." In her western way of talking Eve said, "Theresa let me tell you Mabel was right. OO-wee!

When those bills start coming in you'll wish you had stayed longer."

Theresa smiled and said, "Eve maybe your right, I can wait awhile."

Just then Mabel came out on the porch where they were talking and asked.

"What are you girls talking about?"

They answered in unison, "Nothing important."

Well, lets go inside and have a cup of coffee because you're both working tonight."

Tom arranged everything with Mabel to have Theresa available every month when he visited Las Vegas. Of course that scheduling would cost Tom extra but to him Theresa was worth every dollar spent. So it went on right up to Christmas. It was Theresa's and the girls first Southwest Christmas, it certainly would be different from Christmas back in Bensonhurst Brooklyn. The girls adapted nicely to their new idea of Christmas but for Theresa all the old haunts started to creep in. She began to think of Joey and how it was when they were kids, her mother and father and all her friends back in Brooklyn. For some strange reason she even thought of Chaz and what a good and loving father he was to the girls. It was a thought she had suppressed in her heart for a very long time. The closer time got to Christmas the more she dreamed of Joey, every time he'd come to her his message was the same, "It's not what you think it is."

She really didn't understand what it meant, so she didn't give it much thought. Mabel put the girls in charge of decorating the tree, hanging all the wreaths and lights and anything else you can think of. The next day after breakfast Lenore and Ashley went to get a Christmas tree with Doug Johnson, Mabel's foreman and best friend. They had known each other for years, back when Las Vegas was a real shoot-em up cowboy town. They headed up into the mountains leading to California. Their destination was about an hours ride due west from Mabel's. On the way Lenore and Ashley were quite talkative and asked Doug many questions about the old west. He was full of information because he had grown up in the West. He was almost as old as Mabel was, he was a real deal cowboy who carried his own six-shooter and had ridden horses most of his life. Lenore asked, "What was it really like Doug?"

"Well, honey, life was simple back then. Men were honest and gallant. Ladies, were' soft and well, lets just say they were proper and pretty."

Ashley chimed in. "What about Mabel?" Doug smiled at the thought and then he said. "Mabel, yeah she was a gem, a very beautiful Lady!"

Lenore wanted more. "Come on Doug tell us." "Okay, I lived on a ranch and tended the cattle and horses. We'd get paid once a month, and take our salary and head down the valley to a little town call Las Vegas. It had two saloons with gaming casinos, a hotel with a steak house, a barbershop with a bathhouse and a general store. We would blow a months pay in one or two nights. It was there that I met Mabel. Don't tell anybody, she was a saloon singer!"

Then just as the story was getting good, Doug stopped the station wagon and said, "Okay little Ladies, were here, lets get going I'll grab the axe."

Ashley looked out of the window and said. "Where's the stores?"

"We don't need no stores!"

It took a minute for Lenore and Ashley to close their mouths that had opened in amazement. "We thought we were going to buy a tree" said Lenore.

"Hell no, out here we cut down our own Christmas tree, It's more fun that way, you girls do know how to cut down a tree?"

Ashley responded," You mean we have to cut down a tree!"

"Sure it's easy, I'll show you how."

They started walking up the mountain to the best trees, Doug was just toying with them, there was no way he'd let Ashley swing an axe.

He pick out a great looking tree about seven feet high and said." How does this one look to you girl?"

The girls had never seen such a beautiful, bushy tree. It was perfect.

"Okay who wants to take a swing at her."

Ashley said, "I can't even pick up that axe!"

Lenore bravely offered, "I'll give it a try, but I never did this before."

"Okay give her a whack Lenore."

She tried to pick up the axe but it was heavy, she remembered moving her hands up a baseball bat made it lighter to swing, so she did the same with the axe handle. Using all her strength she hit the tree but hardly made a dent. Doug said, "Do her again, Lenore."

She hit it a second try, then a third and a fourth. Finally Lenore said, "You better do it Doug, I'm afraid if I keep trying we'll miss Christmas!"

"Step aside girl and watch a real western man bring down a tree."

Although it was winter, the girls did not quite understand why they were so hot. Trying to swing that axe had worked up a sweat Lenore turned to Ashley and said, "I'm dying of the heat, I'm sweating bullets. I have to take off my jacket."

"Me too." Ashley echoed.

Doug stopped them. "Oh no, you want to get sick? Never take off you jacket or coat after you've worked up a sweat. Right now the sun's rays are hot, especially because we're up so high on a mountain. It will get cold mighty fast and before you know it you'll be freezing. Just take off you hat and gloves and open your jacket zippers halfway, till you cool down then you can zipper up again."

"Doug I'm hot." Whined Ashley.

"Listen to this old cowboy, I know about the mountains."

Then Doug took his own jacket off and handed it to Lenore.

"How come you can take your jacket off and we can't?"

"I'm not sweating, and I won't be while I'm cutting down this tree."

The girls looked at Doug, his long silver hair that peeked out of his cowboy hat shimmered in the sunlight.

## LENORE'S NIGHTMARE

His leathery skin showed his age and the years of a hard cowboy life. When he swung the axe it was obvious he was still strong and healthy. Both girls loved his deep rough voice yet gentle way and his blue eyes sparkled when he told his tall tales. He was a glorious combination of tremendous strength and unfailing kindness. They could tell Doug brought down many a tree in his life.

Every swing was true and deep and the chips flew as he carved a deep gash in one side of the trunk. Despite the hard work, his ever present Stetson remained perfectly angled on his head and not a hair in his handlebar mustache moved out of place. Before they knew it, the tree had fallen. Then Doug said. "Shoot! I forgot the rope to tie around the branches so they don't get damaged dragging the tree down the mountain. Can you girls go back to the station wagon and get it? Look on the floor and bring the rope back here."

"Sure Doug we can do that." Said Ashley.

"Just stay on the path girls, it leads straight to the wagon.

Lenore shouted, "I'll race you, last one there is a stupid nerd!"

They both raced down the path. Doug yelled back at them, "Slow down you two, before you fall and break a leg or something!"

Half was down the mountain they stopped running. They spotted a baby deer snuffing and grazing on the grass that wasn't cover by snow. The little fawn pushed the snow and then nibbled on the tender shoots of exposed grass. It suddenly bolted and ran a ways, then leaped into the air and stop to resume it's quite foraging. The girls were mesmerized, they stayed very still and quite. They smiled and giggled to each other covering their mouths. Lenore put her finger to her lips to warn Ashley to be quite and as she turned back to watch the beautiful fawn she was still grazing. Ashley took a step closer to get a better look, as she did she stepped on a dry branch. It sounded like a cannon shot when it cracked under her weight and shattered the silence. The fawn was gone in an instant, leaving nothing but it's footprints and snuffle holes in the snow.

"Oh Ashley you scared it half to death, where did it go?"

"I don't know, but if we stay still and very quite, maybe she'll come back."

They searched in vain for the fawn, there disappointment swiftly disappeared and the path began to get covered as a light snow started to fall. They looked for the first time at the unbelievable beautiful scenery of the mountains, they realized the majesty of their surroundings. The snow was pure and white, not like the dirty snow streets of Brooklyn. It was so quite on the mountain not like the noise of New York City. They fell to the ground and started to make snow angels, Lenore liked the simplicity of western life.

It was helping to heal her mentally of all the past memories and pain she had gone through. Their senses sharpened as they smelled the scent of fresh pine. They felt the soft cold snowflakes on their faces.

As the snow fell on their ski-jackets, they saw the incredible blueness of the sky. They both stuck out their tongues to taste the snow. When they turned to each other with there tongues still sticking out they began to laugh. Then they remembered Doug and the rope so they ran to the path and continued down to the station wagon. When they found the rope they ran straight back to Doug. This time they made no stops, when they got back to Doug with the rope he said, "What took you two so long? I thought I'd freeze my buns off!"

"We saw a baby deer and stopped to watch it."

"Come on help me tie up this tree and get it down the trail to the woody! I sure could use a hot cup of coffee and a big piece of Mabel's apple pie."

His mention of food spurred them to get busy. When they returned to the woody, Doug said. "Okay girls give me a hand lifting this tree on the roof. Hold it so I can tie it securely to the rack." As they rode down the mountain Doug put on the heater. "If you girls get to hot let me know and I'll shut the heat off."

Ashley chimed in. "Please leave it on, my feet are numb and my toes are frozen. Doug finish your story we want to her more!"

Doug played coy, "What story are you talking about?"

Lenore said, "The story you were telling us on the way up the mountain. You know, about Mabel and the saloon."

"All right, I'll tell but you girls have to swear not to repeat it or Mabel will skin me alive."

In unison they said, "We swear to God not to say anything!"

"Like I was saying, in the old days I was just a young cowboy who came to Las Vegas to spend a month's salary. A hot bath and shave was always first on my list. After all sometimes I'd spend weeks out on the range, sleeping under the stars with my horse and cattle everywhere. You couldn't tell who smelled worse, my horse, the cattle or me! So if you wanted any female companionship, you had to get cleaned up and put on a fresh set of clothes. I remember walking into the Belle Star Saloon, feeling young and handsome with a month's salary in my pocket. I thought I was Tom Mix or Johnny Mack Brown!"

Lenore interrupted," Who on earth are they!"

"I can't believe what you girls don't know! They were the most handsome, "Root-in-Toot-in" Cowboys at the picture show!

Everybody wanted to look like them, so I moseyed up to the bar and there she was singing her heart out. I guess it was LOVE at first sight."

Ashley said. "I bet she was real pretty. Wasn't she Doug?"

"Down right beautiful, and she could handle herself too. The boys would get a little rough, but Mabel could shoot the eyes out of a snake and everybody knew it. She always carried a small two shot Derringer. Nobody messed with Mabel, except them that didn't know her.

Lenore asked, "What made her carry a gun?"

"Well, it happened one time when I was out on the range on a cattle drive. Some stranger came into town and stayed till closing time at the saloon. He got a little drunk, seems he fancied Mabel and asked her to join him for a drink. She obliged, but he wanted to take her to a room upstairs. She told him she was only a singer not a house girl. You know what that means, don't you girls?"

"Yeah Doug we know what that means."

Well he didn't like being refused and got mean and rough, he started to beat her real good. He accused her of leading him on so he would buy more whiskey. The bartender tried to stop him, but the stranger pistol whipped him and turned back to beating Mabel. I heard about it when I got back in town and I helped nurse her back to health. That's when I taught her how to shoot a six shooter which she wore when she wasn't working, but it was to big to wear with her show dress. So I gave her a small pearl handle two shot Derringer. Damn if she didn't become a better shot than me! Anyway about a year later don't this guy comes back to town and gets drunk and waits for closing and outside the saloon he starts to get rough with Mabel only this time she takes out her Derringer and shoots him right between the legs. She turned him from a bull to a heifer in a wink of an eye! We never saw him again, I've been with her ever since you know like a guardian angel so there you have it. Now don't you girls speak of it."

"No never!" Then after a while Lenore asked, "Doug will you teach me to shoot like Mabel?"

"Heavens child, what makes you want to shoot a gun? That was way back when men got liquored up and did bad things, it was a rough time back then.

"Doug men do bad things today too, will you teach me please!"

Doug didn't answer, Ashley warned. "Mom would kill you if she knew you wanted to shoot a gun!"

"Ashley shut up! Doug will you?"

Again Doug didn't answer, he only looked into Lenore's eyes and saw the desperate need. He picked up on her pain immediately and when Ashley wasn't looking he gave Lenore a nod indicating that he would. He raised his finger to his lips to signal her to be silent about it. Half way home he stopped for gas at Whiskey Pete's a local favorite watering hole, restaurant, bar, gas station small casino. As he pulled up to the pump he said, "Who's hungry? All that tree chopping somebody's got to be!"

Ashley replied quickly, "I'm starved!"

Well they have the best burger and fries ever, little girl!"

Ashley opened the door and suddenly stopped, darn! I don't have any money."

"That's no problem just go in, the woman behind the counter, is a friend of mine. Just tell her that Doug from Mama Mabel's is outside and he wants his favorite. Then order what ever you like."

Ashley hot-tailed it in not waiting for Doug or Lenore. This gave Doug a chance to talk to Lenore in private. "What's this about Lenore? Why do you want to learn to shoot a gun? What's gotten into you little girl, come clean if you want me to teach you?"

"Doug I'm afraid my stepfather is going to fine me. We've been running away from his evilness, your like a grandfather I've never had. I feel close to you and safe, but your not always going to be there and I need to protect myself.

"Why are you so afraid of him, what did he do?"

"He raped me and made me do horrible things with other boys so he could take pictures and movies. I never told my mother everything, I never told Ashley anything. I was scared and confused, he robbed me of my self-esteem. He made me feel like dirt, I wanted to kill myself I wanted to die. Then when my mother found out he hurt me we ran as far as we could. Please help me, please don't tell anyone. Only you and my mother know, please help me."

"Don't you worry as long as your under Mabel's roof, you have nothing to fear. We know how to deal with men like that, I'll shoot him dead myself if he comes near you."

## LENORE'S NIGHTMARE

Lenore thought for a minute, "It's not right to involve you. Just teach me how to shoot and I'll kill him myself."

"Okay Lenore, I'll teach you"

"I knew you would help me, I feel the good in you. Thank you for understanding."

"I'm off on Saturday afternoons, I'll take you to the range it will be our secret Okay?"

"Okay Doug." She grabbed his hand and kissed him on the cheek, "Lets go eat! I can smell the burgers and coffee from here."

Lenore smiled and Doug could see in her eyes that she had a great load taken from her shoulders. Lenore had finally told someone who had great respect for her about her story, she was filled with a new sense of hope. She was sure that with Doug's help Michael would never hurt her again. They both joined Ashley and ate the best damn burgers west of the Mississippi. Afterwards the drive back to Mabel's was very quite. Not another word was spoken about Lenore's request or her private talk with Doug. When they got back they couldn't wait to tell Theresa about their new experience. Doug took the tree off the roof of the station wagon and brought it inside.

"Where do you girls want this tree to stand?"

"You mean we get to choose?"

"Yes you do!'

"Over by the fireplace, no wait a minute. In the corner, no by the couch, wait a minute definitely in front of the window. This way you can see it as you drive up the circular driveway."

Ashley said, "Definitely!"

Theresa and Mabel agreed, "The window it is!"

## JOSEPH SQUATRITO

Doug got the stand and he had it all set right in the middle of the window then he said," We'll just let the branches fall overnight and tomorrow you girls can start decorating, but first I have to get the ladder and cut a foot off the top. It fits in the room now but we'll never get the snow angel on top.

Theresa said," Go up stairs and start your homework, dinner will be ready in an hour. I have to work tonight so don't give Mabel any trouble."

Theresa came home after work about two o'clock and found Lenore sitting on her bed in the dark, "What's wrong honey?"

"Nothing mom, I just couldn't sleep. I keep thinking about what a great day we had on the mountain. It was so beautiful, and Doug is such a warm, and kind man. I had immense fun helping with the tree." She did not reveal her secret with Doug about learning to shoot a gun. "I can't wait to decorate the tree and the house, I'm so glad we're here."

Theresa gave her a hug and kiss, because it was the exact way she felt about being here under Mabel's wing and roof. She left Lenore after she tucked her in and went to her own room to undress and take a shower. As she was taking off her makeup and earrings she realized how lucky she was to have met Eve. She got into bed and started thinking about Joey, Chaz and the 18th avenue gang. She thought about sending Mary a Christmas Card, even though she knew it might be dangerous but she knew she was seeing one of her gentlemen calls tomorrow night who lived in the state of Washington. She would ask him as a favor to mail it from his home city of Seattle. The next evening as promised the girls got busy putting lights on the tree and around the window, it keep them quit busy as Theresa when to work. Doug made a wreath for the front door with the extra branches he cut off the top of the tree so they could get the snow angel to fit. When the angel was put in place to crown the tree, she looked over the cheerfully decorated room. The Christmas ornaments were not the same as the ones back east in Brooklyn, Santa riding a horse! Shotguns and six-shooters painted on Christmas balls, some had famous western hero's like Wild Bill Hitchcock, Buffalo Bill Cody and Calamity Jane. Ashley looked at the finished work, it looked a little strange to her. Lenore recognized Ashley's look, because she felt the same way but she said, "This is Nevada not New York. We have to get use to the fact things are different out here, I like it! I like it a lot, especially Santa riding a horse!"

"Me too, lets go decorate he porch

Mabel caught them before they had a chance, "Wait a minute, you girls have done a beautiful job here but you both have school tomorrow so go up and do your homework."

Ashley protested, "Do we have to? Can't we just do a little bit more."

Lenore chimed in, "Just give us a half and hour, I'll help Ashley with her homework. I promise!"

Mabel saw the happiness they were having so she gave in and said," Okay a half hour then upstairs, no if, and or buts. Your mom would have my hide if she knew I let you stay past cutoff time. So it went right up to Christmas Eve when Theresa and the girls brought down all the gifts they had wrapped and had hidden in their bedrooms. They placed all the presents under the tree. Eve was there with her children, Doug and of course Mabel. This was her new family, many of Mabel's friends drop in for eggnog and some Christmas cheer. Even Tom stopped in to see Mabel

He was on his way to spend the holidays with his father, who lived in California but when you own your own jet making a quick stop is just a way of life. He brought Mabel a huge basket of fruit and the most beautiful bouquet of flowers, and a bottle of brandy for Doug. It seemed Tom's dad, was Doug's boss and Mabel's friend when they were all young. Tom's father owned the biggest cattle ranch in three states. Although he didn't stay long he had enough time to privately wish Theresa a Merry Christmas by giving her a small gift. Theresa was taken aback she never expected a gift. She said," What's this, I never."

"Just a little something, when I saw it, I thought of you!"

"But, I haven't got a gift for you."

"Sure you do. Good night everybody, Merry Christmas! Walk me to the door." When they got to the door, he kissed her on the lips smiled and left. Theresa was lost for words it was unexpected yet very pleasurable. After dinner they all went into the living room to sing Christmas Carols accompanied by Mabel on the piano. At midnight Mabel played

"JOY TO THE WORLD, THE LORD HAS COME!"

Theresa felt Joey's presence as she walked to he front window. She caught her breath as she saw a shooting star. In her heart she was sure it was a sign from heaven and that Joey was with them that night. When Mabel finished playing the piano, Ashley jumped up and yelled," Merry Christmas! Let's open our presents, she ran over to the tree and started handing out the gifts. It was a joyous night for all of them, Theresa was most curious to the gift Tom gave her. When the time was right and she was alone she opened it. She could not believe her eyes a gold bracelet.

Christmas Day it was quiet and peaceful, the girls had a week off from school, so Theresa took them up to Mount Charleston to go sleigh riding and to have some fun in the snow. At an elevation of ten thousand feet, there was plenty of snow in December. It was only an hours drive away.

After fortifying themselves with a hearty breakfast they made their way to the snow. The drive seemed shorter than they thought it would be. They all loved to play in the snow. The memory of Chaz playing with his tiny daughters and his wife, whether conscious as in Theresa's case or long buried as in the case of the girls was probably the basis for their keen anticipation. They made snow angels, had a snowball fight and made a snowman, all before they stopped for a quick lunch at the ski lodge.

As they walked to the mountain top lodge Theresa said, "I think it's time for a hot chocolate with heaps of whipped cream!"

Lenore responded with, "Make mine a double!"

Afterwards the went to the station wagon and got out their sleighs, and had the time of their lives. The day flew by so fast, soon it was time to start for home. They started down the mountain on a winding stretch of road. In some cases the bends in the road were very sharp. The day almost ended in a disaster when a group of boys, in an old pickup truck took a wide turn and forced Theresa off the road and into a ditch. It scared the life out of all of them, Theresa checked with the girls to see if they were all right. Then as she got out to see if there was any damage to the old woody, the boys just drove off leaving them stranded there.

Theresa looked things over and called to the girls," Come on, we have to walk down the mountain to that lodge we passed on the way up. We can probably get help there, I think all we need is a tow truck to pull us out of the ditch. So the trio started down and arrived just before it got dark and the wind kicked up. Theresa went to the front desk and explained their problem. She decided to call Mabel and explain what had happened and to let her know they would be late. Mabel told her to call AAA for help, tell them her wagon was on file as a member, and that she lent the wagon to her for the day. Theresa said, "Okay that sounds like a good idea. Theresa made the call and AAA, told her to wait in the lodge someone would be there to help within an hour. They had some dinner in the lodge restaurant while they waited. When help came the tow truck driver told them to stay in the lodge while he got the woody out of the ditch and check for damage. When he returned and had checked everything out he said," It doesn't look like there's any real damage, I think it's safe to drive I looked under the body and checked the wheels but to be sure I'll follow you for a while. I get off at exit 15 for Las Vegas by then you'll know if there is a problem. Just let me unhook the auto, sign here and we'll be on our way."

They got back to Mabel's safely, but they were totally drained. As they entered the driveway Theresa could see Mabel waiting at the front window. By the time they parked and got out of the woody Mabel was standing on the porch. When the girls ran up to her she gave them a big hug and said.

## LENORE'S NIGHTMARE

"Thank GOD, your all safe." She looked at Theresa shook her head and said," I arranged for Eve to take your escort appointment tonight. Just go inside relax, take hot bath and unwind."

"When your ready I'll bring up some hot chocolate with a mountain of whip cream."

A very grateful Theresa said," That sounds wonderful. Tomorrow we'll stay home and take in a movie."

Lenore and Ashley hid their emotions and agreed that a movie sounded great. Both girls tried hard not to express the fear that had filled them after the day's experience. After they had fallen asleep, Theresa went down to Mabel and broke down in tears, "I forgot that it's only been a short while since we fled that monster, this minor incident today showed me that our fears are not buried very deeply. When those boys forced us into the ditch I almost lost it, my whole life flashed in front of me. I tried so hard not to show the girls how scared I was, I refused to cry in front of them. I've always been their strength but thank GOD your here for me and the girls."

"Honey, don't worry. I've got broad shoulders and they're here anytime you need them.

Theresa hugged her and said, "Your the best, a true angel from heaven."

The next day was very quite, they watched a couple of tear-jerk movies that masked the emotion they were able to unleash thinking of the day before. Theresa had to get ready for work that evening she told the girls," Don't give Mabel any trouble. You can stay up a little later because there's no school tomorrow, but not to late. As she dressed for work she knew her girls were safe with Mabel. The limo driver picked her up at nine to take her to her date in Las Vegas. Carl Ingram had become a regular customer and always asked for Theresa's company. As she sat in the limo en route to her date, her thoughts drifted back to Brooklyn. She thought it might be time to call Sal Brancato and touch base. A feeling was growing inside her, urging her to reach out to Chaz and let him know the girls were all right. Now that she was away from Michael's influence, she knew in her heart that Chaz just could not have killed JOEY!

# THE CONFRONTATION

Back in Brooklyn Michael was losing his patience. His ego lead him to believe Theresa would be back after she calmed down. After all how could she possibly walk away from him and all he did for her. Surely after her money ran out she'd come home. When Christmas came and when he started to get crazy, he couldn't speak of this with any of his so called cronies. His ego would not allow it. He started to think she could not have pulled this off on her own. Who would she turn to for help, it had to be someone she knew and trusted, a life long friend" Sal Brancato."

He walked into the reception area of my office. My receptionist Meri Black inquired," May I help you?"

"Yes,' I'd like to see Sal Brancato!"

"Do you have an appointment?"

"No, just tell him Michael is here, he'll see me!"

Meri didn't know Michael from a hole in the head, so his reference to his name meant nothing to her, "He's with a client just now. Have a seat and I'll tell him your here."

Michael sat, but not for long he was losing his patience. He walked over to Meri and said," How much longer, I don't have much time and you haven't even attempted to let him know I'm here."

Before she could act, Michael barged into my office and said," Get rid of this guy Sal, I want to talk to you!"

I turned to my client excused myself and apologized for the sudden interruption, "I'm sorry about this, will it be all right if we continue this meeting tomorrow?"

My frightened client agreed and left the office. I said."What do you want MICHAEL!"

"Where are they?"

"Where is who?"

Michael really got pissed, "Don't play games with me Sal. I'll ask you just one more time, where is Theresa and the girls?"

I stood my ground, it was the only way I'd have a chance, to make the rest of my statements believable, "Why are you asking me? I have no idea what your talking about."

"Don't make me have to hurt you, so talk!"

I looked him straight in the face and said," I don't know what your talking about it time for you to leave my office."

"Your the only one she would turn to for help, the big deal lawyer. She told me, "She ran into you and your cunt, wife' a few time and had a wonderful stroll down memory lane about the old neighborhood. Did she ask about Chaz, that righteous son of a bitch mister do-good high and mighty. Did she send her love to him?"

"You're way off base Michael! We never talked about Chaz, if you have a problem with Theresa don't bring your shit to me. Now get out of my fucking office, you prick!

Michael was furious at my reply and lunged at me. He pulled me out of my chair and smacked me in the face repeatedly until I was bleeding from the nose and mouth and threw me to the floor. I lay there stunned as he began

## THE CONFRONTATION

to wreck my office. He picked up my chair and threw it through the window to the sidewalk below, he pulled down a heavy bookcase filled with scores of my thick leather bound law books. Like a madman he broke everything in sight. Meri came in and shouted. "I call the police!" "I am the police sister! Now beat it." He came back to me picked me up from the floor I throw a punch at him landing in his stomach then another to his face. He punched me repeatedly. "You just hit a detective, that's assault counselor! Where are they, I'll kill you if you don't tell me."

He punched me again and repeatedly, even if I wanted to tell him I don't think I could have. I was out on my feet the only thing holding me up was him. His firm grip on my jacket keep me from falling to the floor. Thank God two uniformed cops came running in, Michael let go and I crumpled to the floor. Immediately he flashed his gold shield, the two cops backed off.

"What's going on here detective?"

"This shit ass lawyer assaulted me."

"You want us to cuff him and bring him in. I'll read him his rights."

"No need I kicked his ass good. I don't think he'll ever try that again." "What do you want us to do for you?"

"Just leave us alone, he won't talk about this I'm not going to arrest him. Besides he's an old friend from my neighborhood, we were close when we were kids but an argument here got out of control. I'll take care of things here myself."

"Okay you look like you have everything under control." With that the two boys in blue left not wanting to buck a gold shield detective.

After they left, Michael stood over me, my face and shirt were blood soaked. He bent over me and lifted my head and shoulders to get his full attention and said," Your lucky those boys in blue showed up, next time I'll beat you to death."

He let me go and my head slammed back to the floor, then he stomped out of my office. Despite my pain and injuries, I considered myself lucky this time. I now knew in no certain terms, that Michael was not only crazy he was reckless and very dangerous. He feared no one, including the law. In his fanatical quest to find Theresa and the girls, no one was safe if they got in his way.

At the same time I was literally taking a beating, Theresa was fighting with herself. She was sure Chaz must be innocent. She had what could only be called, a visceral urge to call Brooklyn and find out about him and the old neighborhood. She could no longer stand to fight the feelings, and decided to call my office. Making that phone call was one of the hardest calls she had ever made. Meri answered," Salvatore Brancato's office. How may I help you?"

"Hello, is Mr. Brancato in?"

"Yes he is, may I ask who's calling?"

"Just tell him that it's long distance, from Theresa. I'm sure he'll understand and take the call."

Theresa heard the usual Musak playing while she waited and then a brief message cut in, announcing my office hours. While she waited Meri informed me, "There's a long distance phone call for you, somebody named Theresa. Do you want to take the call?"

"Thanks Meri, yes I'l take the call."

# THE CONFRONTATION

I wasn't sure if Michael was playing tricks, so I answered with my usual phone greeting." Salvatore Brancato, may I help you."

"Sal it's me Theresa!"

I recognized her voice immediately, "Oh my God Theresa, where are you! NO! Wait, I don't want to know where you are or where your calling from.

Why are you calling me after all this time? Is everything all right, are you and the girls okay?"

"Yes, Sal I can't stop thinking about home, my friends, the neighborhood and Chaz."

I paused for a couple of seconds, I could not believe what I just heard," CHAZ! After all this time, Theresa you got to be ( I paused).

I mean your thinking of Chaz. I can understand friends the neighborhood but not Chaz."

"Sal I can't understand it myself, I feel. I mean, I keep dreaming of Joey. It's like he's taken a knife from my heart and removed a veil from my eyes. I can feel and see clearly that whatever I thought happened that terrible night is simply not true. I know in my heart, Chaz could never have killed Joey. Being away from Michael and his influence he had over me, I can believe in people again. Joey has brought me to a place where love, compassion and loyalty are a way of life. Like you and Mary, you've always been there for us only sometimes you have to take a step back to see it.

It's a shame what human nature takes for granted. Sal you have to tell him, tell him the girls are all right. We've found a good place to hide from Michael."

## JOSEPH SQUATRITO

"Theresa, Michael is out of his mind, he was here in my office a week ago. Looking for information about your whereabouts. I mean he's totally nuts he wrecked my office and beat the crap out of me all the while screaming that I knew where you are and how it had to be me who helped you to run from him. Theresa, please where ever you are forget about Brooklyn. I just hope one of Michael's partners in crime does all of us a big favor and kills that bastard, and may his soul burn in hell forever!"

"Sal I'm sorry I've caused you so much trouble, please tell Chaz I know he didn't kill Joey. Ask him to forgive me!"

"Okay Theresa, I'll relay the message."

She hung up and I thought to myself that things had not yet come full circle. A week later on the drive up to Attica, I couldn't come to terms with myself about what to do about Theresa's phone call. Another of Chaz's appeals had been turned down. Bad news seemed to be the reason for each of my visits, but would letting Chaz know that Theresa had a change of heart, really help. Would I be giving him false hope? What kind of friend would I be if I hurt him unnecessarily? How could I tell him about my call from Theresa, without telling him the whole truth about her marriage to Michael. Telling him about Michael's abuse of Lenore, I was afraid it would kill him. How could he live with himself knowing there was nothing he could do to help her? What if he blamed himself for not being there for Theresa and Lenore? What if he did something stupid to release his anger and jeopardized his protection at Attica? As the first set of iron-bar doors slid back to give me access to a holding room I made my decision.

# THE CONFRONTATION

Leaving him in the dark was best for him. I sat down at a table and waited for him to be escorted in by a guard. I looked up as he entered, the look on his face seemed to say he could use some good news. I had nothing to offer him in the way he needed, I smiled and asked," Chaz how are you?"

"Sal, I can tell by the look on your face we've been denied again!"

"Is it that obvious?"

"Yes, I could always read you like a book. You never had a poker face, but a better friend I could never have!"

"I tried Chaz, I really did. I told them you were a model inmate, there were recommendations from the warden and the captain of the guards. It just seems as if the parole board turns a deaf ear when it comes to you."

"I'm going to have to do twenty-five years before I get out?"

"I really don't know, the parole board may change. People step down and others step up. There's always a chance that a sympathetic ear may emerge, I'll keep trying that you can count on.

"Sal, I honestly don't think I can do fifteen more years!"

"Don't give up, I'm going to keep fighting you have to keep fighting too. Just hang in there, keep the faith."

"Okay I'll try, I really will!"

We started to talk about the old neighborhood and my family, Mary and the kids. After an hour of conversation, Chaz through me a curve ball he said, "Have you heard from Theresa lately? I don't know I can't explain it, it's just a feeling I have. I dreamed of Joey the other night and when I woke up I couldn't be sure what he was telling me.

It's been really bugging me, I wish I could let it go something about Theresa and the girls."

"No Chaz, I haven't heard from Theresa! It will pass, you were just upset about this parole appeal that was coming up." Chaz said. "Maybe your right."

Then I told him, "I'm going to talk with Warden Stankowitz before I leave today. Maybe he can give me some in sight as to our next appeal?"

"Sal thanks for being my friend! If it wasn't for your help I'd probably be dead. Mastori's protection in here only came because you keep his nephew out of jail."

Using Warden Stankowitz as an excuse to leave, I said my good-byes and left Chaz. I was afraid if I stayed any longer, I'd tell him I heard from Theresa and that would open some can of worms. Actually. Not worms, more like a can of snakes.

Later as I drove back to Brooklyn, a thousand thoughts whirled around in my head. Since I started to try to get the dirt on Michael my personal life has been filled with pain and despair. Unlike Chaz, I was free to go anywhere and do anything I wanted. I could only imagine what it must be like for Chaz. When I got home, I related the day's events to Mary. She soothed me by telling me that doing my best to help was all I could do. I began thinking that maybe I had made a mistake by not telling Chaz about

Theresa's phone call. I asked Mary what she thought I should have done.

Mary answered by saying, "Sal you did the right thing. If you told Chaz about Theresa's phone call he would have gone crazy. Don't torture yourself, you've been his only friend. What more can you do?"

# THE CONFRONTATION

"I feel so unsure about everything Mary. There's the physical altercation with Michael, the mental strain about trying to help Chaz and the nervous worry for all of us including Theresa and her girls. I think I'm coming apart at the seams."

"Maybe we should get away for a while. You need a vacation."

"Yeah but where should we go?"

"How about Las Vegas? You could rest at the pool during the day, then at night we could eat a good meal, take in some shows, gamble a little and if your not to tired have some great sex. Let me give you some TLC. what do you say?"

"I guess the answer is, yes."

"Great I'll make all the arrangements. Don't worry about anything. Is this coming weekend too soon?

"No, book the trip. I'm ready."

The next day Mary went to the travel agent and booked a week in Las Vegas at Caesar's Palace. I got home before her, I just couldn't get my head into my work. When she got home we were all set. She had us booked to leave on Sunday. J.F.K. direct flight, nine a.m. and I was getting excited with only three days to tie up loose ends in the office, I put my clients on hold until I returned but left Meri in the office just to answers phones, take care of mail and walk in future clients. By one o'clock Vegas time we landed, checked in at Caesars, unpacked and was having lunch at the pool side cafe. The days flew by, we started each day with a late breakfast, took in the sights and visited other hotels. To me they just didn't compare to the majesty of Caesars. When we would get back to our hotel, we take in a swim and feel the warm sun penetrate and sooth our bodies.

At night after a wonderful dinner we would see a great show. We chose a show at a different hotel each night and every show was fabulous. We could see why Las Vegas was known as the entertainment capital of the world. Each hotel tried to out draw the other with it's headline superstar or production extravaganza. The idea was draw the people in to see the show and hope most would make a pit stop at the casino, it amazed me the strategy of lining the wall with slot machines and having the show line which moved slowly right in front of them. Boy did that idea work, people played those slot machines while they waited, not me after the show I always liked to go back to Caesars to gamble. Mary was right, it you ever want to take a hiatus from the real world then Vegas was the place to visit. After five days of whirlwind activity, we realized that the T.L.C. had been left out. Mary took care of that by planning for a Room Service', dinner, a good bottle of wine, soft music and a lot of sexual pleasuring. She told me, "Tonight you are the King of this Palace!" Now I knew why she took it easy on me with no shopping or sightseeing just a leisurely afternoon at the pool. She didn't care how much money I had lost at the casino, or weather or not I had maxed out our credit cards. Kiddingly I told her, "You just want me to be your sex slave!"

"You got that right big boy and you better be good or I'll just have to hurt you."

Now this kind of talk from my wife was not part of her soft demure personality. Las Vegas had turned her into a sexual tiger. I replied by saying, "I was one of the Italian Stallions or did you forget?"

"That was a long time ago, I'm going to take a shower and slip into something very sexy."

When Room Service' arrived Mary was not yet out of the bathroom so I took charge and told the waiter where to set up the table. It was covered with a white and gold table cloth, the china was decorated in gold leaf with the Caesars logo, a rose in a crystal vase with a candle on each side. Mary had ordered the food from the "Spanish Steps Restaurant" one of the best Caesars had to offer. I signed and tipped the waiter and he left, when Mary heard him leave she came out dressed in a black lace teddy, covered by a silk and lace peignoir her hair freshly done, red lipstick smell of sweet perfume. I thought it couldn't get any better than this, boy was I wrong. I looked at her and just said, "Wow!" She walked over to me gave me a kiss and slowly touched my crotch then she said."Shall I light the candles, sir?"

"Yes, please." I was shocked, I sat down and she served dinner.

I uncorked the wine and poured both glasses, we tapped the glasses and toasted to a fabulous time together. We started with shrimp cocktail, then Caesars salad. Mary bent over opened the warmer and took out two prime rib dinners the signature dish of the Spanish Steps. As she bent over most of her breast we exposed. I couldn't decide which looked more inviting her cleavage or the end cut prime rib with baked potato my favorite. Maybe it was the wine but I said to her.

"You even remembered to get and end cut, your the best sweetheart." She reminded me that I was the king that night, she top off the dinner with peach melba laced with Chambord liquor. By the end of the meal I was worried my performance would be hindered from to much wine and Chambord. Then I decided to take a shower and freshen up Mary yelled out, "Don't get lost in there, I'll be right here waiting for you on the bed."

They say that after you've been married for more than a couple of years, sex is not as good as it was when you were young. It wasn't that way with Mary and me. Mary was better than ever, because we truly loved each other. We didn't have sex, we made love. When your a kid, it's wham-bam "thank you, mame" five minutes later it's lets do it again. We showed our love with our bodies. My only thought was to satisfy and please Mary and her only thought was to satisfy me. It was an unbelievable session. After more than an hour of incredible pleasure, we just lay there totally spent. Looking lovingly into each others eyes, suddenly we both said in unison, "Casino!"

And burst out laughing. We both ran into the bathroom took a shower together got dressed and left the room in record time. As we were riding down in the elevator, I looked at Mary and said, "What's our hurry, it's not like the casino is closing."

"Well, I have a slot machine with my name on it, it's calling me."

The elevator stopped at the casino floor, when the doors opened, we headed in different directions. "I'll be playing blackjack."

Mary yelled back," I'll be the woman screaming her head off when I hit the jackpot!"

# THE CONFRONTATION

Although we went our separate ways, we were closer than ever to each other. About an hour later Mary was in the Ladies, bathroom. Entering a stall when from the corner of her eye she thought she saw Theresa. She turned to get a better look but the woman had her back to Mary. She only got a good look at the skintight red dress she was wearing. Mary yelled out "Theresa" but the woman kept walking, without turning or stopping.

After finishing in the Ladies room she came looking for me. When she found me at the blackjack table, I was really excited because I was on a winning streak. I saw her and said. "Hi honey, look I'm finally winning! Your T.L.C. must have brought me luck, among other things." Then I whispered in her ear. "I've got most of our money back."

"Sal I thought I saw Theresa!"

"Theresa, what do you mean?"

Then she got very frazzled, "Theresa! I was in the ladies room looking for a stall, I walked right by her but from the corner of my eye I swear it was her. When I turned and called out her name, she just kept walking away. Never turned her head or looked back."

"So go look for her!"

"I did all over the casino, where could she have gone?"

"Anywhere, this place is huge, maybe she went in a restaurant or the showroom. I'll tell you what, the show gets out in an hour we'll wait by the box office. If she comes down the stairs we'll be sure to see her. Just give me forty-five minutes and I'll meet you there, here take a twenty-five dollar chip cash it in and go play the slots."

"Sal if that was Theresa, she looks incredible. The outfit she had on had to be worth well over five hundred dollars, what a gorgeous dress and those exquisite accessories but being a woman I was looking at what she was wearing. Wish I would have looked more at the face."

I gave Mary a kiss before she left for luck, but I couldn't concentrate I keep thinking about Theresa. I lost a few hands I should have won so I decided to cash out and go looking for Mary. This time I found her winning at the slots. Mary turn to me and said, "Sal I hit a jackpot for a thousand bucks! Didn't you hear me screaming?

"No, I'm afraid not. I couldn't concentrate on the game after what you told me so I cash in my chips for six, five hundred dollar chips and with the thousand you just won we have a free trip. Now lets go to the casino cage and turn these tokens in to money, then we'll go look to see if that really was Theresa."

"Okay help me fill my bucket!"

The bucket was so heavy that I thought I might get a hernia lugging it to the coin redemption window. Mary was still playing with extra coins that didn't fit in the bucket. The grand total was one thousand two hundred fifty dollars more than we both though.

When I got back to Mary she had filled yet another bucket hitting her second jackpot of the night. I looked at her in amazement and said, "Holy shit Mary were going home winners, nobody wins in Las Vegas do they? Maybe we should forget about Theresa and stick with this machine."

"No! I want to find Theresa!"

I handed her money and took the second bucket to the coin redemption window, even the woman behind the cage smiled and shook her head in disbelief. This time the count was thirteen hundred dollars. I thought to my self

## THE CONFRONTATION

she really is trying to get me a hernia. Mary was flushed red with excitement when I returned she was still playing so I told her," This machine love you, you are on a roll woman! Don't leave this machine, I'll walk over to the box office and look for Theresa."

I stood at the foot of the red carpeted stairs just left of the box office, waiting for the Circus Maximus Show to end. I was getting nervous as the room let out, if she was there wearing that red dress I was sure I'd spot her. The Circus Maximus Showroom was almost completely empty when I saw her. There she was at the top of the stairs. I was astonished to see her, she looked even more beautiful than I remembered her.

This was not the Theresa of Bensonhurst, not the Theresa who played stickball with the boys and not the Theresa who hung out at Dom's candy store playing the jukebox. She looked magnificent in that red dress, she could still turn heads she could turn a man into a babbling idiot. I asked myself how a woman on the run with two children could become the vision I was gawking at. There were many pieces to this puzzle that I had yet to discover. As she got to the bottom of the stairs I realized she was not alone. She was on the arm of a very well dressed man, who definitely was no slouch. His suit must have cost a thousand dollars and his shoes were imported maybe from Italy. He had his arm around Theresa and I could see he wore a diamond pinky ring, the stone had to be at least three carats. This was no wise guy or pickup, he was a moneyman a CEO of a large corporation. I said, "Theresa!" then I grabbed her arm to stop her from walking by, "Theresa it's me!"

"Hi Sal what are you doing here?"

"Mary and I are on a vacation, she said she saw you in the ladies room. How are the girls?"

"Sal I have to go!"

"Wait we have to talk."

"I can't, I have to go."

I held her arm tighter, I couldn't let go."

"Sal, your hurting my arm!"

The guy she was with then pushed me back and I let go. He stepped between Theresa and me, ready to do battle and defend her. She held him back and whispered something in his ear. He stepped away, Theresa put up her arm with her palms in my face a sign to back off.

"Theresa please, we have to talk!"

"Sal, forget you saw me. It's better for both of us, especially for you. You know what I mean." Then she reached out for me, pulled me close to her, hugged' me and kissed me and said, "Give my love to Mary, I'll never forget that you were there for me and my daughters!"

I stood there totally stunned, as she turned and walked away with the stranger. They disappeared into the crowd as if the chance meeting had never happened. I was so startled, that if it hadn't been for the delicate scent of her perfume clinging to my jacket, I might have believed she had been a figment of my imagination. I went back to Mary who was still playing her slot machine. Mary stopped playing her machine. She turned to me and asked," Sal, did you find her?"

"Yes, you were right, it was Theresa you saw."

"Did you get a chance to talk to her? Where is she?"

"Talk? No, not really. She said it was best not to, she was with a man and wanted to be left alone. They disappeared

## THE CONFRONTATION

in the crowd. Theresa was dressed like a high price call girl and the guy she was with was obviously a high roller. I wish we could have talked, I wonder where the girls are tonight and who's watching them?"

"Sal they're not babies anymore. If she has become a prostitute, well a mother has to do whatever she has to do to survive and provide for her children. I'm sure knowing Theresa that whatever she's doing it for the good of the girls."

"You're probably right, she does have to make a living. What a bummer, this was a great vacation now it's going to drive me nuts not knowing the truth.

"Sal you were doing so well leaving your troubles back east. just forget it. Please lets enjoy our last day here tomorrow. What ever you want to do we'll do. Lets go back to the room and finish off the rest of the wine."

"I say lets order another and really finish the night."

Tears flowed from Theresa's eyes as she climbed into the back seat of the limo, that was waiting out in front of Caesars. Even though the tinted windows darkened the interior of the limo, Tom Shanks her companion for the evening saw her tears and said. "Okay Theresa, come clean. What was that all about and who was that guy?"

"He was just someone from my past, a friend. His wife has been my best friend since we were kids, they helped me and my girls when I needed help the most."

"It didn't look that way to me!"

"Tom I can't involve him in my troubles, he's already been badly beaten just because my husband thought he might be the one who helped me. My ex-husband is a bad-ass gold shield detective. Who's looking for me and my girls, did I mention he is totally insane."

"Then let me help you!"

She couldn't even look at him from embarrassment. Staring out the the blackened window she said, "Believe me you don't want to get involved. My ex-husband is truly evil. Maybe only God can help us, I honestly hope and pray that some drug addict shoots him dead!"

"Listen to me, I have been seeing you every chance I get. Your not just an escort date to me, I really care for you. Can't you tell that I'm falling in love with you. I have money and power, please let me help you!"

"Tom your great, the gentleman in every girls dream. You treat me like a lady and I know you mean what you say, I've seen it in your eyes for a long time and I really love you for it. You've given me back some of the self-esteem I lost. Only right now my girls need me, and for now their needs come before mine."

"Theresa if I help you, I'd also be helping them!"

Tom reached for Theresa's hand in complete sincerity, but Theresa knew that there was no way she could involve him, "Just be my friend for now. Can you do that with no questions asked. Lets just be you and me, with no ties. I need for you to be someone I can talk to, someone that makes me feel good about myself. You're someone I respect and admire. Just the thought that you want to be with me makes me feel like a new person."

"All right, I'll play it your way. The ball is in your court, maybe in time you'll change your mind you know how I feel. I just know that I can't stay away from you and that I want to get closer to you." He pulled Theresa to him and kissed her with all the passion of a lover.

## THE CONFRONTATION

After a few seconds Theresa sighed and pulled back and said. "I'm not ready for this, it will only lead to other things. You want what I'm not free to give to you."

As the limo turned into Mama Mabel's driveway their conversation had turned to a quiet lilting exchange. The limo driver opened the door for Theresa. Tom grabbed her hand as she was about to get out and said, "Wait a minute, Theresa. I'm taking my private jet back to California tonight. I don't want you to think I'm leaving because of what happened tonight or because of our conversation. I have an important business deal in Asia, I have to attend to. You may not hear from me for a while, if you need me, call my secretary and she'll get in touch with me. The office always knows how to reach me. Let me give you my private office number. I'll leave word that you might call, just ask for Sue Penetta. She'll know where I am if need be I have local men here to protect you and the girls. They can be here in a moments notice."

He handed her the usual envelope for her nights work. She waved him off saying, "Tom this is not necessary, I don't take from my friends. Your friendship to me is more than money."

This time she leaned into him and kissed him goodnight saying, Maybe someday things will be closer to what you want them to be."

As she pulled away to leave, Tom slipped the envelope into her handbag. The limo started down the driveway and Tom lowered the window to get a last look at her. She climbed the stairs to the front door, he thought to himself that she looked as sexy from behind as she did face to face, what a body! He knew that body was just the start of her charms, he had to have her. When she turned back to wave to him, she could only see the taillights of the limo as it turned out of the driveway.

Two days later, Mary and I left Las Vegas. We still didn't know anything more about the chance meeting we had with Theresa. Back at Mabel's the days turned into weeks and the weeks turned into months. Before long spring had arrived and the warm weather was a welcomed delight. The girls had settled into their new school and were finally feeling comfortable, making friends. It was a little easier for Ashley than it was for Lenore. She still had that fear, Michael had instilled in her. Still afraid to totally open up to people. When she was asked to try out for cheerleaders no one was more surprised than her. Rene' Wheeler her new friend, and classmate felt Lenore was a shoe in to be picked.

"Lenore, you just have to try out. You're the perfect height and weight and you certainly have the looks. You have to climb out of your shell and be more outgoing." Lenore looked at her and smiled saying," Why don't you try out, I don't think I will besides I have to watch my younger sister after school. I don't know how they got my name, hardly any one in school knows me."

"Wrong, I told the cheerleaders about you and they saw us together at lunch. They agreed that you were perfect. I couldn't make it but there's no reason why you can't. Besides if you make it, it will be like me making it."

"I'll have to think it over and talk to my mom about it."

On the way home that day Lenore began to get excited about the idea of becoming a cheerleader. Only the prettiest

## THE CONFRONTATION

and the most popular girls got picked. She thought about some of the boys on the football team, they were real foxes! At dinner Lenore told Theresa that she had been asked to try out for a spot on the cheerleading team.

"Lenore I think that's great. Are you going to try out?"

"What about Ashley, Mom? The cheerleaders practice after school and right through the summer. Maybe I shouldn't."

Mabel chimed in, "Nonsense! A girl of your age needs to be with girls her own age. I was a cheerleader of sorts in the old days, at the El-Rancho Saloon. We did a lot, of cheering in that place! I was a beauty and could high step the Cancan!"

Theresa gave Mabel a "look" while shaking her head no and rolling her eyes to heaven. She felt the girls were not ready for saloon stories.

"Well that's another story, maybe when your older."

Everyone looked at each other around the table, and then they all burst out laughing. Lenore waited until the laughter died down and said, Maybe I will try out I can high step, but I certainly can't Cancan!"

A week later at try outs, it's obvious that Lenore was sure to make it. She could have passed for a cheerleader in the NFL. There was no way you would pass her by, in her short skirt and sweater. In fact, when she jumped around during cheerleading tryouts she stopped football practice.

Quarterback, Troy Hansen went back to throw a pass downfield. He saw Lenore out of the conner of his eye, turned to look at her and forgot to throw the ball. After the defense knocked him to the ground, he got up and,

"Who the fuck is she! Did you see those tits bouncing in the breeze?"

The football coach yelled," Hansen, what are you doing out there?"

Lenore's gym teacher, Nancy Dawson blew her whistle and shouted, "Okay girls, first full practice is Monday, Wednesday and Friday. We meet at three in the afternoon right after school. You can change in the girls locker room. Your pompoms will be distributed at practice. Welcome to the team Lenore!"

All the girls gathered around Lenore to welcome her to the team. For the first time in a very long time she felt good about her self. This time it was because of recognition from the age group that mattered most. She secretly desired to belong and to be accepted. She got even more excited on her way home, by the time she reached the front door her heart was racing. She threw open the door and yelled, "I made it, I made it I'm a cheerleader! She found what she thought was an empty house, so she started up the stairs to the second floor when she heard Mabel come out of the kitchen and call, "What's all the yelling about child? I could hear you way back in the kitchen, even with all the pots and pans clanging."

"Mabel I made the cheerleading team!"

"Didn't I tell you so? I said all you needed was a little encouragement."

Then Lenore asked, "Where's Mom and Ashley?"

"I'm not sure, your mother went to pick up Ashley after school. She said something about shopping."

"I guess I'll go up stairs and practice my cheers. Two, four, six, eight" as she bounced up the stairs.

## THE CONFRONTATION

"That child is going to give some boy a run for his money. I never had a body like that and I killed them!" Mabel said to herself as she walked back into the kitchen to tend to her apple pies. A smile crossed her face as memories came flashing back. She could almost hear herself in her prime as she dazzled the men, "Well howdy boys, welcome to the can-can review!" Those surely were good times in her younger days.

Later that afternoon when Theresa and Ashley returned from shopping, Lenore was still as high as the proverbial kite. Her excitement hadn't diminished one iota. When she heard them come in she flew down the stairs. "Mom, I made it! I'm part of the team."

"That's great honey! See I told you you'd make it."

"Mom that's exactly what Mabel said, come on Ashley I'l show you my cheers so when you get older you can make it too."

Theresa went up stairs with her packages and went directly to her room.

She walked over to her front window, tears were flowing from her eyes. She dried her eyes as she raised them to heaven, "Thank you, oh Lord! Thank you for answering my prayers and giving my Lenore a second chance. Please Lord, help her forget the cruelty and evil pain she has suffered." Almost immediately she thought of Joey, again she felt, as if he were standing by her side. She could feel his presence saying, "Joey, I know you're her with me. Thank you for sending my prayers to our Lord! I love you and miss you very much.

During the rest of the school year Lenore kept up with her grades and practiced very hard. Through it all, she never let her friendship with Rene' falter. She always made sure she made time to include Rene' no matter how busy her schedule was. This developing friendship gave Theresa more time to spend with Ashley. Ashley was always confused about why they had to leave their home and their friends in Brooklyn. She still wasn't really old enough to understand what had happened to Lenore. She would ask Theresa, "Aren't we ever going to see Daddy again? Why can't we go home?"

Theresa would answer, "Mommy and Daddy don't love each other anymore. Daddy is very mad at Mommy and he might hurt me if he knew where we were. You wouldn't want that, would you? Aren't you happy here at Mabel's sweet heart?"

"Yes, I love aunt Mabel."

At times like this, Theresa would always distract Ashley and change the subject without Ashley being aware of it. So far Ashley hadn't caught on to her mother's ploy, but Theresa knew it wasn't going to work forever. She worried how she would handle all this when Ashley got older. Theresa felt that all she could do in the meantime was to build a strong bond between her and her daughter. During the day Theresa devoted her time to her girls but at night she did a great job earning a living as an escort. Mabel took her share plus rent, food and car expense right out of Theresa's earnings. Theresa never questioned how much she took, as far as she was concern the money she was receiving far surpassed what she could have earned nursing. Paul Ingram requested her company most often, he was wealthy and very influential. Like Tom Shanks, he wanted more than Theresa was willing to give. Like

# THE CONFRONTATION

Tom he was hooked and his ego would not take no for an answer. He requested Theresa's service for a week not just at night but twenty-four hours a day. Mabel was taken aback!

No one had ever requested that much of time before from one of her girls. Her answer was," first I have to talk it over with her and second do you have any idea what that is going to cost you?"

His answer was, "I don't care what it cost, Tell her there will be a five thousand dollar tip for her and that we'll be going to Italy. She'll have her own room at the Excelsior in Rome, during the day she can shop, and take in the sights. All expenses paid and each night, there is a dinner party. I'm counting on you Mabel!"

He hung up the phone and Mabel started to think how she was going to present this request to Theresa. As a business woman that side of the coin was a bonanza. She could charge twenty times the six hour nightly rate plus extra. As Theresa's friend she feared for her, so far away and helpless.

Paul had always been a gentlemen but she was to slick not to see he wanted more from Theresa. That night she talked to Theresa about Paul's phone call and all the perks that went with it. Theresa knowing Paul's intentions said, "He's dangling the proverbial carrot just to get in my pants, I don't need his money so I don't want to go to Italy. He's a very nice, man but no I'm not leaving the girls for a week and I'm not having sex with Paul. Mabel said, "Okay, I'll explain it to him as you just can't leave your girls for that length, of time. Lets just hope we don't loose him as a client."

"I'm sorry Mabel. You know I'd do anything for you, but this is not what I signed on for." Mabel looked at her and said, "Don't fret honey, it's only money we'll make more some where else."

The next day it was like from Mabel's mouth to God's ears. Who should call but Tom Shanks he was back from Asia and hadn't seen Theresa in months when he told Mabel he wanted to see Theresa every night for a week she said," Sorry Tom her calendar is filled for the next three weeks!"

"Mabel can't you do an old friend a favor and rearrange her schedule for me. I'll pay double what your usual rate is."

"Now Tom you know it doesn't work that way, I have to be fair with all my clientele." Mabel knew Theresa was only booked for a night in the middle of the week. After a pause she said, "Only because of the relationship I had with your father, as old friends, I'll move things around and free her service for you. Now remember your paying for those cancelled appointments so double is more than fair. I can't cancel tonight it's too short notice and I don't have any other girl to replace Theresa. Tomorrow night she's yours for a week, is that okay with you?"

Tom answered in a flash," Better than okay, Mabel your the best. I'm just going to have to hug and kiss you when I see you."

"Well, if you start that kind of stuff with me and my engine gets revved up, you might have to give me more sugar honey!"

Then they both started to laugh and said goodbye. Mabel knew she just made some of the money back she lost on the deal with Paul, But she was smart enough to know

# THE CONFRONTATION

not to try it again. Tom was no fool and she certainly didn't want to lose him as client or a friend. Later that morning she asked Theresa how she was getting along with Carl her date for the evening.

"Fine why do you ask? Has he complained about me? Is something wrong?"

"No honey, it's just that Tom Shanks is back from Asia and has requested your company for the next week after tonight."

Theresa was very nonchalant as she replied, "That's great, I like Tom. He and Carl are both gentlemen, they treat me with the utmost respect. I feel very special when I'm with either one of them."

Theresa had never told Mabel about the conversation she had with Tom in his limo the night he left on his trip to Asia. How he professed his love for her and was willing do anything to protect her.

"So you don't mind spending a week straight with Tom?"

"I don't mind if he don't mind."

"Good, very good."

"I'm going to the movies with Ashley, I'll be back in time to dress and be ready for Carl's limo. See you later Mabel."

Mabel enjoyed the monetary side of her business, to her it was a money game and she played it well. There was now a bidding war for Theresa's service between three very rich men. They all wanted her at their beck and call, they all could well afford to play the game. So Mabel saw no reason why she shouldn't make them pay her, and pay well. Theresa was totally unaware of the game Mabel was playing, so conducted herself with her usual class and gentle demeanor. Her beauty spoke for itself, this made Tom, Carl and Paul want her more. Mabel was a master when it came to knowing men and what made them tick. She had spent her whole life filling their desires. When she was young and quite a beauty herself, she learned how to fill a man's desire. Now as an old woman she still filled their needs even if it meant hiring a stable of beauties. She combined knowledge of men, with her shrewd business sense and was making a fortune.

She knew how to wheel and deal and Theresa was her number one asset. She told Theresa all the time. "You've come a long way, just be yourself and let Mama Mabel worry about all the details." For the next week, Theresa and Tom saw each other every evening, It didn't seem possible, but each evening was better, renewing their friendship and working out their relationship. Theresa could see Tom wanted more than the casual escort date. Although she truly enjoyed being with him and if there was anyone she would give into, she was not ready to take that step or lower her guard. There were always to many demons whirling in her head, no matter how hard she tried the fear of Michael was always there haunting her. Lenore had new friends and her cheerleading practice. Ashley showed signs of growing up. As the summer flew by, Theresa still keep a close eye on her girls. September rolled around and school was again in session. Ashley had graduated and now both Lenore and Ashley attended Henderson High. This gave Lenore more to worry about, but it also made it easier for her to keep an eye on her younger sister. She still watched over her like a mother hen. Although Ashley voiced her

# THE CONFRONTATION

opinion to their mother, Lenore still got her way and continued to keep tight reins on her. Ashley was beginning to resent Lenore, she couldn't understand why Lenore was on her back but then again she didn't know the dark secret Lenore kept inside. Ashley just like her mother and sister was blossoming into a very beautiful young woman. She also started to spread her wings and show her sexuality. Ashley now almost fifteen had a larger bra size than Lenore. She wanted to wear tighter clothes, her awareness of boys was becoming very obvious. She had no reason to be shy, when she talked about boys, she referred to them as hunks. This made Lenore crazy, to Ashley it looked like a fierce case of sibling rivalry. To Lenore it was a battle for Ashley's protection and happiness. Theresa tried to talk to Lenore about giving Ashley some space, "She has to learn on her own Lenore, she has to made her own mistakes."

Lenore wouldn't hear of it, "Mom you should see how the older boys at school look at her. Incredible, and she stares back at them smiling shaking her ass or expanding her bust. Before you know it they'll be wanting her to do things she's to young too do. You know exactly what I mean, well not if I have anything to say about it."

Theresa understood Lenore's concerns all to well, and she didn't want to open any old wounds. Lenore was happy about herself and seemed to have left her demons behind her. Ashley was another story.

As the months went by the fighting and arguing increased, Ashely became more brazen and obnoxious. One morning as the girls were leaving for school, Lenore noticed Ashley was wearing no bra under her top. Her nipples were standing at attention on high beams, a girl with the size of a D-cup should never go braless even though she thinks her breast are firm and do not hang. Lenore said, "Your not going to school looking like that! Did Mom see you? Go inside and put on a bra, what do you want to be ex-spelled from school!"

"Your just jealous, mine are bigger than yours and the don't flop around like yours.

"Are you crazy! Go get a bra on before I drag you in by your hair!"

"I like to see you try, your not my mother!"

Lenore grabbed Ashley by the hair, and started to pull her into the house. Ashley started to scream, "I hate you, your always bossing me around. Let me go." Ashley started to fight back, kicking and screaming at the top of her lungs. Theresa came running down from her bedroom, Mabel came in from the kitchen even Doug heard the screams from the back garage. Theresa was first on the scene, by this time Lenore's firm grip in Ashley's top had ripped open and more than half her breast were exposed. Theresa said, "What in God's name is going on down hear!"

"She wants to go to school braless!

Mabel rushed in and when Doug got look at Ashley he turned away and said. "Oh lord, what are you thinking little girl!"

Theresa pull them apart, "Up stairs now, put on a bra and a different top!"

Ashley covered up as she went up to her room. "I hate her Mom, I hate her."

"Don't you ever pull a stunt like this again, your grounded for a week!" "Mom she's such a little bitch, she did this just to start a fight."

# THE CONFRONTATION

"Well, now you both missed the bus for school and I'll have to get dressed and drive you both."

Theresa rushed to get some clothes on and check on Ashley's attire, Lenore waited and did a slow burn. Mabel tried to calm her by saying, "You were right to do what you did. She's just at that rebellious stage give her time. She don't mean what she said."

When Theresa and Ashley came down they were both dressed, Ashley had a new top on and most importantly a bra for support. The ride to school was very quite, neither sister was talking. Theresa was besides herself!

She knew Lenore was obsessed with Ashley's behavior, and Ashley was determined to act grown up even if she really had no idea what that entailed. Theresa did not know how to defuse the situation. She was at her wit's end and told Mabel so. Even Mabel didn't have an answer sibling rivalry was not something she had experienced in her younger days. The football season was coming to a close and Lenore would have more time to be on Ashley's back. She just couldn't help herself. It was time for Theresa to have a heart to heart talk with Lenore. One afternoon before she got ready for work, Theresa took Lenore outside on the porch and told her, "Lenore you have to stop this obsession with your sister's well-being. She has good family values, you must trust her to make her own decisions. You're causing her to pull away from you when she need you the most. Do you want her to lose her love and respect for you? I'm afraid I don't know how to handle this without telling Ashley what happened to you!"

"Oh no Mom, please don't tell. I'd never be able to live with myself if she knew."

Theresa understood all to well why Lenore acted the way she did. "Okay I won't say anything if that's the way you want it." "You have to try to help the situation by not fighting with Ashley all the time." "I promise I'll try!"

Theresa gave Lenore a big hug and kiss. "I love you baby, more than you'll ever know. Tomorrow is Saturday, let's go to the movies, just the three of us, and start to heal our problems."

"Okay and I promise I wouldn't fight no matter what she says."

Things seemed to calm down after that. Lenore kept her word and stopped the fighting and the remarks to what she was wearing or doing. She left it up to Theresa to police the situation and Ashely was able to accept the constructive way Theresa explained things to her. On Thanksgiving Day the football team played their last game of the season. Lenore was cheerleading for the last time, until next spring. Ashley went to the game with her friends from school. Theresa was helping Mabel in the kitchen with the traditional turkey dinner. She told the girls to come straight home after the game and they both agreed. It was a beautiful day for Henderson High versus it's old rival Boulder High. The weather was perfect not a cloud in the sky and the temperature was in the high sixties. It turned out to be a great football game and Henderson won 28–21!

After the game, Troy Hanson made a point of stopping Lenore.

As she was leaving the field he yelled out, "Hey Lenore, got a minute?" "Hi Troy, great game!"

"Lenore now that the football season is over, I don't have to practice every day and you don't have cheerleading

# THE CONFRONTATION

practice. I'd like to see you maybe we can go to a movie or a dance?"

Lenore was surprised and hesitated for a moment. Then a smile lit up her face, "Okay sure, maybe we can talk about it when we get back to school on Monday! I have to meet my sister now and get home. Have a nice "Thanksgiving" bye Troy!"

"Bye Lenore, you have a wonderful, Thanksgiving too."

She spotted Ashley waiting by the exit, as she walked away she turned smiled and waved to Troy. Troy let out a loud yell of excitement as he ran to the locker room. All of a sudden the winning touchdown pass seem unimportant. The team was cheering and singing their victory song. Troy wished the next four days would fly by so he could make plans with Lenore.

When the girls got home they entered the house yelling and cheering, "We won, Henderson High won!" Theresa came out of the kitchen and said, "They can hear you two clear over in Las Vegas. I'm glad we won but now go up stairs and get dressed, dinner is almost ready and company will be coming in an hour." They both ran upstairs no question asked.

Thanksgiving dinner at Mabel's was wonderful. The usual friends gathered around Mabel's table, Eve was there with her kids, Doug, Theresa and the girls and two new friends Sally-Jo and Maryanne. Who had just started working for Mabel. Everyone agreed Mabel had out done herself with dinner but all were waiting anxiously for dessert. Mabel's hot apple pie with ice cream, peach cobbler, fruits and hot chestnuts. As they were enjoying their delicious treats they had an unexpected visitor. Doug's nephew Billy-Bob Johnson stopped in to wish everyone a Happy Thanksgiving. Billy was twenty-one years old and as wild as a West Texas Wind. Trouble always seemed to follow Billy, and rumors were he had just gotten out of jail for who knows what this time. At Mabel's, everybody got a second chance and with Billy, Mabel didn't care if it was a third, fourth, or fifth chance. She love him to death, "Well look who stopped in for dessert, This is Doug's nephew BILLY! Now come and give old Mabel some sugar."

"Hi everybody, Happy Thanksgiving!

He took off a broken down cowboy hat that matched his worn out boots and planted a big kiss on Mabel.

She smiled and said. "Now that's what I call dessert. Make some room give this boy a chair, why your so skinny a good strong wind could carry you away. I'm just going to have to keep you here and fatten you up." Billy took a piece of pie and said. "It's just as I remembered it. Best apple pie in all the Southwest!"

"Have some more, put some ice cream on it. Wait a minute did you have a proper meal today?"

"I grabbed something on the road, but I was dreaming of this pie the last fifty miles."

Billy was a very handsome young man, he may have been enjoying Mabel's pie but he couldn't keep his eyes off Lenore. Ashley couldn't stop staring at Billy. Mabel didn't miss a trick. She thought there's going to be trouble if Billy sticks around. Then Billy said. "Mabel could you use an other hand around here. I sure could use some work, I'm flat broke. Used whatever I had left on gas just to get here."

# THE CONFRONTATION

"You'll have to talk to Doug, he does the hiring and firing around here." "Well, uncle Doug, can you use me?"

Doug looked over to Mabel and she gave him a nod as if to say, okay.

"Okay you got a job. You mind your manners, and be sure to give me a day's work for a day's pay. You get me boy?"

"I sure do. If I'm staying for a while where do I sleep?"

"Out back with me in the bunkhouse. Tomorrow we'll start to get ready for Christmas. We have cleaning up, painting, washing windows and some fixing up to do. There's also a well that's broke, she needs new pipes and then there's all the Christmas decoration to get down from the attic."

"With all that work ahead of me, I think I need another piece of pie."

Everyone laughed, old Doug was on a rampage. He was going to make sure Billy was so tired at the end of the day he wouldn't be able to get into any trouble.

Ashley chimed in," Can I help Doug?"

"No honey this is man's work."

"What about a tree? Can we cut one down like we did last year?"

"Sure we can Ashley, maybe in two weeks. We can't go to soon. We want it to be fresh for Christmas. If you remember last year we want for the tree a week before and it was fresh right through New Year."

Ashley asked, "Billy will you be here for Christmas?"

Billy looked at Doug and said. "I don't know, I sure would like to be here for the Holidays." Doug replied. "I guess we'll just have to see how long the work holds up."

## JOSEPH SQUATRITO

For the next two weeks Doug kept Billy real busy getting the house ready but the work was getting harder to find and a need for an extra hand was not necessary. Mabel told Doug. "Slow down with the work, keep Billy here through New Year's."

"Don't have much more to do except,' cutting down the tree and putting up the decorations for Christmas. Last year Lenore and Ashley helped with all of that."

"So this year let Billy do it with the girls. Let him clean out the garage and paint it. He can get rid of all the junk that I've been accumulated over the years. If need be let him paint my bedroom. I want it freshen up I'll sleep in one of the spare rooms at the back of the house. This way, when he leaves he'll have a good stake to carry him till he gets a new job."

"Okay your the boss!"

The next day Billy started cleaning out the garage. Doug told him to through all the junk in his pick up truck and together they would bring it to the junk yard. So before Billy started painting the clean up would take a few days. By the time the painting was finished in the garage, it was time to cut down the tree. Doug thought better of letting Billy go up to the mountains with the girls so he decided to go too. The mountain roads were dangerous with no guard rails. The way Billy drives that old pick up truck he was afraid he'd drive clean off the mountain and kill someone. The morning they were leaving Lenore asked Doug, Is Billy taking us up the mountain for the tree? Mabel said at breakfast he was."

"No were all going up in the woody, I'll do the driving and Billy can do the cutting, and you girls can do the

# THE CONFRONTATION

picking. Besides he'd scare me half to death the way he drives.

Ashley said," I'm not afraid to drive with Billy in his pick up truck."

Lenore smiled and said," I don't think so, your to eager to be alone with him. Your hormones are working overtime, you heard Doug we're all going in the woody. On the drive up the mountain Ashley never stopped talking or asking questions. Billy was trying to be as much of a gentleman as he could with his answers. Ashley threw him for a loop when she flat out asked if he was in jail. Billy turned beat red, and put his head down and didn't answer her. Lenore blasted her for having the Gaul to say such a thing.

Billy said. "Yes I was, I served ten months for a barroom fight I didn't start."

Just then Doug said. "Okay where here this is as far as we can go with the woody." They unloaded the trunk and took the axe and the rope and started their climb, up the trail to the best trees. When the found a tree the girls agreed on, Billy went to work chopping it down. Doug looked at the sky took off his hat and scratched his head, then he said," I've seen this before those dark clouds are coming fast and the wind is picking up. Work faster Billy I think a snow storm is on it's way. Billy got the tree down in a couple of good swings. They tied it so the branches were secured, and they made their way back down to the woody. This time there was no time to look at any deer grazing, or enjoy the sight of a beautiful sky. As Doug and Billy tied the tree to rack on the roof of the woody the snow began to fall. At first it was light but as the wind increased so did the snow. The mountain roads were dangerous enough without the snow to make them slippery. A wrong speed on one of the curves and you could slide right off the mountain. Billy said. "Let me drive old man your eyes aren't what they use to be."

"My eyes are just fine, besides you drive like a madman.

"I promise to take it slow, you know my reflexes are faster than yours." Doug gave in and said. "If you do anything stupid, I'll kill you before we all die."

"Then who's going to be driving the wagon?"

Everybody started laughing, Billy kept to his word and took it real careful driving down the slippery roads. By the time they got to the lower elevations the snow mixed with rain and the ride home was easy. When the woody turned into the circular driveway and stopped the girls were first out of the wagon. Ashley ran into the house and yelled, We got a beauty, wait till you see this tree." Then she ran back outside and said. "Lets bring it in the house so Mom and Mabel can see it."

Doug and Billy had it down from the woody when Doug said. "Not so fast little girl, this tree is to wet to bring into the house. It's going to have to stand out on the porch for a few days and dry out. Then we'll bring it in cut the rope and let the branches fall out."

Ashley was very disappointed so Billy said, "Until then we can decorate the rest of the house."

The next day Billy got down the decorations from the attic, but when he started to help the girls Doug told him, "Let the girls start. We have a bigger job out back. The roof on the garage is leaking with last nights rain, just lucky I went in to get some tools."

# THE CONFRONTATION

The first order of business was to clean out everything that got wet, and wipe dry all the tools so they wouldn't rust. Billy had forgotten how large Doug's tool bench was, and if there was anything more important to Doug than his tools he wasn't quite sure what it might be. Doug said, "Check the draws and make sure rain water didn't get inside." Billy knew those draws held, screws, nails, bolts and wrenches. He prayed they were dry because Doug would have him dry every one. When they checked only half the draws were wet, so Billy's job was half what he had feared. Doug told him, "Take care of this bench, tomorrow we'll start bright and early on the roof."

The garage had an old fashion A line roof with a very high walk in loft. In the old days it was a barn and the loft was used to stock hay for the horses.

At six A.M. Doug woke Billy and told him, "Wake up sleepy head it's show time. I made some coffee and when the kitchen is opened, I'll bring you breakfast. Come on lets go I got everything you need ready to go."

"Doug you got to be kidding the sun is barely up, why do we have to go up on that roof so early?"

"I'm too old to go up on that roof, you're going up on the roof!"

"I never worked on a roof before!"

"Well, it's easy, all you do is look for loose shingles and nail them back down. If you find any that have splits or tears, you tar the shit out of them. If you find some are missing we have new ones to replace them. Now don't that sound easy? Get up, get your pants on before it gets too hot up there, It's going to be a very sunny day and by noon it will feel like a hundred degrees up there. Work from the back to the top and down the front."

Billy got dressed, had a cup of coffee and started. He climbed the latter and brought up all the tools and materials needed and began his roof repair. By eight o'clock he reached the highest point of the roof, he surveyed his surroundings. He realized he could see into the second story windows of the big house. Being a Peeping-Tom was never his style, but when he caught Lenore coming out of the shower just wrapped in a towel he could not look away. Her clothes were laid out on her bed and when she removed her towel and her naked body was more than he could dream about. As she slipped into her panties and reached for her bra he began to get an erection, his heart was pounding as if he just had sex. He ached to reach out and touch her, but all he could do was look. Her body was young and firm, her breasts pushed up out of the black lace bra she was wearing. It looked like the bra was to small for the size of her breasts.

It created a cleavage that would turn on any man, let alone a stud like Billy. He began to think what it would be like to break her cherry and give her the fuck she would never forget. Then Ashley walked into the room wrapped in a towel. He realized the sister shared the same room. He could see Lenore and Ashley were having a heated conversation but he could not hear what they were saying he could only stare. Lenore left the room, Ashley was standing in front of a large mirror beside her dresser. Her back was to Billy and when she let her towel fall to the floor revealing her totally naked body. This was even better than Lenore, Ashley turned slightly and

# THE CONFRONTATION

Billy could see the side of her shapely breast. Then she turned completely around so he got a full front view. He almost fell off the garage roof. Ashley was shapelier than Lenore, she had a body to kill for. Billy realized she was too young, at her age she would be known as jail bate. That was one thing Billy was not ready to go back to. If he ever touched her he'd go to jail for a very long time. He watched her as she lovingly touched herself. She stroked her breasts and her nipples got hard and grew triple in size. Billy closed his eyes an imagined what it would be like having his lips around them. When he open his eyes, she was moving her hand down to her beautiful patch of hair. She brought her fingers up to her mouth and licked them as if they were dripping with nectar. Billy had a hard-on that he could hardly keep in his pants. His tight jeans were no place for his eight inch penis that was getting bigger and harder as he watched Ashley's tantalizing display. Like a bolt of lightning it suddenly stuck him that Ashley could see him looking from the roof of the garage. She was giving him a show she hoped would be impossible for him to forget. Ashley had the hots for him and she planned on Billy being the one to take her virginity. At fifteen, Ashley felt she was a woman. She certainly was built like one, Billy was going to her first. He was going to be the one she'd never forget. As she stroked herself, she pictured how it would be with Billy. She was sure she would remember forever the feelings, the excitement, the trill of that first penetration. She walked closer to the window and looked right at him. She licked her lips, smiled and then she slowly wrapped herself in her towel and disappeared.

## JOSEPH SQUATRITO

Doug yelled out, "Boy, I don't hear no hammering! I don't smell no tar drying in the hot sun! What are you doing up there? Daydreaming? We don't pay you to dream!"

"Okay, I was just taking a little break. The sun's mighty hot up here!"

As he began to work again, that little devil in him thought maybe I'll fuck both of them and take off for Mexico or Canada. Two days later he over heard Lenore talking to her mother, "Tonight I'm going holiday shopping at the mall with some of the girls. I've got some money saved but I could use another twenty-five dollars can you help me out."

"Sure honey, I'll give it to you right after dinner."

"Don't start worrying, Rene's mom will drive us there and then pick us up later."

Billy thought that maybe he needed to do a little shopping too. It would be a perfect way to start a relationship with Lenore. That night Lenore and Rene' met up with a few of the girls from the cheerleading team.

Barbie Flagg asked Lenore, "Is it true what I hear? Does Troy Hanson have the hots for you and he asked you out?"

"I don't know about the hots but he did ask me to go out with him."

All the girls chimed in," You are going out with him, aren't you?"

"I'm not sure."

Rene' said," You have to go, Troy is the best looking boy on the team!"

Lenore smiled and kept walking. All of a sudden, she saw Billy leaning against the lamp pole, just twirling his cowboy hat. She waved to him, and Rene' immediately

## THE CONFRONTATION

said, "What a hunk." When he saw her, he walked right over to her and her friends and said, "Hi Lenore got a minute."

"Sure Billy." She excused herself form the girls and walked a few feet away for some privacy. "What's on your mind."

"Need a ride home, Lenore?"

"I came with my girlfriend and I wouldn't want to leave her behind."

Then he smiled and said, "I have room in my truck for both of you. Does she live on the way back to Mabel's?"

"Yes, she does, but I don't think so. Rene's mom is going to take us home and maybe some of the other girls as well."

"You scared to ride with me!"

"No, even if uncle Doug thinks you drive like a maniac. I think you wouldn't drive fast with me in the pickup, would you?"

"No, I wouldn't I swear to God!"

Lenore looked him in the eyes and said," You only get one chance. If I accept your offer it's all up to you."

"Well, then it's settled, I'll being hanging around window shopping. Look for me in the food court having a cup of coffee."

Lenore walked back to her girlfriends and said, "He wants to take me home, when we're done shopping. I told him it was up to you girls and that it depended on how you're getting home."

Barbie said, What a fox, don't be crazy just go. Don't worry about us I'll call my mom or we can share a cab."

Lenore said," Rene' I came with you, do you want to ride with us?"

"I don't want to be a third wheel."

"Actually, I want you to come. I've never been alone with him so I'd feel safer with you there. Please say yes!"

"You haven't told us who he is? Where do you know him from?" "He's Doug Johnson's nephew. He's doing odd jobs at Mabel's house. I think he's a little wild."

"He's wild about you Lenore, look at the way he looks at you. I wish he'd look at me that way, I'd give him anything he wanted. If you know what I mean."

"Stop that talk Rene'! What have you lost your mind?"

"Tell me you wouldn't give yourself to him if he asked. They say you never forget your first time. I sure wouldn't mind having him as my first."

"What are you saying?"

"Lenore if you're still a virgin, he would make a great first! Wouldn't he?"

Barbie said," The first time I did it was in a pickup! It wasn't the greatest, to tell you the honest truth. It was very uncomfortable, things were so cramped that gear stick was up my butt and I almost broke my neck. When he finally stuck it in, it hurt like hell. I'll never forget it, not because it was great or romantic. It was the more like the worst sexual experience I ever had. If your going to loose your virginity do it in a bed!"

Lenore cringed and interrupted," I don't want to hear anymore Barbie. Lets finish shopping."

Billy kept a keen eye open to see the girls every move. When they were finished, and about ready to call for their ride, he came over and again asked Lenore," Do you want that ride home?"

"Lenore turned to Rene', "What do you want to do? Do you want to call your mom or take a chance with the wild man?"

# THE CONFRONTATION

"Lets take potluck with Billy."

"Okay Billy we'll ride with you. Remember no crazy driving, promise?"

"Scouts honor, cross my heart, hope to die!"

They all laughed and walked to Billy's pickup. There was just enough room for three in the cab. Billy insisted Lenore sit in the middle and she had to sit on an angle because of the stick shift on the floor. This put Lenore at a disadvantage. Every time Billy down shifted his elbow and arm brushed against Lenore's left breast. Billy keep his word and didn't drive like the maniac Lenore painted. Rene' was a little disappointed she was hoping for a wild ride so she had something to tell the girls the next day. When they got to Rene's house, and let her out that's when Lenore moved over towards the door and then she began to tense up. Billy could sense she was nervous, "Relax Lenore. I'm not going to bite, you could sit a little closer. I love the smell of your perfume'."

"Did you love the feel of my left breast too!"

"I'm sorry about that I thought there would be more room with the three of us than there was."

"Really, just drive Billy!"

Lenore began to relax when Billy turned into Mabel's driveway. He shut off the engine and his conversation was suddenly quite different. The exuberant cockiness Billy had displayed while Rene' was with them was gone. Billy got very personal he reached for her hand and said," How old are you Lenore?"

"I'll be eighteen next year."

"When next year?"

"July 25th.

Then Billy asked, What are your plans in June, after high school?"

"I want to go to college!"

"Back east?"

Lenore thought for a while and said," Probably not. I really like it out here, I was thinking maybe University Nevada Las Vegas."

"How would you like to go down to Mexico with me after you graduate, maybe for the summer?"

"You must be nuts! My mom would never let me go, not with you or any other boy."

"You won't need permission, if your over eighteen. A girl is plenty legal at that age."

"You don't know my mom, she's Italian. She'd kill both of us!"

"Listen Lenore, I really like you a lot and if I'm going to stick around for eight months, I want to know that we have something to look forward to."

"Eight months is a long time form now and we would have to know each other a whole lot better."

"How about kissing me for a start?"

Lenore smiled and said, "I don't think so, when I kiss you for Christmas, you'll know whether you should stay or go. You got two weeks to let me get to know you better, if I were you I'd start tomorrow. Pick me up after school we could go for a soda or coffee maybe an ice cream and talk."

Lenore got out of the truck and said, "I'll see you tomorrow three thirty in front of the school, wait make it around the corner less confusion. Good night Billy."

"I'll be there waiting Lenore, Good night."

# THE CONFRONTATION

As he drove around back to the bunkhouse, he saw someone standing in the shadows. He couldn't tell who it was so he reached for a tire iron he had hidden under his seat. He got out of the truck very cautiously and walked towards the bunkhouse. Before Billy arrived at Mabel's he had done enough stupid things to produce a number of people who might be mad enough to come after him. As the mysterious figure emerged from the shadows, Billy raised the tire iron in self-defense thinking it was someone from his past.

"Oh my God! It's you Ashley. I almost bashed your brains in. What the hell are you doing back here? You scared the shit out of me!" Billy could feel his heart pounding as the adrenaline surged through his body. He bent over and put his hands to his knees and took a couple of deep breaths.

"I saw you looking at me from the roof top, I turned you on didn't I? You liked what you saw, I have a great body. Don't I? You want me, I'm still a virgin you can be my first!" All the time getting closer and closer until his upper arm was feeling her firm breasts and his hand could feel the heat from between her legs. Then she took her hand and reached for his cock, it was already getting hard. The little vixen knew what she wanted and how to get it. "Don't worry Billy, before the year is over your going to want me bad. Your my Christmas Wish and I always get what I want for Christmas!"

"I'm no Santa Claus and you're no Christmas Angel! Your nothing but trouble, what are you fifteen? To me your jailbait. I just got out of jail and I'm not going back. I don't care how big your tits are or how hot you are."

She pushed him away and said," Don't tell me you have the hots for Lenore. She's such a wimp-ette, she'll never satisfy you!"

Billy turned his back to Ashley and walked into the bunkhouse alone. He couldn't stop thinking about how Ashley looked totally nude in the window. He knew life wasn't going to be easy with Ashley around. The next afternoon Billy made sure his work was finished early so he had no problem being at school on time waiting for Lenore. When she got out of school she walked around the corner as planned and saw the truck parked. Walking toward the truck her heart started pounding with excitement. It was a long time since Lenore had this kind of feeling. They went to a local bakery cafe and sat outside under an umbrella table. Billy had a coffee and pie, Lenore had an Ice cream soda. The conversation was light when Billy said, "This is not like Mabel's pie!"

"Order something else, don't eat it if you don't like it."

Lenore call over the waitress," He really doesn't like the pie can he get something different." The waitress said, "Sure what would you like?"

"How about a cheese Danish? Sorry about that but the pie is just to sweet."

A couple of minutes later she came back with the Danish and took the pie away. Lenore smiled and said, "See you don't have to eat something you don't like, after all, your paying for it."

"I'm not use to sending back food I don't like. Where I've been, if you don't eat it, you starve."

The more they talked Lenore started to see a softer side of Billy, he was trying to be a gentleman and not the wild

## THE CONFRONTATION

man everyone thinks. She asked him if life in jail was a bad as they say. Billy answered by telling her it was worst than she could ever imagine. He told her sometimes things are done to you there that you have to live with for the rest of your life, and how he believed everyone deserves a second chance. She didn't know if Billy was talking about her or himself. She wasn't sure if he looked into her soul through her eyes and saw her pain but she was sure there was more she wanted learn about him. The next week every night Lenore went Christmas Shopping, Billy was there to take her home. They always stopped off on the way home to share a pizza, or have a burger. Their conversation became more intense and personal mostly on Billy's part. Lenore could not yet talk about what happened to her and all the evil things that were done to her. She was to afraid Billy would change the way he felt about her once he found out she was used goods and not a virgin. Every night they stayed out a little longer and talked about what was important to each other.

Billy wanted to know all Lenore's likes and dislikes. He wanted to know what kind of man she saw in her future. One night as they sat in the pickup parked outside on the driveway Billy asked," Lenore could you ever see yourself with the likes of me. I mean you have up bringing, and class and education. I'm only a broken down jail bird."

Billy don't bring yourself down like that, I don't like it when you talk about yourself that way." Lenore was starting to get a crush on him. She was flattered by his constant interest in her views and values. The two of them were like water and fire, she was the calming influence on his wildness. He in turn, gave her the confidence she lacked. The more Billy listened to Lenore as she told him about what was important to her, the more she believed he really cared. He never got bold or tried to push himself on her, Lenore brought out a side of him even he didn't know existed. What started out as a conquest on Billy's part was turning into a real relationship. About five days before Christmas, at night, Billy was waiting for Lenore when Ashley spotted him in the mall. She broke away from her friends to talk to Billy, "Hey Billy, what are you doing Christmas shopping?"

"Just waiting for a friend."

"How about a ride home later?"

"Sorry no can do, my friend is a female and she wouldn't like it. You know what they say, "Three' s a crowd"!

"I'd show you a really good time, if you weren't such a chicken shit. A wild jailhouse cowboy, my ass! Are you a fag, or just a virgin like me. You probably wouldn't even know were to put it, next time you jerk off think of me." She turned and walked back to her girl friends.

Billy walked away and got lost in the crowd, Ashley definitely knew how to push his buttons and she was beginning to really get to him. He wasn't used to some little bitch talking to him like that. When he found Lenore he said," I have to leave right now." She could see he was very upset, but she didn't know why. She agreed to leave immediately without asking any questions. As he drove out of the parking lot he headed for the freeway and Route 15 north. Lenore asked." Where are we going?"

"Up north a ways, I know a really great spot, a high ridge that overlooks the valley. Talk about Christmas Lights, the view is incredible! The lights jump up at you, they twinkle and sparkle in every direction. Besides I need your calming influence. Someone really got to me tonight. He drove faster than he ever did before with Lenore in the pickup.

Ashley's words really got to him and his dark side started to show through. At the top of the ridge near Mount Charleston, Billy pulled over and shut off the engine. He was right, the view of the valley was spectacular. Then Billy asked Lenore," Ever been here before?"

"It's my first time, you were right it's beautiful!"

Billy looked at Lenore, not the lights and said," They're not as beautiful as you." Then he moved closer to her and whispered in her ear. She began to giggle and smile. He kissed her gently, but passionately and she responded for the first time. The truck windows began to steam up as he slid his hand under her blouse and unhooked her bra. Her breasts fell free and he could feel her flesh. Lifting her blouse he saw her pink nipples. Her breasts were firm yet soft. He put his lips to her nipples and as he sucked they got bigger and harder. Reaching down between her legs he began to stroked her through her pants. Billy could feel the moist heat of her coming through. The harder he rubbed the more she responded. Her passion overwhelmed her, at the same time it caused her to panic. She put her hand to his lips and said," Please stop, I can't. Billy please stop!"

When he looked up at her tears were flowing down her cheeks. He knew if he had any real feelings for her, this was not the time or the place to force himself on her.

"Stop crying Lenore, I would never hurt you. I won't do anything you don't want me to do. You know I'm falling in love with you!"

Billy pulled her close to him just to hold her and comfort her.

"Please don't be mad at me. Billy I want to but I'm very scared!"

"Every girl is scared her first time. It's okay, lets go home."

For Billy this was a first. The first time he ever showed compassion and consideration for someone else's feelings. Being a gentleman had never been one of his talents, not when he had a girl all hot and bothered. Tears never got in his way before but where Lenore was concerned he was different. He couldn't explain it. This new found gallantry felt right, when he was with Lenore it just seemed natural. Was it because she didn't throw herself at him or offer her body, just because he smiled at her or showed some interest in her? Lenore was very confused as they drove home. Billy had aroused feelings in her that she had never experienced before. She couldn't believe how wet her panties were just from letting him touch her breasts and rub her "down there" while they kissed. She felt like she was in a sauna. She realized that this was probably the way sex should feel.

It was passionate, sweet, rewarding and fulfilling. She couldn't help making the comparison with her former experiences. The feelings she felt with Billy were not disgusting and guilt-ridden like the feelings she had when her stepfather molested her. Lenore didn't know how to explain to Billy about what had happened to her, would he understand her pain? Would he be horrified, would his love turn to hate? She tried to force these questions aside not only because she was afraid of the answers, but also

## THE CONFRONTATION

because she wasn't ready to relive the horror of the past by telling Billy all there was to tell. Lenore began to think that perhaps she could fool Billy and lead him to believe that he was her first. Realizing she could reenact the pain of losing her virginity and she would be able to produce the telltale blood by waiting until the beginning of her period. It always started lightly and the effect of staining would fool even the wisest of men. She was aroused to the point where she really wanted to try.

Billy asked for a goodnight kiss when they reached Mabel's driveway. Lenore was very willing and kissed him quickly, but passionately. Billy felt he may have made his move at the wrong time and place, but he was sure Lenore would be worth waiting for. Theresa's busy schedule kept her from realizing how much time Lenore was spending with Billy. That night Billy wouldn't even take off his shirt to go to sleep, all he keep smelling was Lenore's lingering perfume and the memory of their passionate night.

With only three more days until Christmas he made sure he was available to help with any added decorations or the wrapping of presents. The more he stayed close to Lenore the more Ashley did the slow burn. The night before Christmas Eve was the last night to shop and pick up any ordered presents. Lenore told Billy not to look for her or think about taking her home. She made up a story that she wanted to spend time with her friends before the holiday break from school. He told her he had to pick up a few last minute gifts himself. Christmas Eve was finally here and Doug and Billy had a list of last minute things to do for Mabel. They had to go to the market and pick up her order, a stop at the florist and get the point setters, and go to the candle store. Mabel wanted red candles for the centerpiece on the table and for the mantle on the fireplace. As usual Mabel out did herself with dinner. The evening was quite festive and all the regulars were in attendance. At midnight Ashley yelled, "Let's see what Santa left under the tree." This year the gifts were piled higher than ever before, Lenore and Ashley started to call out all the names on each present.

There was a present for everyone who was there. Of course Lenore and Ashley received the most gifts. Billy made sure he had a present for Mabel, Doug, Theresa' and the girls. He was the most surprised when the biggest box was taken out from behind the tree and Lenore said," This one is for Billy from a secret Santa." When he saw the size of the box he said, "What in the world can that be?" As he ripped off the wrappings and opened the box his jaw dropped. It was a new black cowboy hat with a silver coined band. He looked at it and said, "Oh my GOD!" Everyone yelled try it on. Lenore asked, "Do you like it, does it fit?"

He elegantly slipped it on his head, "Fits like a glove!" He knew the gift came from Lenore and he thanked her with the passionate kiss of the night. No one was more taken aback than Theresa and Ashley, but for very different reasons. Theresa was surprised, Ashley was just plain jealous. She was even more determined to have sex with Billy no matter what the cost. She knew Billy's work time at Mabel's would be over after the New Year Holiday.

If she was going to make her move it had to be soon, but she still couldn't figure out how to persuade him. Christmas Day was a very quite and relaxing day and it gave Ashley time to ponder her sexual fantasy. Christmas Day fell on a Friday

# THE CONFRONTATION

and every Saturday night, Doug would visit a lady friend and stay out all night. Ashley knew this would be a good night to put her plan into motion. She waited until every one was asleep. She sneaked down to the bunkhouse after steeling an extra set of keys that hung on a rack on the kitchen wall. Wearing only a robe and Lenore's perfume, she entered the bunkhouse. She quietly climbed into bed with Billy. The room was dark and she stroked him into an erection. He was more asleep than awake. Climbing on top of him she gently began kissing him. His first sense as he started to wake, was the familiar smell of Lenore's perfume. He reached for her breasts and since both sisters were quite buxom, they too seemed familiar. He was thrilled that Lenore had finally conquered her fears and he tried to position her so he could penetrate as gently, as possible. Billy was well endowed and as he slid deeper and broke through her membrane, Ashley yelled," Oh it hurts! It hurts bad!"

He pushed her off him as he gained his full senses," You little witch!"

Looking down at his penis which was covered in blood he panicked, grabbing her by the shoulders he shook her, "You don't know what you've done! Fucking Bitch, get out of here now."

"I told you I always get what I want for Christmas, and you were it!"

"Get out I said I have to think,"

"You'll want me again. When you do just call and I'll be there anytime anyplace."

Early the next morning Billy went looking for Lenore. He packed everything in the back of the pick up and drove to the front of the house. He called her out to the porch and said," I have to leave, I can't wait until the end of the holidays. I got a job offer down south but it starts it two days and if I want it, I have to be there then."

"Why didn't you tell me sooner? Billy are you in trouble?"

"What makes you say that?"

"There's something in your voice and eyes, they're not sincere you can't look me in the eyes your lying."

Billy kept looking down, "I'll keep in touch, you're the only girl I'd ever wait for. You have no idea what our time together has meant to me."

"Why do you have to leave? You can find work around here, I thought you really cared for me. I would have given you what you wanted, Billy give me a chance, I'm falling in love with you. I see a different side of you now. Don't shut me out. Please don't leave!"

Billy turned and started down the stairs," Lenore you don't understand I'm in trouble, big trouble it wasn't my fault. I just can't go to jail again, I can't face what happened."

"Tell me what happened?"

"I can't you'll hate me forever, I'll be back after graduation in late June or early July. Please don't give up on me until then. I love you Lenore!"

Lenore watched her first real love leave, she cried hysterically as uncontrollable emotions raged inside her. She didn't know if he would ever return to her. When Billy didn't show up for dinner everyone wondered what had happened to him. Mabel asked Doug, "Where's Billy? Isn't he coming in for dinner? I baked him an apple pie his favorite."

## THE CONFRONTATION

"I'm not sure what's going on with him. He left me a note thanking me for always being there for him but he had a offer for a job down south and that he had to leave. Billy is a wild spirit. You never know what to expect from him. No matter how hard you try to help him, you can't always predict what that crazy Son of a Bitch would do. Pardon my language, Ladies."

Lenore blurted out," That's not so, you're all thinking things about him that are not true."

Doug said," Lenore why are you so upset? You take a liking to him?

"I told you my nephew is as unpredictable as a Texas Windstorm!"

Lenore tried with all her might to hold back the tears, but her eyes filled and the tears spilled over and down her cheeks. Ashley turned to her sister and said," What's wrong Lenore? Did you lose your lover boy? He's not the man you think he is. He's a chicken shit scared rabbit."

"What do you know about him Ashley, all you ever do is throw yourself at him, but he loves me not you! He never wanted a baby like you Ashley. You're just a spoiled brat who always wants her way."

"Maybe if you had given him what he wanted, he'd still be here.'

Lenore lashed back," You don't know what your talking about. He was falling in love with me. He said so."

Ashley barked back," Oh yeah! I guess that's why he slept with me last night not you."

Lenore was in complete shock at what she had just heard," I hate you Ashley! You little tramp!"

Lenore picked up a bowl of mashed potatoes and threw it across the table at her sister. Then she ran around the table and grabbed Ashley by the hair and pulled her right out of the chair she was sitting on, "I'm going to pull the hair right out of your head."

Theresa got between them and pulled Lenore away from Ashley and Mabel held on to Ashley. Lenore screamed, "I hate her mom! She made Billy leave, she's jealous of what we had together."

For the first time the sibling rivalry that had been smoldering for years erupted in a way that Theresa never expected. Lenore cried uncontrollably, only her mother knew how important Billy must have been in Lenore's life. It could have been the best medicine to help Lenore get over the horrible abuse Michael had inflicted on her. Theresa took Lenore upstairs to comfort her, "Don't worry baby if he really loves you, he'll be back. Ashley doesn't know how much he meant to you."

"She does, I hate her! I wish she was dead!"

"You don't mean that Lenore."

"Yes I do, I hate her!"

Theresa put Lenore in her bed and locked the adjoining door to the girls room. She thought that the best thing she could do at this point would be to let Lenore cry herself to sleep. Ashley couldn't believe that her mother had left her there and had gone with Lenore to comfort her. Her mother had simply ignored the confession she had just blurted out.

She, at the tender age of fifteen had just told everyone that she had lost her virginity and no one seemed to notice. Ashley sat there defiantly and said to no one in particular,

# THE CONFRONTATION

"You see, I don't matter at all. Nobody cares what I do or what I say. Nobody cares about me, not even my own mother!"

She sat back on the chair brought her knees up to her chest and clasped them with her arms. Then she buried her head in disgust. After a short while she jumped with surprise when she heard her mother calling her name. Theresa came down the stairs to deal with her." Ashley where are you?" She called from halfway down the stairs, "Ashley" the tone of her voice got more intense. Theresa confronted Ashley in the dinning room.

"You said you had sex with Billy? Your only fifteen! Did he forced himself on you? Did he rape you?"

"No. I raped him!"

Theresa slapped her so hard that she fell to the floor. Mabel ran over to Ashley and helped her up. Ashley's mouth was bleeding and her lip was split open. Theresa could still pack a wallop. Then she said, "Your grounded for a year, go up stairs before I, not Lenore beat the crap out of you." Mabel stood between Ashley and Theresa, took a clean napkin from the table and wiped the blood from her face and applied pressure on her lip.

"Let me see honey."

Ashley jerked away from Mabel's help, and ran upstairs to her bedroom.

Theresa said to Mabel, "I can't go out tonight. Please get one of the other girls to take my place, my world is falling apart."

"Okay don't worry I'm sure one of the girls will be happy to take over for you. They'll just say that you got sick at the last minute and that they had to step in and replace you."

Theresa was overwhelmed with guilt and helplessness. She didn't know what in the world to do. This seemed like a problem the best of mothers would have trouble dealing with, let alone solve. Without knowing what to say, she went upstairs to have a talk with her youngest daughter. She realized that teenagers, her daughters age, were far more promiscuous than when she was in her teens. Not only were they more free with their sexuality, they were well trained in most schools about how to prevent pregnancy and sexually transmitted diseases. Although Ashley may have enough information about the physical workings of sex, she didn't know anything about the emotional workings.

Theresa realized she had been so busy running and hiding from Michael and trying to keep Lenore from being crushed by the past, that she had never discussed love or sex with either of her daughters. She felt that she couldn't bring up the subject with Lenore because it would remind her of the things Michael did to her. As for Ashley, in Theresa mind, no matter how developed her body was, she was still her little girl. Discussions about love and sex were not on Theresa's list of priorities, and after divorcing a man she truly loved, and marrying a monster she didn't feel like much of an expert. When she finally faced Ashley, she said," I don't want to fight with you. I just want to know the truth. What really happened between you and Billy? Did he rape you? Ashley it's important you tell me the truth. Don't try to cover for him. Ashley paused for a minute and thought to herself. It was time to own up to what she had done. "Mom, I tricked him. I stole the key to the bunkhouse and let myself in while he was asleep. I wore Lenore's perfume it was dark. I took off my robe and

## THE CONFRONTATION

slipped nude into his bed. He thought I was Lenore. I knew he'd never give me what he wanted from her. I didn't care, I wanted him to be my first. When he realized it was me he freaked and pushed me off him, It was too late he had already broken my cherry. I bled all over him, that's when he told me to get out. He ran away because I'm underage. He was afraid he'd go back to jail. I never would have talked or gotten him in trouble, I swear!"

Theresa told her," Things like what you've done always find a way to surface. Your only a baby, you don't know what you've done."

"Look at me mom, do I look like a baby with this body?"

"Your body may look mature, but you're not grown up enough emotionally or mentally to handle sex yet. Now I'm afraid, I can't trust you to go out at night."

"What do you think I'm going to go to bed with every boy I meet? Billy was special to me, I love him, if I was older he would have loved me, not Lenore."

Ashley broke down and started to cry, when she cried she looked like the fifteen year old she really was. Theresa found herself with two problem daughters, both dealing with their sexuality but at different ends of the spectrum. She reached out to hold Ashley and comfort her. As her first step in an attempt to solve her daughter's dilemma, she decided to give all her time to both Lenore and Ashley. She knew that she was the only one who could smooth out their differences.

She prayed that the spirt of Christmas past and the New Year Holiday somehow could bring them, closer together. All she could do was to give them a mothers love and understanding, and pray for the best. Theresa remembered her mother saying, "Little children, little problems. Big children big problems." It certainly described her situation.

New Year's Eve came without the familiar good cheer and love Theresa was so used to. Although the girls were civil to each other they stayed at opposite sides of the room. Still the tension between them was unmistakable. The holiday spirit did not soften their hearts as Theresa hoped. They hadn't talked since the night Billy left, and no matter how hard Theresa tried, she couldn't tear down the wall between them. For the next six months they keep as much space between one another as they possibly could. Lenore went to school and never looked for Ashley during the day. After dinner they did their homework in separate rooms. Lenore let her friend Troy know that if he still wanted to go out with her it would be only as friends. She told him her boyfriend was working down south and that he would be back after graduation. She told him if this arrangement was acceptable to him, when they dated as friends, it would be" Dutch Treat." There would be no way she would take advantage of their friendship. Troy was hoping for more but he agreed. After all, Lenore was the most beautiful girl in the senior class. Just being with her made him look like the big man on campus. Secretly he still wished he could win her over, and he had six months to do it. Ashley thought she was the stronger of the two sisters. She had seen and heard Lenore at her weakest moments. She didn't know about the ghosts that burdened her and caused all those nightmares. She didn't know how Lenore had prevented her being seduced by their stepfather and why Lenore had been so protective.

# THE CONFRONTATION

On the night of the prom, Troy came to pick up Lenore in a limo provided by Mabel. He was dressed in a tuxedo and held the most beautiful corsage for Lenore. When he rang the door bell, Mabel let him in, Doug was standing at the foot of the steeps giving him the once over. "Hi I'm Mabel and that old cuss is Doug. Come on in, Lenore will be down in a minute."

They could both see he was nervous and unsure of himself then he said, "I want to thank you for sending a car, I mean a limo to pick me up and provide it for us tonight. That was very thoughtful of you."

Mabel said, "Well we couldn't have the best looking couple go to the prom in a broken down pick up truck. Now could we?"

Troy kept looking around at the interior of Mabel's house, after all, there weren't many houses around that had the old world charm of the old west. There were so many antiques inside it could have been a museum, certainly something for a young man to behold. Theresa came down the stairs and introduced herself, "Hi you must be Troy! I'm Theresa, Lenore's mother!"

Troy looked at her and said," I certainly can see where Lenore gets her good looks from, a pleasure to meet you."

He held his breath as Lenore descended the stairs. She wore a beautiful pale pink satin gown trimmed in delicate lace. The satin clung primly to her perfect figure, and the sweetheart neck line reveled her cleavage that he couldn't keep his eyes from her. After a minute he said, "WOW, Lenore you look beautiful." Then he paused, "I have a corsage for you but I don't know how to pin it on."

Theresa said," Here let me help you with that!"

Lenore had her hair swept up off her neck into a flattering up-do, she looked exquisite and sophisticated. Just before they were ready to leave Mabel said. "Wait a minute honey, we can't let you go out with a bare neck. I have something I want you to wear tonight, It's very special to me but it's the finishing touch you need." Then she put a gold chain around her neck with a hanging heart that had a diamond in the center. "Now that's perfect!"

Lenore ran over to the mirror in the living room to see what Mabel had just put around her neck. "Oh Mabel! It's beautiful" Then she gave Mabel a hug and a kiss, then Theresa and even Doug. They all walked to the door and watched as the limo drove away.

Even though Ashley pretended not to care about what was going on she watched from the top of the stairs. She felt happy for Lenore. After they drove away she told her mother how beautiful Lenore was and what a great couple Lenore and Troy made. Theresa smiled and said. "Why didn't you come down and tell her yourself?"

"I don't think she wanted to hear from me or even see me. She's a lot stronger than I ever thought she was."

"Ashley this feud has got to end."

"If Lenore is willing to forgive and forget, so am I!"

Theresa opened her arms and hugged her daughter, "That's wonderful news! I'll be sure to tell Lenore, maybe we can be a family again?"

It was a wonderful night for Lenore, she danced and partied till the sun came up. It was the first night she didn't dwell on Billy's absence.

When their dates finally took them home, Lenore and Rene' were totally exhausted. The foursome were so glad

# THE CONFRONTATION

they had a limo waiting. When they got in for their ride home they kicked off their shoes and relaxed. Lenore went straight to bed after she was brought home and slept until the early evening. Theresa was eager to talk to her and tell her about what Ashley had said. Knowing it was a big night for Lenore and remembering how tired she was at her own prom she let her daughter sleep. Lenore slept for fifteen hours, being up for twenty-four straight hours was more than she could handle. When Theresa finally got her chance to talk to her daughter, her first order of business was to find out all she could about Lenore's night. Theresa asked. "Did you have a good time? Who was the best dressed, what about the hall?"

"Mom, everyone looked great! The catering hall did a fantastic job with the food, the music and the decorations in school colors were unbelievable. Afterwards almost everybody went to that disco on Boulder Highway. It was opened to prom kids only and served soft drinks, (no-alcohol) and provided music. The atmosphere was all disco. It was worth the twenty - five dollars a head. They let us dance ' until four in the morning and then we all went for breakfast and watched the sun come up."

"I'm really glad you had such a good time. There's something I have to tell you. Your sister has had a change of heart, she wanted to let you know how beautiful you looked and that she wished you well at the prom."

"Why didn't she tell me then, herself?"

"She didn't want to spoil your night."

"Since when does she care about my feelings?"

Theresa grabbed her hand, "Please Lenore, she's trying to make amends. Can't you ever forgive her?"

"I really don't want to. I lost Billy because of her, she can go to hell for all I care!"

"Please Lenore for me! I want us to be a family again."

Lenore pulled her hand away, "No mom, I can't. Never!"

"Honey she made a mistake, granted it was a big mistake, but she doesn't know what happened to you back home with your stepfather. She thought that all the attention I was giving to you was because I loved you more than I loved her. It's more my fault because I didn't tell her the truth. I thought she was to young and wouldn't understand.

I should have explained why you were getting all I had to give, my love, my time, my understanding and my tenderness. I was so worried about you, I forgot about her needs."

"Stop mom! Your trying to confuse me."

"No Baby, never I love you both. I'd give my life for either of you."

At that point Theresa backed off. She was afraid of bruising Lenore's very fragile ego. She knew it would take time for Lenore to think about all she had told her, and she hoped Lenore would soften in time.

Graduation was only two weeks away, Theresa could see her conversation was weighing heavily on her daughter's mind. A couple of days later as the three o'clock bell rang out and the school day was over, Lenore was walking out, not paying much attention to her surroundings, a familiar voice called out to her. "Hey Lenore, need a ride home?"

She knew in an instant who it was, she turned in the direction of the voice and there was Billy. Standing waving his black cowboy hat, she couldn't believe her eyes she was speechless. He smiled and his eyes opened wide, they were bluer than ever. His hair was bleached blonde from the sun, and his skin was a golden bronze tan testifying to the outdoor life he must have been leading. He opened his arms wide and Lenore dropped her books and ran to him. He hugged her as tightly as he could and lifted her in the air. They kissed as he put her down and said," I told you I'd come back for you."

Then unexpectedly, Lenore slapped him as hard as she could.

"What's that for?"

"For leaving me." She hauled off and hit him again, "And that's for sleeping with my sister!"

Billy reached for his cheek. Like her mom Lenore could pack quite a wallop.

"I can explain. Didn't Ashley tell you what happened?"

"No, I haven't spoken to her since you left."

Then Billy started to tell the truth about what really happened that night, "I thought Ashley was you that night. I swear to God! She came into the bunkhouse while I was asleep, she was wearing your perfume, it was dark. She started to rub herself on me, I had an erection before I woke up, She was on top of me when I reached for her hips to control my penetration, she was so tight that I knew she was a virgin. I thought it was you. When I broke through she screamed, that it hurt. I immediately knew it wasn't you because I recognized her voice, I pushed her right off me. I panicked because of her age. God, she's only fifteen! I was afraid of going back to jail. Please try to understand. I know I love you Lenore. After graduation come with me for the summer, we'll go up to Canada. I saved enough money for us until you come back for college."

"Billy please, you appeared so suddenly. I have to think, your going to fast."

"Tell me you don't hate me."

"I don't hate you, now that I know the truth."

"You love me, tell me you love me."

"Maybe, I love you."

"I know you love me, and you missed me say it. Come on, say it."

Lenore smiled and said, "Okay yes, I missed you."

Billy grabbed her and kissed her again, "Meet me to night and we'll really talk, I'll tell you what I've been doing."

"We need to talk, I have something to tell you. I'll meet you at the South entrance of the mall at eight o'clock.

"I'll be there."

At eight sharp, Billy pulled up to the South entrance. Lenore was waiting just inside. She saw him and came outside. In her mind Ashley was no longer lurking in the shadows. Lenore truly believed that Billy had come back for her. Now she had to find out if he could handle what she was about to tell him. Her confession would soon let her know how much he really cared. Was he man enough to understand and realize the horror she had endured at the hands of her evil stepfather! She was beaming as she got into the pickup, "Hi Billy" she leaned over and gave him a kiss.

"Hi Lenore. Are you hungry? I'm starved, how does a burger and a frosty root beer sound?"

"Great, but I already ate. I'll just have a frosty and fries."

"Is that drive-in-car hop place still open on Decatur?"

"It's still opened."

They drove over to Decatur and pulled in and ordered. Eating in the truck always seemed more fun and private.

## THE CONFRONTATION

Billy started eating like it was his last meal, Lenore just played with her fries and sipped her frosty. She couldn't find a way to start telling Billy about her past. "Billy slow down, you're eating to fast. You'll give yourself indigestion."

Billy smiled and said, "You're right, what's my hurry? See, I need you around me,"

After Billy finished eating, Lenore said, "I have something to tell you about me. Before we start a relationship, you have to know. I'm not the girl you think I am. Please understand that this will be very hard for me. If I didn't care so much for you, I wouldn't even be telling you."

"Lenore your talking, but your not saying anything, I'm here for you."

She took her hands and covered her eyes and began to cry. She couldn't find the words or the courage to begin. Billy grabbed her hands and pulled them way from her eyes saying, "You can tell me anything, I love you."

"I'm so ashamed, I can't. I want to Billy. I love you!"

She hung her head down and cried harder than ever. Billy lifted her chin and turned her face towards his. He kissed her wet cheeks and whispered, "No secrets Lenore."

"Billy I was raped by my stepfather, that's why we ran away from Brooklyn. He's still looking for us, but my mother has hidden us away from him. Please don't hate me, you probably wanted a virgin. Well I'm not a virgin. Sex terrifies me, I want to make love to you but you have to be patient and gentle. Just give me time and I hope I can make it worth the wait. Please don't leave me again, I couldn't bare it if you were not in my life."

Billy was not prepared for something like this, he was shocked by the news.

The image of Lenore he had created was shattered, he was very quite for a short time and then he hugged and kissed her. At last, her deep dark secret was out in the open.

Billy did understand the pain she was feeling, he had bad things done to him in jail. He was a pretty' boy and those were the ones the lifers wanted.

He had been raped many times and had his own demons whirling around in his head, maybe they could heal each other. "I don't care what happened before we met, I only care about now! I know you're right for me, I'll give you all the time you need, just let me know we will always be together. I love you Lenore, the past is dead there's only the future." Lenore reached out and touched Billy's face, putting the palm of her hand on his cheek. She tried to hold back the tears as she looked deeply into his eyes. What she saw helped her to believe his words, then she took his hand kissed his palm and held it to her face. She intertwined her fingers with his and placed the back of his hand on her breast. Only the tough macho image he had always projected kept him from telling his own dark secret.

They sat for a while and held each other and hugged tightly feeling their rejuvenated loves energy flow from one to the other. Billy started the engine and on the ride home Lenore sat very quietly staring out the window wondering if there really was hope for love in her future. She couldn't understand how just a rough and tough macho guy could be so caring, loving and understanding. Then she didn't know about the skeletons in Billy's closet. As they got closer to Mabel's, Billy became fearful of the event that happened with Ashley. He still didn't know what to expect form Theresa and how she would handle the fact of him being back. He stopped outside the driveway and told Lenore," I don't want anyone to know I'm back but you not even uncle Doug or Mabel. Tomorrow is Saturday, I have to be back to work on Monday. I want to spend as much time with you as I can before I head back to work."

"Pick me up in the morning at nine, mom usually sleeps until noon so only Mabel will be up that early. I tell her I'm spending the day with the cheerleading girls and please let mom know." She leaned over to Billy and gave him a goodnight kiss. Then she opened the door, and as she got out and said "I'll love you forever, just give me time."

Billy knew he had found the love he had been searching for. "Lenore, wait I have something to tell you about me, I." He put his head down and couldn't finish. Lenore could see his pain.

"It's okay Billy, you don't have to tell me what's so hard for you to tell. When your ready you'll tell me and I'm sure I'll understand."

Lenore went straight to her room and went to bed anxiously anticipating her date in the morning with Billy. The weekend was truly a rebirth of Lenore's life and she spent every minute she could with the love of her life. Over the weekend Theresa noticed a change in her. She was smiling, not daydreaming or looking depressed. Her whole general attitude was bright and hopeful. Theresa chalked it up to preparing for graduation, shopping for a new dress and shoes. She even asked Ashley her opinion of her new outfit. Everyone in the house was shocked by the sudden change.

Mabel asked Theresa," What's up, I can't believe my eyes or ears."

"I don't know Mabel, but something's going on."

"What ever it is, it's good. I even saw her talking to Ashley, could it be divine intervention?"

Theresa said. "It's strange you should say that. Recently I dreamed of my brother Joey. He hadn't come to me in my dreams for a long time. When Lenore smiles a certain way she looks just like him. She has the same expression he had. Maybe I should talk to her that's what he's trying to tell me."

"Maybe you should leave it alone and let Lenore tell you when she's ready. You know she will eventually."

"I guess your right Mabel, It's probably just the excitement of graduation. I'm sure she feeling all grown up and excited about going to college and meeting new friends."

"I never went to college, but it feels real good around here lately. Praise the Lord." Mabel turned to go back into the kitchen and started working on her apple pies then she stopped and said, "I'm real happy for you and the girls Theresa, you're a good mother and a fine person."

"I love you Mabel."

Sunday night was Lenore's final time with Billy until after graduation. He told her. Please' take pictures and he wished he could be there with her, but reminded her he would be back for her birthday. She'd be eighteen and legal to make her own decisions about going up to Canada for the summer.

The next afternoon, when Ashley got home from school Theresa asked her, "Did you see your sister in school today?"

"Yes, we had lunch together."

"Really, What happened?"

## THE CONFRONTATION

"Nothing, we ate and talked a bit."
"About what?"

Theresa was bursting inside to hear all sorts of good news, but Ashley was very vague and didn't give her mother any real information. All she said was, "Mom it was just girl talk. I have to go up stairs and study for a test. I'll talk with you later before you leave for work."

Theresa was totally flabbergasted. She had expected to hear details. It looked as if the girls were making up in their own quite way. Each day that passed, their relationship got better. Only Lenore knew about Billy's return and that the time spent with him made for a much happier home. When she finally asked Ashley to come to her graduation, Theresa knew her prayers had been answered. They were a family again. She made up her mind that she didn't need to know what caused this wonderful change. Everyone was happy. It looked, as if letting them work it out like adults, was the smartest thing she could have done. It never occurred to her that Billy was the angel she was praying for.

Graduation day arrived, each graduating senior was allowed four tickets. Theresa, Ashley, Mabel and Doug attended. After the ceremonies they all went out to lunch at one of the finest restaurants in Las Vegas. Later that night there was a fabulous party at Mabel's. All of Lenore's friends were there as well as all the adult friends they had made since coming out west. By midnight most of the guests had left to go home. The day had been filled with happiness, but it was a long day. After the last of the guests left Mabel said, "I'm to tired to clean up tonight lets leave it until tomorrow. Lets just go to sleep, I'm dead, I'm not getting any younger you know."

Everyone was happily exhausted so she didn't get any arguments. The next morning Theresa woke up a little later than usual. She lay in bed for a while, she was still exhausted from all the excitement of the day before. Staring at the ceiling she closed her eyes, and thanked God that her daughters were acting like sisters again. Praying that all the pain they endured at the hands of Michael was behind them. She finally decided to take a hot shower and go down stairs for a cup of coffee. When she got down stairs the entire house was cleaned, Lenore and Ashley got up early and surprised not only her but Mabel as well. Theresa sat with Mabel in the kitchen with their coffee and Mabel said, "Miracle's do happen!"

The day before Lenore's eighteenth birthday Billy kept his promise and returned for her. When she saw his truck parked down the street form the house she knew he was back. She left a note on his windshield to met her at the mall at eight their usual place. They met that night and Billy asked if she was ready to go up to Canada. She told him she was, but it had to be the night after her birthday. She wanted to spend that night with the family because her mother planned a birthday cake with a few close friends. He said he was sorry. He couldn't be there but spending the rest of the summer together was more than he had hoped for. Lenore's birthday dinner was just a few close friends, Afterwards even Tom stopped in before he and Theresa went out on their date. When the cake came out, everyone sang Happy Birthday to Lenore, Mabel baked a triple layer cake with eighteen candles around the edge and one in the middle for good luck. Even with the lights out the glow lit up the room. Lenore made her wish and blew out the

## THE CONFRONTATION

candles in one breath. She thanked everyone for coming and for all the gifts they gave. Almost everyone gave her a card with money telling her to buy what ever she liked. She knew the cash would come in handy up in Canada. When all the guest left she helped Mabel clean up the room.

Lenore was alone in the kitchen with Mabel putting the dishes and glasses way, Mabel finally figured out what turned Lenore around. Theresa wanted to believe it was her brother's spirit or divine intervention but Mabel knew better. That's when she said, "Tell me Lenore, how long has it been, that Billy is back?"

She caught Lenore totally off guard. "What makes you think that Billy is back?"

Mabel was smart and had many years of experience with young women and their broken hearts. It just took a little longer because Billy was so unpredictable, coming back for Lenore was never his style. "You know I'm right, you must be very important to him to take the risk of going back to jail on a rape charge."

"Please don't tell mom, I not sure how she would react about what happened with Ashley. Billy told me the truth, Ashley tricked him into thinking she was me and I believe him."

Mabel had come to love both girls for different reasons, She knew how much Billy meant to her and she could see the difference in her when he was back in her life. "Don't worry your secret is safe with me, besides you can do what ever you want you're of age and no one can tell you your mind. Only remember your mother has to protect Ashley who is still under age so you better be sure what your next move with Billy will be."

"Mom is out with Tom and by the time she wakes up tomorrow I'll be gone with Billy for the summer. I'll write her a letter explaining my reasons for going. With all that's been going on, I forgot to give you back your beautiful golden heart, I left it on top of my dresser."

"I was wondering when you would mention that gift."

"Gift? I thought I was wearing it just for the prom?"

Mabel smiled and said, "I want you to have it, a graduation and birthday present."

"Mabel you hold it for me. It's too expensive to take on the road. When I come back for college, you can give it to me then." She gave Mabel a hug and kiss and said, "I'll miss you, you've been like a second mother to me."

Lenore went up to her room and started to pack while Ashley was asleep. Not really knowing what type of clothes to bring, she decided to bring a few fall and winter outfits and a warm jacket. When she was finished packing, she sat at her desk to write her letter

Theresa got home a little later than usual from her date with Tom, so she slept later. When she woke she stared at the ceiling still feeling exhausted from all the excitement of Lenore's party and her evening out with Tom. As she started to get up, she noticed a light blue piece of paper propped up against her lamp on her night table. She was puzzled because she hadn't noticed it when she had made an earlier trip to the bathroom. Her eyes were still not completely focused as she picked it up to read. She rubbed them but it didn't help, so she went to the bathroom to wash her face and the sleep away from her eyes. Returning to her bed she sat on the edge and began to read the letter Lenore had written her.

## THE CONFRONTATION

It explained why she had been so happy the past few weeks, Billy had come back into her life. Tears rolled down Theresa's cheek when she came to the part where Lenore described how she told Billy about what had happened to her in Brooklyn. She told Billy she was raped by her stepfather and that was the reason they were on the run, her mom wanted to get her daughters out harms way. The letter continued to say Billy comforted her and told her that the past was the past, only the future counted. He said he truly love me. Theresa wiped away the tears so she could read the rest. Lenore wrote she was going to spend the summer with Billy up in Canada and that she'd be back for the start of the fall semester of college. She continued to say, "Mom I really love you but this is the start of a new life for me. Please understand that I felt this was the only way I could tell you, Billy is still afraid to show his face at Mabel's house. He said he could never go back to jail, not for something that was not his fault. I'll see you in a couple of months, goodbye for now. If it weren't for you, I would never have had this new start. Then she signed it, Love you always! Lenore."

The letter was touching she couldn't hold back the tears. She clutched it to her heart well aware Lenore was now eighteen. Legally she could not stop her from going up to Canada, but she feared for her being out on her own. Knowing all to well it was time to cut the cord and let her spread her wings looking for the happiness she deserved. When she came down stairs to tell Mabel the news, Mabel said, "Lenore and I had a long talk last night and she told me of her plans. I tried to stay up and tell you myself but you came in later than usual and I fell asleep on the couch waiting up for you. When I woke up I went upstairs to her room but she was already gone. Things won't be the same the next few months around here."

Theresa asked, "What do you think I should do?"

Mabel answered, "What can you do? She's of legal age, just hope for the best and wish they find peace and love together."

Lenore and Billy drove north. At night they shared a room with two single beds. Billy was getting impatient, their lovemaking consisted of kissing and petting. Every time things got too passionate, Lenore would panic and stop. She was well aware she was running out of time. She knew sooner than later she would have to give herself to Billy totally or risk losing him forever. With Lenore gone, the summer passed slowly for Theresa. Ashley followed her sister and joined the cheerleading team. So without her two daughters to fuss over, Theresa had nothing but time and no one to share it with. No longer did her afternoons include shopping or going out to lunch or seeing a movie with the girls. One afternoon Theresa got a long distant phone call it was from Lenore, "Hi mom, it's me."

"Lenore I was getting worried. It's been a month how are you?"

"Fine, great! It's so beautiful up here."

"Where are you?"

Lenore thought for a second not knowing her mothers frame of mind towards Billy," We're outside of Vancouver. Billy has a friend who is doing a construction project up here and is giving him work. He's working very hard and treating me wonderful. Mom then she paused, mom I have a problem I still can't make love with Billy. I'm so afraid I'm going to lose him, mom you have to help me. Your my best friend tell what to do?"

"Lenore when your with Billy, don't think about what happened to you. Think good thoughts, let the past go. It's perfectly normal to be scared but accept the fact that Billy understands that what happened to you was something you didn't want and couldn't prevent. Let his love for you wash away those awful memories and show you that you deserve love. Just look into his eyes and know it's right loving him."

"Okay mom I'll try, I love you say hello to everyone and tell them I miss them all.

"I will, love you baby remember you can call me collect anytime, Bye."

Theresa put down the receiver and hoped she had given Lenore good advice. That night it was Lenore who began to tease Billy by kissing and caressing his body. She danced around him, she wore a short nightie with a transparent lace top showing her very voluptuous breasts. Billy said, "Don't start something you don't want to finish."

"Maybe tonight I may want to finish it!"

Billy looked at her with suspicious eyes, "Really, are you sure?"

She danced around and began to unbutton her bodice, very slowly exposing her breasts. Billy could hardly control his excitement, Lenore got closer to him and unbuttoned his shirt. She loved his strong and muscular body, she sat down on his lap and began to kiss him with all the love and passion she had stored up inside her. Billy laid back and pulled her on top of him. For the first time she gave him no resistance. He hoped the time he had waited for had finally come. He took off the rest of his clothes and embraced her. As his erection grew he rolled her over on the bed and looked deep into her eyes as he slowly pushed to penetrate her. She was as tight as any virgin he had ever had. When he was half way in, he started to pull back and forth. She was so wet he slipped the rest of his eight inches inside her. Lenore began to moan in the heat of her passion and when she completed her first orgasm, she knew she was not having sex but making love. Their bodies spoke to one another as no words could ever do. Expressing their love and passion. Neither of them had ever had such an incredible experience, Lenore had made love for the first time and Billy knew it. When they were finished Billy never pull out and as they kissed he was ready for round two. Lenore could not believe he was getting hard inside her. Billy told her the first time was for you, this time it's for me and rode her until he climaxed inside her. Every day was a new experience in love and as their relationship grew stronger and so did the bond of love. They began to realize they would always be there for on another. Lenore soon got a job working in the office of a real estate firm. She did what ever was needed, mostly typing, filing and making copies. After a while she began to help with the listings of homes and going out in the field with one of the licensed real estate brokers. She began to fit in nicely with the other ladies in the office, and the job gave her a new sense of fulfillment. The work was satisfying and earning money was a new experience for her. At the end of the week, they would enjoy a candle - lit dinner at a fine restaurant or go dancing at a top nightclub. Billy worked fourteen straight days to get a job finished on time and his boss gave him a long weekend off. It was getting close to the time Lenore

# THE CONFRONTATION

would have to start thinking about going back home to start college. She told Billy that she would do what ever he wanted, this would be his weekend. Billy thought for a couple of minutes and said, "Lets go on a camping trip," He knew Lenore was in awe of the magnificent grandeur of the Canadian forests.

Lenore agreed to a pack enough clothes and food and what ever they needed. Early the next morning they started to pack the truck. There destination was a lake area up north, it was about a five hour drive. Lenore got in the truck cab first while Billy put the axe, tent, sleeping bags and kerosine lamps in the truck bed along with the boxes of food and clothes. Then he secured everything tightly and covered them with a canvas tarp just in case it started to rain. When he finally got in the truck. Lenore said, "Billy was that a gun and bullets you just put under the seat?"

"Yes, just for protection. Don't be scared there's bears and mountain lions up there. We might even see a wolf or two."

"Don't even say that, are you trying to scare the pants off me!"

"I'd love to have your pants off, but I want to have you warm and sexy under the moonlight in front of a crackling fire. Oh I'm getting horny. Maybe we should go inside and take care of a little business."

"Maybe we should drive north."

"Lenore it's a long ride, I'll be nuts by the time we get to the campsite." "No, I'll make it worth the wait I promise."

"Okay but you better keep your promise!"

Lenore reminded him. "I'm a city girl, I'm going to be so close to you tonight your going to think were attached at the hip. Can two people sleep in one sleeping bag? Now kiss me and drive so we can get there before dark."

Billy drove straight north, halfway into the Canadian Rockies. They stopped for gas and lunch. When they resumed their journey, Lenore was very quite as she took in the majesty that nature lay before her eyes. They crossed many small bridges. Beneath each one she saw white capped raging waters, swirling around rocks and occasional downed trees. All around there were new and exciting sights. Lenore said, "It's so beautiful up here. It's really God's country!" Billy smiled, "It gets better, there's a bridge up ahead about two miles where we can stop. It has an overlook where you can see down the natural valley the river has carved through the mountain. It's really breathtaking."

"So you've been here before?"

"Yes, the last time I worked up here, I told you I've worked here before."

"So who did you camp out with back then?"

"Nobody, what? You don't believe me?"

Lenore got sassy, "Tell me another story, you didn't bring one you probably brought two girls at a time up here."

"Lenore! You're jealous!"

This was a side of her Billy had never seen before, and he was quite flattered that she cared so much. Before long they arrived at the overlook. Lenore was like a child, she was out of the truck door before the engine was off. She inhaled the cool fresh air and looked down the gorge. Billy was right it was amazingly beautiful, fall had not yet arrived. The trees were just beginning to change color. Lenore said," I can't believe that all the fall colors are starting already!"

## THE CONFRONTATION

"It happens much earlier up here in the north, I'm afraid it may be cold tonight. I think we should get a motel room and not camp out."

"Don't worry Billy I'll keep you warm."

"Okay if you want to rough it, I'm game."

After a short stay and a few pictures at the overlook, they both got in the truck and rode on without stopping until they reached their destination.

They checked in with the forest ranger at his office and went to the campsite. Billy told Lenore that it was always a good idea to let the rangers know your out their in case of really bad weather or animal trouble with bears or mountain lions. When they got to the perfect place Billy stopped and told Lenore, "Where here let start unloading. They got out all the equipment needed to pitched their tent. They gathered wood and rocks to start a camp fire. Billy finished emptying the truck, Lenore asked," Where did you get all this stuff?"

"Some I had, but I borrowed most from the guys at work."

Then the big question bubbled out, "What about the gun you have under the seat?"

"It's Smitty's, he gave it to me for protection. You know I really can't have a gun with my record. They'd never give me a gun license."

"Why so many bullets?"

Billy hesitated for a minutes and said," I want to do a little target practice, I haven't shot a gun in a long time. It's a man thing!"

"Can you teach me to shoot?"

"What? Why do you want to learn to shoot?"

Lenore smiled her coy little smile and said. "I have my reasons."

With a shake of his head no, "I don't think so. This is a Colt 45! One of the most powerful hand gun in the world. The recoil will knock your arm off."

"Please, I have broad shoulders."

"With big breasts, which are lovely, beautiful, firm, pink and luscious. The answer is still no."

Lenore was pissed. "Stop! Is that all you ever have on your mind, my body?"

Billy said, "Me? Never! Now lets pitch this tent. You hold up the high post at the center and I'll drive in the stakes, then we'll go to the other end and do the same."

Being a city girl, this was all new to her, Then she asked. "How did you learn all this?"

"I'm an outdoorsman, you know a real westerner. Now hold tight while I put in the back stakes. Next I'll show you how to make a real camp fire." Billy picked up the shovel and started to dig a circular hole about a foot deep. He lined all the rocks around the edge of the hole and filled it with kindle at the bottom and two foot logs. Then he explained in case of a strong wind the logs won't roll out of the fire, and you'll still get good heat and light from the flame. He stacked the rest of the fire logs near it and set the cooler and a metal rack that would be used for cooking with the coffee pot and frying pan on top. He criss crossed the shovel, the axe and the boxes with canned food forming a barricade around the front entrance of the tent just in case any animals came wandering by. Then he laid blankets on the floor inside the tent and placed the sleeping bags on top. With a blazing fire outside they settled in, Lenore

## THE CONFRONTATION

kept her promise of making sure Billy was warm and satisfied. The next morning after a night with no animal disturbance Lenore woke to the smell of fresh coffee on the fire. Billy was up at first light and started the fire and placed the rack and began to make some breakfast. Billy yelled out," Wake up sleepy head. I've got egg sandwiches and coffee out here."

Lenore came out and they ate the sandwich and sat enjoying their coffee. The conversation was mostly how wonderful it was feeling the warm sun after a cold night. Even their love making didn't last all night. Then Lenore said. "If I tell you a secret, will you teach me how to shoot?"

"What secret, I thought you told me everything."

"Not everything. Let me practice with you and then I'll tell you."

Billy smiled and said, "Tell me first and if it's good I'll let you have a few shots at a tree."

"No, promise me first."

"Okay you've got my curiosity going."

She still was sure Billy would keep his promise, even though she had no reason to distrust him. It was just a feeling she had about the person involved in her secret, but she put her trust in Billy and said, "Your uncle Doug started teaching me to shoot out on the range, we only went a few times. It was hard to sneak away from my mother or Mabel."

"No way! Get out of town, Uncle Doug would never teach you to shoot a gun. Besides he only carries a small 22 caliber Derringer."

"I swear it's true, when I told him my stepfather raped me and how I was afraid he'd find us and do the same to

Ashley, I told him I wanted to kill the monster if he ever found us. Believe me I would, your Uncle Doug understood how much I needed to protect myself."

She was trembling with tears in her eyes as she told her secret. Billy could see her mind was flashing back to the terrifying ordeal she in counted at the hands of her stepfather. He knew she was telling the truth, so he looked for the biggest red wood he could find as a target. He told her to spread her feet for stability and used both hands to hold the gun. He knew the recoil would knock her back so he stood behind her and guided her hands. Telling her to squeeze the trigger and expect the power of the gun to lift her arms, so try to lock your shoulders. After a few shots she got the feel of the gun and he let her fire on her own. Dame if she didn't put six bullets in the tree all close to each other. Billy took his own practice shots only he set up a few cans and bottles, he handled that Colt 45 like a true cowboy. They went back to the camp got a bottle of water each and a couple of apples and bananas and went exploring the forest. Billy reloaded the Colt leaving one chamber empty at the barrel for safety and stuck it in his belt at his hip. They got back to camp late in the afternoon, Billy started the fire while Lenore peeled some potatoes for roasting as Billy cooked hot dogs over the open flame. Soft music played from a battery operated CD player. By the time they finished eating the night sky glittered with stars that looked close enough to touch. Billy added more logs to the fire because although it was a clear crisp night it was getting much colder than the previous night. Lenore put on her ski jacket and brought Billy his down vest, he was filling

## THE CONFRONTATION

the kerosine heater Lenore asked, "Are we going to sleep with that heater tonight?"

Billy answered, "I'm going to put it in the tent to warm the inside and the sleeping bags. I'll shut it off before we turn in for the night."

Look Billy, a shooting star! Quick make a wish and it will come true."

Billy grabbed Lenore from behind and wrapped his arms around her shoulders and whispered in her ear, "I've already had my wish granted. It's you my love!"

"Oh Billy, that's so sweet. I love you too!" Then they kissed and Billy lead her into the tent for a little love making. Lenore said, "It's to hot in here.

"Not if you take your clothes off. Okay I'll shut the heater and let it cool down a bit. Then we'll take our clothes off and make love."

The next morning with no interruptions from any wildlife, Billy was sexually satisfied and ready for breakfast. At first light Billy started the campfire and put on a pot of coffee and waited for Lenore to come out of the tent. He saved some hot water for instant hot cereal, gathered and washed some wild berries then decided to gently wake Lenore. He went into the tent and kissed her until she was wide awake. "Come on wake up sleepyhead, your missing out on a beautiful day."

She stretched and rubbed the sleep from her eyes. She slowly remembered the lovemaking that put her into such a deep sleep, she said. "What smells so good?"

Billy gave her a clean wash cloth soaked in hot water and a towel. "Here wash your face, get cleaned up, and put on your pants."

When she stepped out of the tent, she could see that Billy had everything prepared. He even pick wildflowers and put them in a bottle with water.

"You did all this? What a guy!"

Billy smiled and gallantly sat her on the big cooler and handed her a bowel with hot cereal and berries. Then he gave her a hot cup of coffee.

Lenore said. "Where did you get fresh berries?"

"I picked them."

"You left me alone, sleeping in the tent and went off to pick berries? Are you out of your mind. If I woke up and you weren't there I would have been screaming my head off. Never mind the heart attack I would have had."

"I didn't go very far, I could see the tent. You weren't in any danger, besides I had the gun with me and, if need be I would have gotten off a shot and scared any animal away."

"You could have left the gun with me and I would have scared them away."

After they ate, it was time to break down the camp and start packing.

Billy poured water on the fire first then started to pack the truck bed with all the equipment. What came out last went back in first, sleeping bags, cooler and finally the tent. With every thing packed away in the truck, Billy double checked the camp fire. He pushed all the rocks into the pit and then poured more water over it. When he was sure it was out, they started on their long drive home. Billy stopped at the ranger station to let him know they were leaving and that the camp site was clean and the fire was completely out. On the way home, Lenore said.

# THE CONFRONTATION

"I've thought it over I'm going to get a small 22 revolver for protection. Just in case my stepfather finds us."

"Lenore, practicing with a gun is one thing. Owning a gun and carrying it is something totally different."

"My mind is made up. If I don't get it now I'll get it when I get back to Henderson. I need protection."

"I'll protect you, your thinking crazy."

"You can't. He uses his shield to hid behind and he'd send you back to jail. He doesn't care who he hurts as long as he gets what he wants."

Billy could see there was no use in trying to talk Lenore out of her crazy idea. Maybe in time she'd come to her senses.

Back home in Henderson, Ashley was practicing hard with her cheerleading team. The summer sun was brutal. Every afternoon temperatures exceeded one hundred degrees. The team practiced every morning from seven to ten o'clock. By the time she got home, she was dead tired and usually took a cool shower and a nap. As the fall term approached Theresa and Ashley went shopping for school clothes. It gave Theresa a opportunity to be with her baby girl, even though Ashley preferred to sleep if given a choice. Theresa would wake her up around three in the afternoon and they went to the mall and had a late lunch together. Theresa thought it was a good way to bond with her daughter and keep her out of trouble. Ashley thought she was helping her mother because she knew her mom was lonely and missed Lenore. The afternoons belonged to mom and the night was Ashley's time to socialize with her girlfriends. She never got into trouble. She had learned a huge lesson from her encounter with Billy. When school started, Lenore had not returned. Theresa was very upset. She feared that something horrible had happened, maybe a car crash on the trip home. Fear turned to panic. Finally the phone rang and it was Lenore.

She was letting her mother know she was doing just fine and the reason she wasn't coming home on time as she promised.

She told Theresa, Billy's job was extended and that she was working in a real estate office and they were happy. She said. "Mom I took your advice about making love, it worked! I can't tell you how wonderful it is, I know you understand. Mom I promise to be back for the next semester, I can't leave Billy now that he needs me the most. I'll see you soon, love you say hello to everyone. Bye."

Theresa tried to get a word in edge wise, simply because she had motherly questions, but Lenore hung up as if she knew her mother would try to talk her into coming back now. When Theresa put down the receiver she began to think like a typical Italian Mama. She thought to herself, "She said next semester, but what about Thanksgiving, Christmas and New Year? Would she be home for the holidays? It may be our first holiday season without Lenore since she was born."

There wasn't anything she could do. Her little girl had grown up and was out on her own. Thank God she still had Ashley at home, she wondered what would happened when Ashley came of age which was not that far in the future. The realization hit her she could be alone out west in a couple of years without any real family around her. She began to think about Brooklyn and the old neighborhood. The only relative she had left back east was her

# THE CONFRONTATION

Aunt Carmalena who lived in the northern part of New Jersey. Aunt Carmalena was only a distant relative but out of respect Theresa always called her "Aunt." As a child she was very close to her and Theresa was her favorite, always saying," My beautiful Theresa." Theresa's parents moved to Boise for health reason, around the same time Carmalena move out of Brooklyn and up to Northern New Jersey. Michael had never met her and so he had no knowledge of where she lived. Theresa had thoughts of hiding at Aunt Carmalena's at first knowing she would be welcomed with open arms, but thought better of it because of her age. Theresa did secretly keep in touch with her through letters and post cards that never had a return address. As always when she started feeling home sick and wanted to return, she'd realized how safe she and Ashley were staying with Mabel.

Ashley was back in school and doing well. After school she was always practicing with the cheerleaders. Theresa was left with more time on her own. Tom Shanks wanted to take her on a long romantic weekend. He tried to persuade her that a weekend away might do her a world of good. Finally she agreed, although she had a different interpretation of his invitation.

Sex was not on her list of activities, Tom was very disappointed when she requested separate bedrooms. Theresa could see Tom was upset with her then he said. "Theresa are you ever going to let me show you how much you mean to me?"

"Tom you already show me every time I'm with you, I can't commit to a relationship beyond just being good friends. We've had this discussion before, if you no longer wish to see me, or if I make you uncomfortable please request another woman for your evenings. I'll understand and so will Mabel."

"No, I only want you! I can wait until you're ready."

Theresa was smart enough to know if she had sex with Tom, it would change everything. Tom wanted love as well as sex, he wanted her completely. If she were a different type she could take him to the cleaners but it was never her demeanor. The more she thought about her life with Chaz the further just having sex was on her mind. So it went, the days turned into weeks, and the weeks turned into months. Before long Thanksgiving passed and Lenore was still not home to share the holiday. Theresa hoped Christmas would be different, but there was still no word from Lenore. It looked as if the night Ashley fooled Billy had created a situation that would keep Lenore away. She wondered how he could face her let alone Ashley after that ominous night. Not knowing if he would have to face the authorities after a sexual encounter with a fifteen year old girl. Although he didn't provoke the act, it would still be statutory rape. That meant a jail sentence for sure, and for someone just out of jail he'd probably receive a stiff sentence. As long as Lenore and Billy were together, there was a possibility that Theresa would never see Lenore again.

All the holiday preparations took place, they didn't seem important. Shopping for gifts were no longer a thrill, and cutting down the Christmas Tree was a task Doug had to do by himself. Even decorating the house seemed boring. The holiday spirit was missing in Mabel's house. Theresa's depression was infectious. As hard as Mabel tried she couldn't create that family joy, she had come to expect since Theresa and the girls had come to live with her.

Christmas Eve dinner began with Mabel saying grace. The table was set with a beautiful Christmas centerpiece. There were red candles at each end of the table. Their light shone on the rich abundance of food. The regulars were all in attendance.

Yet the room lacked the usual lively conversation, the room felt empty to Theresa. Suddenly, a loud festive voice came from the front door.

"Merry Christmas!

Theresa without looking up knew who it was, "Lenore."

Everyone rushed over to Lenore, Ashley was closest to the front door and immediately ran to her sister and hugged her and kissed her. Lenore had two shopping bags filled with wrapped presents. She dropped them to the floor and hugged her back. Then Ashley said," I'm sorry Lenore, forgive me I love you and miss you. Merry Christmas!"

Theresa cried uncontrollably as she hugged her eldest daughter, "Oh Baby, I'm so clad to see you. Merry Christmas, I love you!"

Lenore's ribs hurt from all the hugs she received. Mabel wrapped her arms around Theresa and her two girls. Lenore received a warmer welcome than even she expected from everyone. Then there was a hundred questions, "How did you get here? Where's your luggage? How long are you staying?"

Lenore said, "Wait a minute, wait a minute! Let me catch my breath! I'm so glad to see all of you but I'm afraid I'm starving. I haven't eaten since this morning."

Mabel yelled, "Make a plate for this child! There's still hot food in the kitchen." Then she walked Lenore to the table and sat her in the middle.

While Lenore waited for her food, Doug carried in her luggage which she left on the porch. Then he said," I'll bring this right up to your room."

When her food came out, she was all smiles. She answered all question in between bites. She finished everything on her plate and said," Oh my God! I forgot how good Mabel cooked, everything was delicious and worth waiting for. She took a couple of swallows of soda and continued," I'll be here until New Years, then I'll fly back on the morning of the second."

Theresa asked," What about school?"

"Billy has six more months of work in Canada, and I've got a really good job working in a real estate office. The company he works for will have two years of work in Arizona starting in September. Billy may start as foreman. They really like him. I'll only be an hour away, then I'll think about school maybe night classes to start. Enough about me what have all of you been doing since I left. What's new?"

Theresa said, "Ashley made the cheerleading team!"

Lenore turned to Ashley. "Get out of town." She kidded, "A cheerleader!"

"I'm proud of you. Have you met any hunky football players yet?"

Ashley smiled, "Mom's going to a black tie New Year's Eve Ball. The most beautiful woman at the Ball will be

# THE CONFRONTATION

crowned, the Queen and will win a weeklong trip for two to Hawaii, all expenses paid."

Theresa added. "First I have to win Ashley!"

"Your sure to win mom! Hawaii, I love Hawaii!"

"Maybe if I win, I'll take someone else."

"Who? Tom Shanks, he's so rich he could take you anytime!"

Theresa looked over to Mabel and said, "Maybe I'll take Mabel and put her in a bikini and see what happens!"

Mabel laughed. "We'll watch all the rich men run for the hills!"

"You've still got it Mabel!"

"When I was young I had it, right Doug?"

Doug's face turned red, "I have to say you turned many a head in your day. Look how long I've been after you, and you still haven't invited me into your room for a little sugar."

"I'll give you sugar! I'll give you a bat in the head or a kick in the butt!"

Doug put up his hands in defense. "Wait a minute! Mabel! There's children in the room."

Everyone laughed, it was old times again. The atmosphere in the house was suddenly filled with love and happiness. The Christmas spirit was again at Mabel's house. Then Lenore said. "Did anyone buy me a Christmas present?"

Mabel said. "Presents! We haven't even had dessert yet. Don't jump the gun. I've been baking pies all afternoon. Wait till you see the smorgasbord of goodies I have prepared. Your going to think you died and went to heaven."

Doug chimed in, "I fell that way every night at this table, that's why I ain't never leaving you honey"

"Now mind that sweet talk, I might have to give you some of that sugar your looking for." Mabel kept to her word, when the table was finally set it looked like a cornucopia of festive delights. Everybody raved over all the different selection of desserts. Doug said, "Am I glad I saved room, look at all that stuff. When you get a chance to load the hump you got to go for it."

Mabel shouted back. "Enough with that rough cowboy talk!"

Eve said. "Leave him be, we wouldn't want him any other way."

Then she gave him a great big kiss. Doug smiled, "See women just love a real cowboy."

Later after dessert, they all went into the living room to be close to the Christmas Tree, and watch the logs in the fireplace crackle. Theresa put on a tape of Christmas Carols just loud enough for the right atmosphere while they talked and exchanged gifts. Lenore was pleasantly surprised to find there were presents under the tree for her.

"I was afraid you might have forgotten me." Then she handed out the gifts she had brought home for each of them. Theresa watched as tears flowed down her cheek to stain her red satin Christmas blouse. Her prayers had been answered, Lenore was home and her daughters were again sisters. What more could she ask for than to see the happiness and love of her girls on the most joyous day of the year. In the days that followed, Theresa, Lenore and Ashley spent as much time together as they possibly could. They spent time shopping for the right gown and accessories

## THE CONFRONTATION

for Theresa's New Year's Eve Ball. Ashley was very anxious about going to Hawaii, Lenore just loved to shop. That was one of the things she missed most being in a small town in Canada, No shopping mall. She was like a junkie in need of a fix, she just went from store to store even if it was only window shopping or returning a Christmas gift. Theresa wanted to please Tom and look her best, she knew many prominent people would attend the Ball.

Tom could make good business contacts at this type of affair. She felt she owed it to him for all the help and understanding he had given her and for the friendship they had developed. The girls choice was a wine red dress with silver accessories, Theresa was leaning towards a gold gown but she took her daughters' advice. The Gown was strapless, with a sweetheart neckline that accentuated her cleavage. Her skin was still soft and silky, most woman her age were already showing signs of wrinkles and dry skin. The girls suggested a push-up bra to really wow the men but Theresa thought better of it saying, "This is a classy event, sometimes simple and elegant out weights trampy. She covered her shoulders with a silver fox jacket that barely reached her waist. A deep ruby and white gold necklace with matching earrings and bracelet, along with a silver handbag and shoes completed the outfit. The afternoon of the Ball Theresa went to the hair salon to have her hair and make-up done professionally. The hairdresser suggested a few highlights to frame her face. After the highlights were bleached to the proper level a black cherry toner was applied.

A cherry rinse was applied to the rest of her off-black hair. When her hair was dried the color exploded in the sun or under the lights. It gave her hair the color of a glass of rich red wine, shimmering highlights. She wore her hair half up, with the loose hair cascading to one shoulder, in front a side part formed a one eye bang that flowed past her cheek and accented the streaks of red hair. Her make up and lip color were absolutely perfect. When she finally got home and got dressed the girls as well as Mabel couldn't believe their eyes. She looked like the Goddess-Venus had come to life, even Tom stared in disbelief as she came down the stairs to met him. All the times he had taken her out in his mind she was always beautiful but tonight she out did herself. Ashley reminded her of Hawaii and Lenore said, "Shut up and go up stairs and do some cheers."

Tom helped her with her jacket and they walked out to the waiting limousine. Everyone followed and stood outside on the porch as their limousine left the driveway. They drove to Caesars Palace in Las Vegas. The Ball was in the Grand Ballroom, a thousand people were in attendance. It truly was an affair to remember. Limousines arrived bearing prominent people from all occupations. The red carpet had been rolled out for their arrival. A business

Associate, of Tom's stopped them as they entered the hotel. Tom introduced Theresa to Mr. and Mrs. Howard Mayville. Mrs. Mayville said," Howard put your eyes back in your head. Theresa you are very beautiful!"

Mr. Mayville said. "Tom, you have very good taste in woman. It makes me wish I was twenty years younger." His wife suggested that maybe it should be. "Thirty years younger!"

It was all said in good humor and they all chuckled over it. As the night wore on, Theresa was certainly the most beautiful woman there and she won the title of Queen of

# THE CONFRONTATION

the Ball! Alone with the title was the trip to Hawaii, Ashley's dream come true. Only Theresa had her own agenda for that trip, she donated her trip to Hawaii to the local Children's Hospital by saying, "I'll give the biggest hug and kiss to the man that bids the highest for the trip. Who will start the bidding?

Tom yelled, "One Thousand Dollars!"

Howard raised his hand and showed five fingers, "Five Thousand Dollars."

His wife said. "You old skin flint! Howard bids Twenty-five Thousand Dollars!" Everyone applauded, Theresa yelled. "The bidding is closed!"

All the men started patting him on the back in real apparition.

Mrs. Mayville said. "Howard take out your checkbook and go kiss her, you damn fool."

He took out his personal checkbook and wrote the check, then he handed it to Theresa and accepted his reward, Theresa hugged and kissed him with everything she had. When she finally let him go, he fanned his face with one hand and turned to the audience and said. "What a Woman! Oh my God!"

At the end of the evening, everyone came up to Theresa and thanked her for making the Ball so memorable. Photographers ' were flashing away at her, right until she entered the limousine for the trip home. As they drove home, Tom commented. "That was a wonderful idea to donate your trip. Why did you do it? You were the most beautiful woman there and you deserved the trip."

Theresa answered without any hesitation. "I have two daughters and I wouldn't want to go without both of them."

"How would you like me to send all three of you to Hawaii all expenses paid for a week or two?"

"Tom I couldn't accept that. You're my friend and that would be taking advantage of your good and generous nature."

"What if I tag along and take advantage of your good and generous nature?"

"Oh Tom, really! You know the answer to that. Boy, that Howard knows how to kiss for a man his age. He almost squeezed my left breast flat, he hugged me so tightly!"

"You're changing the subject, my lady."

"You know me so well."

Tom looked at her and sighed, "Not as well as I would like."

"Come over here and give me a kiss, big boy. We're almost home."

Then Tom moved closer and whispered in her ear. "May I kiss you like Howard did?" She pulled back and nodded her approval. He kissed her with, all the passion and love he had in him. Then he said, "You certainly know how to twist me around your little finger." She kissed Tom more passionately than she had ever done before and said. "Thank you for taking me to the Ball. I had a wonderful time. Please, don't give up on me. I'll make it worth the wait, I'll give you everything you've hope for."

This was the first time Theresa gave Tom hope for a future together. When the limousine turned into the driveway and stopped, the chauffeur got out and opened the door for Theresa and Tom. He walked her to the front door. She touched his face and kissed him goodnight and

## THE CONFRONTATION

said. "Thank you, I had a wonderful time." He answered her by saying, "The pleasure was all mine. Can I see you later tonight?"

"Tonight is the last night before my daughter Lenore goes back to Vancouver. I really want to spend the time with her, you understand I won't see her again for six months." Tom was very understanding and said, "No problem, maybe we can all go out to dinner, some place special, I'll call you in the afternoon and you can tell me your plans."

He turned and went back into the limousine. The chauffeur closed the door and they drove off. Theresa went straight to bed, she knew she was going to be up earlier than usual and the girls would have a shower of questions for her. That morning at breakfast everyone wanted to know how the evening had gone at the Ball. Theresa was still half asleep when she sat at the table, Mabel poured her a cup of coffee and passed over a basket of muffins. Theresa sipped her coffee as everyone waited anxiously, Ashley broke the ice with the with the question she could no longer keep inside.

"Did you win, did you win? Are we going to Hawaii?"
Lenore asked. "Was it romantic?"
"Hawaii, what about Hawaii?"
Theresa said. "Calm down and take a deep breath Ashley. Yes, I did win and they crowned me the Queen of the Ball."
"Yea Hawaii. I knew it, were going to Hawaii!"
Theresa tilted her head. "Sorry Ashley, I gave the tickets to the highest bidder. It raised twenty-five thousand dollars for charity that went to the Children's Hospital in Las Vegas."
"No, Hawaii? You gave it away? Say it isn't so, you're kidding mom aren't you?"

Lenore said. "I don't think she's kidding."

Mabel started to laugh. "Now I heard everything!"

Doug came in from the bunkhouse and said. "You think so, well I was listening to the country music station and they just announced. "Mystery Woman, donates twenty-five thousand dollars to Children's Hospital!"

Theresa was shocked at the news. "Boy am I glad that's a local radio station. Not many people listen to cowboy music anymore."

The rest of the day was quite and layback. Most people slept through the early morning local news. New Year's Eve traditionally is a big party night and most everyone is still hung over the next day. Theresa was hoping yesterday's news would be over and done with by tomorrow. When Tom called in the afternoon as promised, Theresa told him she wasn't planning on going out that evening. She wanted to help Lenore pack her clothes and have a heart to heart talk with her about Billy. Tom agreed that was probably a better way to handle things and that he'd see her the following night. After a late lunch, Mabel joined Theresa and the girls to watch a movie in the living room, Doug had started a fire earlier, and by the time the movie started, the fireplace was glowing. The heat in the room accented the smell of pine from the Christmas Tree. It was a perfect ending to a wonderful holiday week for Lenore. Theresa was happy her family was back together yet sad at the same time, Lenore was leaving on an early morning flight back to Vancouver and she wouldn't see her until September.

The void in her heart would be open again but not the pain that was there before the family reunited. When the movie was over Lenore excused herself saying she wanted to take a hot shower and wash her hair and then start packing. Theresa followed her up to finally have that talk they had been avoiding all week, Billy. Theresa told Lenore to tell Billy he had nothing to fear from her in retaliation of what happened with Ashley. She understood it was Ashley who was the culprit and although it would be hard for him to face them both. Coming back to visit Doug and Mabel was okay with her. The next morning everyone was up by six. Mabel prepared a knockout breakfast and a special goodie bag for the plane ride back. Lenore said her goodbyes to Mabel and Doug, they got ready for their ride to Mc Carran Airport. Doug carried out Lenore's luggage to the woody and Theresa and the girls were off. When they arrived Theresa dropped Lenore at the curbside checkin and then parked the car. She met her and Ashley inside the terminal. They walked Lenore to the gate and hugged and kissed to a tearful goodbye. As Theresa and Ashley were walking back to the car, they passed a news stand. Ashley screamed "Mom" she held up the newspaper on the front page of the *"Las Vegas Review Journal"*

There was a picture of Theresa in her gown, the caption read

Mysterious Woman gives big kiss worth $25,000 to local-Children

Hospital Charity! Multimillionaire - Howard Mayville pays for kiss, woman donates. The Money!

"Let me see that!" As Theresa grabbed the newspaper from Ashley.

"Mom it's as big as life, a half page photo. You're a celebrity!"

Theresa dropped the newspaper, grabbed Ashely's hand and ran to the woody. When they got home she ran to tell Mabel but she was sitting having a cup of coffee holding the paper. Theresa looked at it again and read the article in disbelief then she said, "Thank God it's only a local newspaper." Then thought for a while, "I just hope doing something good don't come back to bite me in the ass. If this ever gets back to Michael I don't know what I'm going to do. What was I thinking. How could I be so stupid to put myself out in the open when I've done everything to stay low key and out of sight."

Later that day Tom called and wanted to see Theresa that night but she was in no mood to be fit company for anybody. She told Tom she had a very stressful day. Then she wanted to know if he had seen the newspaper, when he told her he had she told him she should have keep the trip. He told her to stop beating herself up, you can't change the past, and that he'd call her tomorrow to see how she was doing.

The next morning the first thing she did was to look in the newspaper. She was happy to see no follow-up picture or article. She breathed a sigh of relief. She thought to herself, "Thank God that's over."

A few hours later in New York, a Fed-Ex letter was delivered to Michael Cavanaugh. He opened the over night special delivery and saw the picture of Theresa in the *Las Vegas Review Journal.* There was a note attached. Look who's rubbing elbows with the very rich in Las Vegas, your

Theresa! It was signed, Your pal-Dan Fields.

P.S. I told you retiring to Las Vegas would pay off, glad to help!

# THE CONFRONTATION

Immediately Michael arranged for time off and made reservations for a flight to LasVegas. He was determined to find Theresa and the girls. He was going to search for them himself. He would, as they say, "leave no stone unturned." The easiest way to find them would be to check with the Las Vegas Police Department and have them run a check with their motor vehicle department to get an address on Theresa. Without a warrant for arrest from New York and without her having a prior arrest record, he would have to explain it was a domestic problem. That he was looking for a runaway wife, and daughters. He wanted to handle this himself for two reasons. First, his ego would never allow someone to know his family ran off, no matter what the reason might be.

Second, what if Theresa told her side of the story and accused him of child molestation and having sex with his own daughter? He knew that people felt that only a sick, perverted person would engage in incest.

He checked into Caesars Palace, the place where Theresa had been recently photographed. He started showing the picture of her from the newspaper to hotel employees. He refreshed their memories by telling them it had been taken on the night of the New Year Ball. First and for most he wanted to find the doorman who worked that night, he passed out twenty dollar bills like they were play money. He talked to doormen, bellhops, Ladies' restroom attendant and even hotel security, but got nowhere. Some remembered her being there that night, but they had no information who she was or her whereabouts. He was getting very frustrated, a New York Gold Shield Detective and he couldn't even find his wife.

## JOSEPH SQUATRITO

He'd decided to approach his search from another direction, by looking for information about the man in the article, who paid twenty-five thousand dollars for a kiss. No average Joe could afford to pay that much, even if it was for charity. So who was the mysterious Howard Mayville? He was even less known than Theresa. He was obviously a very rich man. Michael tried to find someone who might still have a copy of the guest list from the Ball. His search lead him to a maitre'd who told him to ask the banquet manager. A hundred dollar bill and a flash of his gold shield detective's badge did little to impress the manager. His response was that badge means nothing out here. However in Las Vegas the color of green is king', and money always talks volumes. Michael laid down five, one hundred dollars and said, "Your information better be real good, don't piss me off."

The manager said," Let me see that picture again, yes I remember her. What a body! Hmm, Howard Mayville comes to the hotel every couple of months. He's very rich from California, a real estate, industrial tycoon."

"He must be to pay all that money for a hug and kiss, unless he's got the hots for her big time."

"Hots for her at eighty? Somehow I don't think so. I don't think he could get it up even with all his, 'Do-re-Mi.' Anyway he never travels without his wife."

"You're not telling me anything helpful."

I don't know who the woman is, but she comes in with Tom Shanks another high roller. He's the right age for her and has big bucks. He's always in the hotel. He loves the Sky Room.

# THE CONFRONTATION

It has a dinner-and-dance type of atmosphere and overlooks the lights on the strip. If you come in about eight or nine at night you might catch them. I've seen her with him a lot lately. Be careful, this guy carries a lot of weight in this town. You don't want to fuck with him."

"He'll be one sorry Son of a Bitch if I catch him with my wife in his company." Michael handed him the five hundred dollars and said. "You don't remember me or this conversation get it? If you don't understand, they'll be burying you!"

"I don't know from nothing"

Michael decided to wait outside the hotel from seven thirty every night, for as long as it takes to find them, he was obsessed with finding Theresa. Every though short of murder ran through his head. For the next three nights he positioned himself so he could see who entered the hotel.

Ever time he saw a limousine come down the driveway, he stalked it and waited ready to leap out like a wild tiger attacking it's prey. Night after night he waited, and still there was no Theresa.

Michael was close to exploding with frustration when a white limousine stopped at the entrance of the hotel. The driver got out and ran to open the passenger's door, a middle aged good looking man emerged. He was unaware of what was about to happen. As he stepped away from the car, Michael saw Theresa stepping out and he rushed towards her. Theresa's head was looking down so she could avoid messing her hairdo and find her footing. Before she looked up, her eyes widened and her nostrils flared as an unforgettable odor penetrated her senses; "Michael!"

Whenever Michael's body temperature was elevated, whether from rage, sexual arousal or simply the heat of the day he exuded a pungent smell all his own. This scent was recognizable, no matter what type of cologne he was wearing. The terror and shock of his presence consumed Theresa's mind and body. As she lifted her head, she came eye to eye with him. The red of the hotel's neon sign reflected in his eyes, giving him the look of a disciple of Lucifer! For a moment she thought he truly was the Devil, himself! She was totally helpless and unprepared, when he grabbed her by her hair and threw her to the ground, then he yelled," I found you! You slut!"

Tom pulled him away from Theresa. Michael turned on him with a vengeance, he hit him with a crashing right hand. Blood was pouring from Tom's nose, which she was sure was broken. Just seeing Michael made her cringe in fear, she let out a scream for help.

The limo driver pulled Michael off Tom from behind, they started punching each other and they fell to the ground. Just the sight of Michael made her cringe in fear, her only thought was to run. Her legs felt like lead weights, but she got away while the fight with Tom and the driver distracted Michael. She ran and hailed a cab. Before she got in she turned back to see the hotel security holding Michael to the ground. Tom looked around and called out for Theresa, but she was nowhere in sight. In a matter of minutes, the Las Vegas Police were on the scene handcuffing Michael.

"I'm an N.Y.P.D. DETECTIVE!"

"That don't cut any mustard out here. You want to press charges Mr. Shanks?

# THE CONFRONTATION

"Throw his ass in jail. My lawyer will file formal charges in the morning."

When Theresa got to Mabel's, she gave the cab driver a fifty and said, "Please forget you saw me and where you dropped me off. My husband is crazy. He'll kill me and my daughter if he finds us."

"Don't worry Lady', you're safe with me."

When Theresa got in the house she yelled for, "Ashley, come up stairs with me pack some clothes your stepfather is here. He just beat up Tom Shanks and his driver. They raced up stairs Theresa took off her evening dress and accessaries, She put on a pair of jeans and a pull over sweater. She packed a small suitcase leaving all her gowns, dresses, high heel shoes and her evening accessaries. She helped Ashley pack a carryon just enough clothes to get by. When they came down stairs Mabel asked, "What's going on, where are you both going?"

Theresa explained what happened to Tom and his driver, "Michael is a madman, he's going to kill both of us, I need to hide until the bank opens tomorrow. Please lend me your car, I'll leave it in the bank parking lot and I'll give the keys to the bank manager."

Mabel tried to calm her down by saying, "You don't have to run, your safe here. Doug and I will protect both of you. If he comes on my property. I'll shoot him myself."

Theresa was frantic looking for the keys to the woody," This is not your problem, You've been so good to me and my daughters. You know we love you, but if anything happened to you or Doug, I'd never forgive myself."

She took the keys and they left, as she drove out of the driveway she tried to think where they could hide for the night.

She remembered a small motel not far from the bank. Across the street from it was a local diner where she could get a cup of coffee and Ashley could get a snack. After they checked in to the motel, they went to the diner and got their take out food. While Ashley watched television, Theresa thought where they could go to be safe. The only place she could think of was to go back east to her Aunt Carmalena. She was hoping Michael would stay out west looking for her and never think she would come back east. Then Ashley wanted to know why they couldn't stay at Mabel's, she really didn't want to leave her new friends and school. She started to nag and argue about leaving. So Theresa finally had to tell her what he did to Lenore, and that was the reason she was so protective of you. When I found out what he did, that's when we ran. Ashley said. "Now I understand why she was the way she was towards me. I was such a little bitch to her. Oh mom, I'm so sorry."

The next morning they got up early took their showers got dressed and had some breakfast before the bank opened. Theresa stuck to her plan, she got her money out of her safety deposit box, left the keys with the manager explaining Mabel would come for them later in the day. She called for a cab from the bank and went straight to the airport. She bought two one way tickets on the first flight out to Chicago. At O'Hare airport she bought two one way tickets to Newark In't. From there it was only an hour car ride north on the turnpike to route 80. She called Aunt Carmalena and told her of her trouble and asked if she and Ashley could stay with her. She knew the answer to that question even before she asked, so she took car service a little more costly but no way to trace like a car rental.

Mean while back in Las Vegas, Michael was still being held by the Sheriff's office. They were giving him time to cool off. Since Theresa had disappeared, Tom's accusation that Michael had attacked her would be hard to prove without her to backup his story. Tom refused to press charges. His thinking was just get Michael out of his life and back to New York. Michael was put on a plane back to J.F.K. Airport in New York. He was told," Only because your a N.Y.P.D. Detective, consider this a courtesy from the Las Vegas Sheriff's Office. Without your professional connections. I would have busted your ass."

Michael barked back, "But she's my wife."

"Just get on the plane and don't come back!"

Michael was furious when he got on the plane going back home.

He had not accomplished what he set out to do. He had been close enough to grab her and now she had disappeared again. On the flight back home all he thought about was where would she hide. Would she stay out west with all her new friends and their powerful connections or just run and start over? Michael knew she had keep herself out of the limelight for all those months and then she made one mistake that almost cost her. She wouldn't make that big of a mistake again, and he knew it.

Theresa was smart enough not to let the car service' bring her to Aunt Carmalena's house. Instead she went to a small Italian Restaurant called Santorri's. It was known as the best Italian food in Pomton Lakes New Jersey. Her thinking was to have a meal and continue on with a local Car Service'. While she and Ashley were eating a man came over to her and said, "Don't I know you? I'm Steve Johnson from Las Vegas. I do business with Mr. Mayville, I met you at a dinner party once. You were with Tom, can't think of his last name."

"I don't know you, so leave us alone."

"Oh but I certainly do know you, Your a call girl!

"Your mistaken! Now leave me alone before I call the manager."

"Don't act so high and mighty! You're nobody special, sister!"

The manager noticed what was happening and came to the rescue, "Excuse me! You'll have to leave, you're disturbing the lady."

"Buddy, she's no lady!"

Theresa broke in, "We're leaving, may I have the check please?"

"It's on the house, please don't fault the establishment."

Theresa went to the coat check where she left her luggage and called for a car. The man who created the disturbance went to the bar. Theresa was lucky he didn't pursue the conversation. The car showed up a few minutes later and they were on their way. When they finally got to Aunt Carmalena's house, it was just as Theresa knew it would be. She and Ashley were welcomed with open arms. Theresa sat down and explained what happened to them and why they were running from Michael. Aunt Carmalena responded by putting her hand, palm down, in her mouth and biting.- An Italian Curse Sign! Then she said, "Bastard! Motha!" ( death in Italian) She followed with more curses

## THE CONFRONTATION

and said," I'll kill him myself! Don't you worry, you're safe here my Theresa!"

Aunt Carmalena was a real Italian Matriarch. She had come to America on a freighter to escape the Nazi invasion of Italy.

In her younger day. She'd cut her heart out before she would give up a family member. She was from the old school family honor meant everything to her way of life. Carmalena wanted to know where Lenore was and if she was safe. Theresa told her she was in Canada with her boyfriend who loved her very much. She went on to tell her about her time out west and the friendship she made with Mabel, Doug, Eve and Tom. Theresa told Carmalena that Mabel was just like her, strong with wonderful family values and that she would go through the fire to help a friend. Doug was her foreman and a life time friend and secretly he was in love with her since they met forty years ago. Eve was a good friend who helped her and brought her to Mabel's. Tom was a wealthy businessman she met through Mabel. He's been very good friend who wants to marry me. Right now I'm so confused and scared I don't know what I'm going.

# FOURTEEN YEARS OF HELL

As the reunion continued, Theresa told increasingly more of her story. The emotional and physical strain of her flight with all it's twists and turns had taken it's tole on both of them. A good nights sleep and a hot bath would work wonders and in the morning Theresa hoped that with a clear mind she would come up with a game plan as to stay in hiding from Michael. How long would her money last and what to do about Ashley's education? The next morning with a cup of coffee in hand a slice of toast with butter and jelly in front of her Theresa. said. "Aunt Carmalena coming here was wrong, in a panic I ran and at your age you don't need all this heart ache"

"You're wrong at this age I shoot the bastard, who cares!"

"I care, you were always the strong one of the family. The one everyone could count on for help, the matriarch with all the right answers. Your wisdom always shown through, but this is different if I stay there are to many lose ends, an eventually Michael will find us again."

"So what have you decided, my beautiful Theresa?"

"I'm going back to Henderson, if I stay out of Las Vegas, stay low key, live off the money I have, who knows maybe this will blow over and Ashley can go back to school.

The next day Theresa and Ashley were on a plane out of Newark Airport back to Henderson. The flight was long and the time just seemed to never move. Theresa keep pondering weather she was making the right decision. She just hoped that Tom and Mabel could keep their word as to there safety. A couple of bloody Mary's helped to calm the nerves, but what would be the reaction to her phone call when they arrived at McCarran airport. She could only hope for the best and that she and Ashley would be welcomed back with open arms. As the plane landed Theresa's nerves were getting the best of her. After getting the luggage it was time to make her call. Theresa found a phone at the far end of the baggage claim, there she went and preceded to dial.

"Hello Mabel, hi it's Theresa! Mama can I come home. Please let me come back. I know I've make a terrible mistake by leaving and not believing in you, but I was so scared for me, for Ashley for you but I know now I can't make it on my own. Please let me come back."

"Slow down child and tell me where you are?"

I'm here in Las Vegas at the airport, we've just come back from my Aunt Carmalena's home in New Jersey."

"Your getting yourself all upset, I can hear it in your voice. I'll send Doug out to get you."

"No, it's all right we can take a cab, I just wanted to hear it was ok to come back, I don't want to put anyone out of their way."

"Nonsense, I won't hear of it and besides do you know what it would cost. Go get something to eat and Doug will be there in a half hour or so. He'll meet you at the main pickup area just passed the cab station."

"Ok, we'll meet him there. Thank you Mabel as always your an angel."

After a quick burger they make their way to the main pickup area and sure as shooting there is Doug leaning against the old woody wagon waiting like a papa bear. As they got closer Theresa could see a big smile on his face welcoming them home. Ashley ran over to Doug and gave him a big hug and kiss.

"I'm so glad to see you Doug, I'm so happy to be back!"

Theresa followed suit and gave him a hug and kiss.

"Wow, you girls are going to ruin my reputation. Never know when one of my lady friends might be around. Hell they'll be thinking I'm your papa or something."

"Well you are like a grandpa to me"

"Hum, ok, ok let's get your stuff in the back and head home."

On the ride back to Mabel's, Theresa was kind of quite she didn't know how to break the ice with casual talk so she mostly stared out the window, then she said.

"I almost forgot how clean and beautiful it is out here. Back east was nothing as I remembered it."

"Well where almost home, I'm sure you and Mabel will have a lot to talk about,"

Five minutes later the old station wagon turned into the driveway and there was Mabel waiting on the porch like a mama hen. When Doug stopped and turned off the engine, Theresa took a deep breath with a sigh of relief before getting out, Ashley quickly jumped out ran around the woody and up the stairs to give Mabel a big hug and kiss.

"I'm so happy to be back. Can I go up to my room, can I please can I?"

Like a bat out of hell she was in the house and up the stairs, Doug preceded to bring the luggage up stairs. He knew Theresa and Mabel wanted some time a lone to calmly talk out Theresa's problem. They sat on the porch swing. Theresa grabbed Mabel's hand and started to cry.

"Why all the tears? Aren't you glad to be here?"

"I'm so confused and scared. I wanted to get away so I wouldn't bring my troubles to you. I thought going back to my Aunt Carmalena and hiding there was the answer, but my memories of her being the strength of the family was long gone with her age. What I found was a sweet, kind, loving old woman who could hardly take care of herself, let alone take on the burden of my troubles. Maybe Tom with all his connection and power can help. I know he's in love with me, but now that he knows what Michael is really like does he still want to be with me and have to confront my problem again. Is it fair to him or so selfish of me. Mabel what should I do?"

"Lets go in and get you settled, we'll have a cup of coffee and think this through. Later that afternoon over coffee, and Mabel's homemade apple pie. Tom's name finally came up.

"I think you should call Tom and let him know that your back. He's been calling from time to time to see if I've heard from you. He's been very worried and very sad about the way you left without giving him a chance to help.

"I know your right, I haven't handled things the right way. Do you think he still wants to be my friend after what happened with Michael?"

"The only way to find out is to call him and let him make that decision. Here's his number call him."

Mabel hands Theresa a card with his number. After all this time she never really needed his number he always got in touch with her through Mabel when he was setting up a working date or he just showed up at Mabel's door. Theresa takes the card half hearted knowing this is what she came back for but in her heart feeling it was wrong. If she truly was in love with him and wanted to make a life together then facing Michael and getting him out of her life was a bridge she, no they would have to cross. But was she, really ready to love again. Even she could not answer that question honestly. Theresa takes another look at the number.

"Call him."

"I will, when I go up to my room. It's been a long day and I'm still on eastern time and to me it's bed time, but I promise I'll make the call first."

Theresa finishes her coffee and goes up to her room, opens the door and sits on her bed trying to get the courage to call Tom. Finally she sits at her small desk and dials the number on the card.

"Hello."

"Hi Tom, it's Theresa."

"Theresa how are you, where are you?"

"I'm back in Henderson, at Mabel's. Please don't be mad at me I'm so sorry What Michael did to you. Tom please say you're still my friend, I'll do anything to make this up to you!"

"Anything?"

"Well, most anything, your getting away from my apology. Be serious."

"Don't worry I've taken a few punches in my day, no big deal I'll live.

"It was so wrong of me to leave like that. You didn't deserve that behavior you've been very good to me and my girls. I just wanted to call and come to a complete understanding between us."

"Ok, so how about the next time I'm in town, we have dinner together like two old friends."

"I'd like that, I'd like that a lot. Thanks for still being my friend see you soon. Bye Tom."

"Bye Theresa."

The next morning Mabel asked. "How did your phone call go last night?"

"Good we came to a complete understanding between us. Tom wants to take me out to dinner the next time he's in town. As old friends. Maybe I can lay low for a while and not work. I can pay for my room and board from the money you helped me earn, this way I won't feel like I'm taking advantage of you and you won't start to resent me."

"Your talking stupid now, and I know your not a stupid person. Quite the opposite, I know your a very intelligent warm loving and caring woman. I'll let you in on a little secret, Tom had an army of private investigators looking for you all over the Tri-State area. He figured that's where you ran off to, so eventually he would have found you. I know Tom since he's a little boy, he's not letting you go.

So no more about this room and board stuff. What we're going to do is take out an order of protection for you and Ashley against Michael. Then we will have the law on your side and out here Michael's gold shield won't be worth donkey crap if he comes near you."

Theresa followed through with Mabel's plan and had no trouble getting an order of protection against Michael. After it was documented, he had caused the fight in front of Caesars Palace. At same time Michael was hatching his own plan on how to get even with Theresa for making him look like a fool in front of his friends and humiliating him with the Las Vegas Police. He no longer cared about getting her back. If he could not have her he'd make sure no other man would want her. A week later after his four to twelve shift was over Michael walked into Hugo's Bar still a favorite watering hole for off duty cops. Most of the cops there were in his command and under his thumb, so when he gave the bartender a signal of his pointer finger in a circular motion it was understood a round of drinks were on him. He casually said his hello to each of his cronies as he made his way to the back room. Sitting at one of the tables in the rear was Dan Fields. Michael gave him a big smile as he walks to the table and pulls out a chair and sat down.

"What's the big urgency that you send me airline tickets and a note to meet you here of all places?"

"What no hello, no hugs or kisses. Is that anyway to greet me?"

"I know you Michael you have something up your sleeve."

"I want you to help me with Theresa."

"Michael I found her for you, I sent you the newspaper article and told you where to look. I'm sorry it didn't go well for you when you went out there, I heard through the grape vine the Las Vegas Police gave you a hard time. Put you on a plane and sent you back but at least you got a pass no jail time what were you thinking starting a brawl in front of Caesars Palace. Did you think you were in New York City where you own the streets. Come on Michael get serious here."

"That's why I want you to find her and fuck her up for me. She's not coming back so if I can't have her I don't want any other man to have her. Find a low life and cut her face, bust her face up."

"The last time you said that you wanted someone fucked up they were murdered. I thought you were going to send the spicks after Joey, give him a beating break his knees but you had your own agenda with framing Charlie to get Theresa. Now you want this. No way, I'm out!"

Dan gets up from the table only to have Michael grab his arm to stop him. Dan pulls away knocks over a chair and starts to walk to the front of the bar, Michael gets up and follows after him. Dan storms out the front door with Michael in hot pursuit. Michael catches up to Dan as he is entering a park car. Michael pushes Dan and slams the car door shut then he punches Dan in the face breaking his nose. Dan goes down on one knee blood pouring from his nose and mouth, Michael then takes his head and slams it against the car door. Dan falls back sitting on the pavement choking on his own blood. As he applies pressure to his nose to try to stop the bleeding. Michael grabs him by his hair and stands him up.

# FOURTEEN YEARS OF HELL

"I own you, when I say jump you say how high. If it wasn't for me coving your ass you would have lost your pension. I took the heat by saying, "I ordered you to stop Mastori's nephew and you got to retire and move out west. You like the little envelopes I send you each month with play money for the casinos, you're in until you die or I kill you and that can be arranged."

Just then Michael's cell phone rings.

"What, oh it's you I wasn't expecting a call until tomorrow. Your right, this is tomorrow I forgot you Latin guys start your day at midnight, yeah I know party all night sleep all day. So what's the good word, Friday night, pier fourteen RedHook the Vargo Eclipse about midnight, how big. Tito you're the man we're going to make a fortune on this hall. Later."

Michael hangs up.

"Now get to the ER. Tell them you fell and hit your head and let them fix your nose. Oh and never talk back to me again."

As Dan drove himself to the nearest hospital he began to think about all the evil that Michael got him involved in. Sure shaking down the bad guys on the streets was no big deal or taking a bribe or two or looking the other way when money was taken in a drug bust or a bookie raid. After all it was Mafia money. Every cop knew about the widows and orphans fund. As Michael got deeper and deeper involved he liked the power of control. Money really didn't mean that much, it was power that turned him on. Dan knew there was no way he was going to see Theresa hurt and if he turned his back on Michael like he knew he would, he was a dead man. He was screwed no matter which way he turned but Michael had to be stopped conclusively. Somebody had to step up to the plate and make the move that makes a difference. Dan got lucky the ER, was very quite as he entered the hospital. A nurse brought him into a small room. As he waited for a doctor to examine him, she took all his information and vital signs then the doctor sent him for x-rays which revealed he had broken nose and a fractured cheek bone. They kept him for several more hours just to make sure he didn't have a concussion. By the time he was released the sun was shining and the city was again filled with the traffic of people on their way to work. Dan drove back to his old apartment that his son is still living in. He goes to a steel lock box and opens it.

Inside there was his snub nose 38 still in his ankle hostler a thousand dollars in cash and a yellow envelope all filled out with the address of one Salvatore Brancato Attorney at Law. He put the envelope on the table with a note to mail ASAP then he phoned the D.A. office and asked for Mr Monroe telling him that he'd come in after a few hours of sleep and tell him a story that would bust the city wide open. Four hours later Dan Fields was spilling his guts telling D.A. Monroe.

"Michael Cavanaugh is behind the biggest drug ring in South Brooklyn. He's into video porn with young girls he picks up in Manhattan, kick backs, extortion. He involves other cops until they can't get out. He murdered officer Joseph Tamborelli and framed Charles Batista because he wanted his wife."

"How do we know your telling the truth, those are mighty tall accusations. We're talking about a gold shield captain here it's your word against his."

"Look at my face, he did this to me last night because I won't help him deface his wife and if that's not enough for you, how about a signed confession of a dying man."

"Who's dying?"

"Me, I'm as good as dead right now."

"We will keep you in protective custody!"

"No because you haven't heard the rest of it, if I tell you what I know that will nail Michael's ass to the wall cut and dry. Do I get immunity."

"How involved are you?"

"The same as a few other cops, maybe a little more I received an envelope of money for keeping my squad car out of a certain area while Michael conducted business. Keeping my mouth shut about Tamborelli."

Suddenly there's a knock on the office door as a small man with a brown attaché' enters the room.

"Samuel Katz, Mr, Fields attorney. Say nothing more, I like time alone with my client thank you very much."

"Okay counsellor you've got ten minutes."

Ten minutes later, DA. Monroe returns to his office with two Internal Affairs Detectives, Quinn and Hogan who want to interrogate Dan Fields. "Wait a minute, do we have a deal for full immunity, because what your about to hear believe me it's worth what my client is asking for."

I haven't heard anything yet, but I do know we have him on obstruction of justice, graft, accessory to murder, drug involvement. Have I left anything out? Oh yeah how about twenty-five to life."

"Lets get real serious here. Do you want justice, do you want to stop crime. Not to mention nailing one bad ass gold shield detective."

"Five to ten, out in three."

Katz leans over to Dan and whispers in his ear. Dan stands up.

"Five, ten, three who cares I'll be dead in a day or two because for this to work Michael has to think everything is okay and he's going to continue with his plan. Friday night about midnight, Pier fourteen the Vargo Eclipse is bringing in about a million dollars worth of coke and enough automatic rifles and C4 to start a war for Tito Perez. The spics want to take back Harlem and east New York. Michael is right in the middle of the Columbian Cartel and Perez. He's brokering this deal stands to make a fortune.

Well, that's one hell of a story but I need proof. What do you have that is hard copy, black and white. You want me to move on a gold shield captain, I don't think so, not yet. Get him out of here, and take your two bit lawyer with you."

As they leave the office, Dan and Katz can hear DA. Monroe shouting with the two internal affairs detectives. They walk out of the building and get into Katz's car and drive to Dan's old apartment.

"You are one lucky man they didn't arrest you right there and then. If you only had that hard copy their looking for then I'm sure they would make a move against Michael."

"But I do!"

"What, what have you got?"

"I sent a tape I made of Michael spilling his guts about Tamborelli. It was after the fact, he called me one night got me out of bed to meet him at Hugo's Bar. Said it was urgent, so I went. When I got there he wanted to talk and have a drink. He was so jacked up about nailing Theresa Batista. How she was the best piece of ass he ever had, about how many times she climaxed that if she was a man she'd be a stallion, how unbelievable her body was how firm her breast were. He just went on and on, then he said she was worth killing Tamborelli and framing Batista for the murder. That if he had to do all over again he would she was that great a lay."

"So why didn't you give them the tape, that would have back up your story. Where's the tape now?"

"I sent it to Batista's lawyer, Sal Brancato, he'll know what to do with it. I couldn't take the chance that if Michael decided to kill me they would find the tape on me or even worst if I gave to Monroe the tape would disappear. Who knows if Michael has his hooks into anybody in the DA office."

"So what your next move, if I were you. I'd make myself invisible.

"If I do that Michael will think somethings wrong, I have to wait until Brancato gets the tape. Then I'll tell Michael that I'm going back to Vegas to do as he has asked me to do and hope he believes me. Brancato should get the tape day after tomorrow, so I'll leave that morning.

The next day Dan called Sal Brancato's office and explained to expect a package by mail, inside he'd find a tape and a signed confession of all the wrong Iv'e done and all the evil Michael is a part of. Also instructions to listen to the tape and make a copy and keep it in a safe place, then call DA Monroe and let him listen and make sure he moves on Michael Friday night. Dan never left his room that night. The next day he called Michael and told him he was leaving the next morning and that he would do as he was told. Michael told him to meet him at Hugo's about ten that night just to show there were no hard feeling and to have a fair well drink or two. Dan knew he had to play it Michael's way but this time he was going to pack a gun for he's own protection just in case Michael got rough and didn't believe him. That night Dan went to his steel box opened it and removed his snub nose 38. No ankle holster he'd keep the gun in his jacket pocket with his hand on ready to start blasting at the first sign of danger. Dan was sitting at the end of the bar nursing his favorite tap beer boiler maker when Michael walked in.

"I see you started without me, bartender I'll have what my friend is having. Boiler maker, only make mine with Canadian Club."

Michael gets his drinks and signals Dan to the back room for a private conversation. They sit at a back table.

"Why the change of heart Dan?"

"Listen Michael I'll do this but my hearts not in it, a broken nose, a fractured cheek bone a black eye I got the message loud and clear. So okay, I'll get someone to do it just like you want."

A smile came to Michael's face as if he had conquered the world. The self gratification he aspires too. You could see in his eyes his mind was spinning to the tune Michael is the Champion. When Dan was finished with his boiler maker he excused himself because he had an early flight in the morning and he hadn't even pack his clothes. Michael walked him to the front door and returned to the bar, this was a load off Dan's mind because he was afraid of another confrontation with Michael not buying his obedience. Dan got into his car and drove to he apartment, he found a parking spot about two blocks from his brown stone walk up. Thinking to himself how lucky am I, parked the car and walked slowly he started to think that was to easy tonight with Michael and was getting a queasy feeling as he got to the front steps. He was looking down fumbling with his keys as he started to climb stucco stairs, suddenly a young columbian man came out of the shadows and Dan heard "bang" clutching his chest he fell backwards onto the sidewalk. The last thought was Michael! The man stood over him and fired two more bullets, Bang, Bang! Dan was dead. The man ran to the corner to a waiting car and sped off. The next day the Newspaper head line read. "Retired NYC Police office Murdered!"

DA Monroe knew he had made a big mistake by not listening to Dan Fields. For just as he predicted, he was dead before the Friday night delivery of drugs, explosives and weapons. Later that morning Salvatore Brancato walked into Monroe's office and handed him the package Dan Fields sent him. He did not turn over the extra copy of the tape he made just as Dan had instructed in his note. They listened to the tape together and Sal said.

"What's your next move mister District Attorney?"

"I'm going to alert the NYPD Swat Team and follow through on Dan Fields confession and warning, a good man gave up his life to finally be on the right side of justice. I'm going to tell the state prison authorities to start the paper work on getting Charles Batista out of prison."

They shake hands and Sal leaves and returns to his office pondering weather to tell Mary the good news or wait until the next night events unfolded just as Dan described.

The next twenty-four hours would pass with the weight of the world on Sal shoulders. Even as he conducted his daily work schedule his mind was on the midnight hour and his imagination was running wild, what might happen or what will happen and how will it all play out. Even the bottle of wine Sal and Mary shared couldn't take the edge off Sal's nerves. Mary asked several times what was troubling him, but he only would reply just work. Mary knew her husband too well. He never acted this way he'd never bring work problems home.

After the kids were asleep Mary made coffee, she brought Sal a cup with a glass of Sambucca (Italian Liquor).

"Sal the last time I saw you this nervous and upset was when Joey was murdered and Charlie was arrested for it. But that I could understand your two best friends, one dead and the other in jail for it, so what gives."Sal thought for a while and figured telling Mary the truth wouldn't make any difference with three hours till midnight, and it really wasn't fair to put her through any further anguish. So he told her of the events of the past two days, if Michael got caught tonight with his hand in the cookie jar it would tie all that Dan Fields confessed to and lost his life over.

"Mary if this all goes down tonight against Michael, Charlie is a free man. If only we could get in touch with Theresa and the girl to tell them but what's the odds of finding her in Las Vegas again?"

"Sal after we ran into her in Vegas. She contacted me and gave me a phone number in case anything happened she absolutely had to know."

"You never told me."

"It was for your own good, in case Michael came looking for information again. What you didn't know you couldn't tell."

They both sat quietly watching the TV, constantly checking the time as if they didn't know. Every so often Sal would look at Mary with anticipated expression raising his eyebrows and taking a deep sigh. Every minute felt like and an hour, every hour felt like an eternity. At the same time the Swat Team moved into position, there were sharpshooters on the roof of the old warehouse across from the Vargo Eclipse and look outs were stationed inside ready to give the call, when Michael appeared. The Vargo Eclipse was a small old freighter, the twenty-thousand ton size not the mega size container ships we see today. Perfect for a small dock like Red Hook with a shallow water draft, a Freighter that could slip into a dock at night with not much notice or interest. The freighter was being unloaded the old fashion way with a crane lifting wooden pallets from its hull and placing them on the pier so a folk lift could load them onto a waiting truck. Most of he crates were stamped machine parts but a few pallets were being held at the end of the pier, those were the ones Michael drove to when he finally got there. They also were under close watch by armed guards. Michael got out of his SUV. carrying an attache' case he looked around for Tito as one of the guards pointed to the ship. There Tito stood giving directions to the men unloading the ship. When he saw Michael he acknowledged him.

Opening his arms like a long lost love he pointed to the pier and started down the gangway, just as he reached the bottom shots rang out. One of Tito's men spotted the Swat Team on the roof line as they moved into a better position.

Just then the look out inside the warehouse called for all Swat Teams to advance onto the pier. Flashing lights and sirens were everywhere, Tito turned to Michael pulling out his gun and said.

"Fucking Cop!"

Michael screamed back, "You got it all wrong Tito I would never" Tito capped off three rounds as the bullets lifted Michael off his feet and through him back against the crates and onto the floor of the pier. With in seconds guns were being fired in all directions. One of Tito's men from the ship was ready to fire a rocket launcher but he was shot. As he fell into the sea below, he fired the rifle and the rocket hit the crates. A terrible explosion occurred and half the pier fell into the sea. With in minutes the gun battle was over. The next day the morning newspaper read, "N.Y.P.D. Gold Shield Captain killed" in drug and arms bust. Again Michael's transgressions were swept under the rug, after all there was no money transfer or recovery of drugs that all disappeared in the explosion. Then again there was the weapons, ammunition and explosives not to mention the capture of drug lord Tito Perez. Every major news network carried the story that day. Sal called DA Monroe to congratulate him on his fine effort. Also to remind him that he had the original tape of Michael's explicate details of why he murdered Office Joseph Tamborelli and how he framed Charlie Batista. Monroe assured Sal, Batista would be free soon as all the paper work was completed. Sal and Mary called Theresa later that night, when they spoke Sal told her it was all over she didn't have to worry again. Theresa said that it was all over the TV, and that she's glad he's dead. He also told her the good news about the tape and how Michael talked about why he murdered Joey and framed Charlie, he told her that in a week to ten days Charlie would be free and that as his attorney he'd be there to bring him home.

Theresa said. "If it's possible to arrange I'd like to be there with the girls when he walks out of prison."

"I'll keep in touch."

It was still early in Henderson because of the three hour time difference. When Tom happened to pay a visit Theresa told both Mabel and Tom about Sal's phone call and that she wanted to be there with the girls when Chaz was released. Maybe seeing the girls would help to heal the terrible injustice, he had endured, not only with the law but the people he loved the most. Getting in touch with Lenore and having her come back from Canada was her most concern. Tom told her just get Lenore back and I'll take the three of you back with my own plane. The day had finally come and Sal walked in to warden Stankawitz office as they reviewed the papers that needed to be signed then they walk to a holding room and waited for Charlie to come in. They walk him to the property clerk and he was handed a large yellow envelope, he opened it and found one wedding ring, a set of keys to who remembers where, a wrist watch that had stopped working years ago and a black wallet. Charlie opened the wallet and looked inside under a flap and there it was his only prize possession a Mickey Mantle rookie baseball card in mint condition. He quickly stashed it back in it's secret place. Charlie signed for the contents of the envelope and put everything back and folded the envelope, and placed it under his arm. They walked through each corridor with steel doors crashing behind them until they reached the light of day. With the sun shinning bright Charlie covered his eyes trying to get focused. As they walked through the last yard they waited for the last door to freedom to open. When it finally did a hundred yards to the street a waiting limousine door opened and Theresa, Lenore, Ashley and Tom got out. Charlie could not quite make heads or tails of it but as he got closer he thought could it really be. The years of stress and strain behind bars had taken it toll. Although still slim he had lost that well built physique Theresa remembered. His hair was salt and pepper and very silver grey at the temples and his clothes were definitely out dated. He stopped dead in his tracks and just steered, Lenore was the first to walk then run to him. Just before she reached him she yelled, "Daddy" and she jumped into his arms and held on tight. When he finally pulled her away to look at her, he shook his head and said.

"My God Lenore you look just like your mother, you are so beautiful let me look at you." Then he saw Ashley he put out his arms and said. "Is this my baby girl all grown up" Charlie hugged both his girls as tight as he could, tears just poured down his face. "Iv'e wait for this for so long, I can't believe it's here, it's the only thing that keep me going just to be with my girls again."

When he wiped away the tears from his eyes and look up he saw Theresa standing next to Tom, Sal walk over to her and nodded his head signaling her to joint the girls but as Theresa took few steps forward she froze in her tracks, not knowing how Charlie would react. He let go of the girls as he reached for Theresa, he took her hand and brought it to his face brushing the back of it from his cheek bone to his lips. Then with tears in his eyes he kissed her hand and whispered "I never stopped loving you or my girls."

Theresa stepped closer and hug him as tightly as she could and whispered in his ear, I'm so sorry for the pain I caused you I hope one day you can truly forgive me."

When they reached the limousine Theresa introduced Charlie to Tom "Charlie this is my very good friend Tom Shanks, he made it possible for me and the girls to be here with you today."

The two men shook hands and Charlie thanked him for bringing his daughters back to be with him. They all got into the limo and the driver drove them to the nearest airport where Tom's plane was refueled and waiting. On the ride there Charlie had a hundred question to ask the girls about what they were doing at this time in their lives. He never mentioned the pass only wanted to know about the now. The fourteen years of hell behind bars had softened his heart and made him wiser. He knew the passed was dead and gone, the future belongs to no one only the present counts and Charlie was going to make the most of it. When the limousine reached the airport the driver did not stop at the terminal but drove right to the waiting jet plane. The limo stopped and the driver got out and opened their door, Charlie was next to last to exit before Sal when he got out and looked he couldn't believe his eyes. He turned to Sal and said, "Holy shit what gives?"

"Don't ask it's my first time on a private jet too, just sit back and enjoy the ride back to Kennedy airport."

"Who's paying for this ride?"

"Not me brother, it's Tom's plane, big bucks real estate guy from California."

Entering the plane Charlie just couldn't believe his eyes, the expression on his face was priceless coming from the bowels of hell to the lap of luxury in a short few hours was more than Charlie's brain could handle. When he asked, "Where is Tom?"

Theresa replied, "Who do think is going to fly this plane!"

"He flies too?"

"It's his passion, but there is another pilot just in case so he'll join us after were airborne. In a few hours we will be landing at JFK. Were all staying at the Hilton just outside the airport. Tonight if you like we can talk just you and I and I'll tell you of my own fourteen years of hell. In the mean time sit with the girls you have a lot of catching up to do. Oh Sal brought you a new set of clothes there at the hotel."

"Theresa who's paying for all of this?"

"Not to worry, it's just like you always wanting to be the man, I guess somethings never change."

They both smile and got a chuckle from it, the healing process was happening without them even realizing it. Charlie sat with the girls at the rear of the plane and Theresa sat with Sal up front, there was something bothering her about Michael's so called death she wanted to talk to Sal about. She told Sal that even though the T.V. news ran the story it really didn't get the big play, so she wanted to hear the details of what occurred that night. Sal told her he talked to DA. Monroe the next day and he said the Swat Team saw Tito Perez shoot Michael point-blank range just before the explosion brought down the pier. Even though Michael's body was not among the dead the N.Y.P.D. was sure Michael could not have lived after the three bullets he took to the body let alone the pier collapsing after the explosion. She thought for a while and said, "Sal that son of a bitch is still alive, Michael is to smart to go to a drug met without wearing a vest and about the pier collapsing Michael is one of the strongest swimmers Iv'e ever seen. I remember one time a young girl got caught in the rip tide off Coney Island and he went in and saved her. He's alive, and if he is I think I know where he might be hiding.

"If you really believe that could be true, let me call Monroe and have him follow through on your idea. I'll give him the location of where he might be."

"First I have to go back to our house in Long Island and cheek on a few things."

"You can't go alone what would you do if he's there when you go back.

He'd kill you on sight.

"He's not there, I'd stake my life on it."

"If you go there alone that's just what you might be doing."

"Don't worry Sal, no one knows Michael better than me. I'll be okay.

For the rest of the trip Theresa was very quite, Sal could see her wheels turning even though he had given her good advice he knew she would not heed any of his warning. She was a woman on a mission. When the plane landed a car was waiting to take them to the Hilton Hotel. As they arrived, Sal told everyone he had to get back to his office for a late meeting with a client but that he would call them in the morning, then he handed Charlie his card and two hundred bucks. He knew the sixty-one dollars he was given when he left prison wouldn't go to far nowadays. Charlie was out of touch with the prices of today, reluctant to take the money Sal reassured him it was only a loan until he got back on his feet.

"Sal I can never repay you for all you've done for me, how about you take my Mickey Mantle rookie card it's the only thing I have of value."

"No, you don't! You have people here that love you and you can't put a price tag on that, I'll see you in the morning."

He got back in the car and left. Theresa and the girls shared a two bedroom suite with a living room in the middle of the bedrooms, while Charlie and Tom were in single rooms across the hall. Tom made reservations for diner later that night in the Steakhouse across from the lobby. So with a couple of hours to spear Charlie went to his room took a hot shower and changed into the clothes left in his room. He quickly put his old out dated clothes in a plastic bag and put them in the garbage bin. Later that night Theresa keep her promise and when the girls were asleep she went to Charlie's room and they sat on the bed and Theresa told Charlie how Michael controlled her with drugs after Joey's death and how he fill her head with lies and misconceptions always keeping the appearance of her knight in shining amour. During the trial still in a state of shock and the more the newspapers said you looked guilty the easier it was to control her, after the trial everyone believed the evidence except Sal and Mary so Michael keep me as far away from them as he could. He keep me under his control until I asked for a devoice and I married him. The two worse things I could have done at the time. He slowly took me off the drugs and the more I came to my senses the more he hated me. When I studied to become a nurse he would drink and beat me, when I stopped wanting to have sex he raped me. The fights got worse and the drinking never stopped. When I found out he raped Lenore I ran, took everything I could pack into my car and left because I knew the next on his list of conquests would be Ashley and there was no way I would allow that to happen. I found really great caring people out west, Mama Mabel was an angel from heaven, I was at my wits end down on my luck and almost out of money. She took me and the girls in and treated us like family. My mother and father died shorty after Joey's death.

Mabel introduced me to Tom he is like the son she never had. These are genuine people who say what the mean and treat you with kindness and love.

"Do you love Tom? Is that why he does so much for you? Are you lovers, it's okay you can tell me the truth."

I'll tell you this there is no finer man in this world than Tom Shanks, I've never slept with him or had sex with him and I know he is in love with me but I don't know if I'm capable of loving anyone again, Michael destroyed my life and my mind."

"Michael destroyed all our lives, you me Joey the girls I often wondered why God turned his back on us. What manner of man brings so much evil to the world and why is it always the good have to suffer."

"Have you any thought what your going to do now that your free?"

"Not really, I never dreamed I'd be hear with you and the girls. When Sal contacted me and said new evidence had been uncovered, proving I was innocent of Joey's murder. I just wanted to get back to Brooklyn and walk the streets of the old neighborhood. What about you."

"Me, well I know I have to list the house with a real estate agent and have them sell everything inside so I guess I'm going back to Henderson. Ashley is in school there, Lenore is living in Canada with Billy. There moving to Arizona because Billy's got a two or three year construction job there. Billy is a really great guy who loves Lenore to death. With the sale of the house, I will be able to buy my own house out there with extra bedrooms for Lenore and Billy to stay or any other house guess. I can even go back to nursing with no fear, I'd be close to Mabel and all my friends. I guess it's a no brainer."

"Sounds to me like you have it all figured out."

"Not everything, Why don't you come back with us and start your life over you've been totally exonerated, you could get a job working security in a hotel in Vegas. Maybe Tom could work you in with his company and you'd be close enough to see the girls. What do you have here except Sal and Mary."

"I don't know, it's all to much to decide on. I need to think it over maybe I should talk to Sal about it and see what he thinks."

"Sure, your right we have bombarded you with a lot for one day. It's getting late, lets talk tomorrow. Good night Chaz."

"Good night Theresa." He closes the bedroom door and thinks to himself. Wow she hasn't call me Chaz since before Joey was murdered. Theresa returns to her room, the next morning she is on the phone with Tom letting him know she needs a day or two to list the house with a realtor and take care of a few loose ends. Toms reaction is no problem as long as their all returning with him to Henderson. After breakfast Theresa goes back to the house opens the door and it's a shambles. Empty beer and whiskey bottles empty pizza and take out boxes everywhere it looked like the place hadn't been cleaned since she left, and it stinks as if the garbage hadn't been taken out in a month. She opens all the windows just so she could stay in the house, went to the pantry got a large trash bag and started to throw everything out when she was finished she went into the kitchen dirty dishes everywhere. She opened the window and put the garbage into the large plastic trash bag, scraped all the dishes and ran a load in the dish washer. She began to think only heaven knows what the upstairs bedrooms must look like, but if she was to sell the house she'd have to make it look respectable for and realtor to show it. So reluctantly she continued to check out the rooms. Much to her surprise they were exactly as she left them, all she had to do was make the beds and air out the rooms. When she was done she'd call her local realtor and ask if they could send someone over for a walk through and to bring the paper work to be signed. She then went into Michael's so call office and started to snoop around, she check every cabinet and draw when she came upon a locked draw she jimmied it open with a letter opener. Inside she found a steel lock box, this time no matter what she tried she could not get it opened. Then she remembered an extra set of keys Michael keep in the garage behind his tool table. She went down to see if they were still there, sure enough when she put her hand behind the table leg there they were. The key ring was hanging on a nail, she was sure a key would fit the steel box. When she opened the box she found Michael's off duty gun and silencer, about ten thousand dollars in an envelope and a key to a safety deposit box. Theresa remembered signing a signature card when they were first married, it was to their local bank where they had their mortgage checking account and saving account. So getting into the safety deposit box no problem. Now all she had to do was wait for the realtor, but first she got a travel carryon from the hall closet put on a pair of white Sunday gloves and placed the contents of the box in the bag, her business with the realtor was completed. She left him the keys with instruction to sell everything. Went directly to the bank and had no trouble getting into the vault and opened the box. Inside was more money than Theresa had ever imagined, there had to be over two hundred thousand. Stacks and stacks of ten thousand packs, Woman's jewelry, diamond rings, earrings, bracelets and a few letters from his Russian bimbo whores. She put everything inside the carryon and told the bank manager to close the account. Driving back to the Hilton, Theresa started to get the guilts about the money how much of it was illegal money and how much of it was earned. After all she worked for years and with her pay and Michael's pay they earned in the six figure numbers. Was she trying to justify keeping what she found and why did he need to have all that jewelry maybe the letters would give her some answers. When she got back to the Hilton she went directly to her suite but the girls were not there so she call Tom's room and there was no answer, so she called Charlie's room. He answered and she asked him to come to the suite, ten minutes later he knocked on the door and Theresa let him in. Her first question was where are the girls? He told her, "Tom took them to New York on a shopping spree and to see the sights, he invited me but I told him a day in New York shopping was as the cliche' goes "Not my cup of tea". I gave the girls a hundred dollars each and told them to buy something you want, from me."

"You gave them the two hundred dollars Sal gave you last night, you do realize Tom is a multimillionaire."

"So what, this was from me their father."

"I have something for you," she hands him the envelope she found at the house. He opens it and looks inside.

"What's this?"

"I found it at the house, I know I can't give you back the years Michael robbed from you but I can give you a start at a new life."

"You do realize this is could be drug money."

"You know that for sure! I don't, so take the money and stop being macho. Let me help you, I want to help you. My business is finished, the house is up for sale and I'll get more than half a million for it, so I think I can afford to give you a start." She put the envelope back in his hands and lead him to the door. "Now go get ready for diner, tomorrow were out of here. I hope your on the plane when we leave ready to make a new start out west."

When the girls got back they were all excited about the new clothes they brought and sights and sounds of he city. Theresa told them to get ready for diner and that they would being leaving to go back home tomorrow. Lenore wanted to know, "What about dad?"

Theresa told them she asked him to come back with them, but it was all up to him now. Later at diner the girls told their father about the clothes they brought with the money he gave them, and that when they wear the outfit it will remind them of him. Lenore told him now that he was back in their lives she hope he would come out west and see how beautiful it was. He just responded by saying. "We'll see."

After everyone was asleep Theresa was determined to really finish her business, she took her extra set of keys her white gloves, Michael's gun and silencer put them in her bag and quietly left the suite. She went down the back stairs so no one would see her leave the hotel. Got in her car and drove to the one place she was sure if Michael was alive he would be hiding. A small rooming house over a block of stores in Brighten Beach not far from the Hilton Hotel where they were staying. Brighten Beach better know as little Moscow was his secret place. She had followed him there many a night after one of their fights he would pick with her, so he could leave the house and stay out all night. She parked around the corner looked at the keys and picked the two that didn't belong to their home. Then she put on her white gloves and the safety to the gun, she then spun the silencer into place locked the car and walked to the rear entrance. She tried one key but it didn't fit so she tried the other and the lock open with a brisk snap. She slowly climbed the stirs to a door marked exit on the other side. Quietly trying the key to each door until she found the lock that opened. Slowly walking into the small apartment, it was dimly lit except for the light from the television where she found Michael slouched in a large leather chair. His shirt was opened and his ribs were wrapped, obviously he had enough strength to contact one of his Russian Whores for help. Theresa could see a large black and blue bruise at the top of his chest. It was obvious to her Michael had on his vest when he took the pointblank range bullets to his chest and ribs. His hair was burnt off and his neck and face were burnt on one side, his shirt sleeve was cut away and his arm and hand were servilely burnt. Next to him was a small table with a bag of white powder, a needle, a spoon, a rubber strap and a cigarette lighter.

All the necessities for cooking heroin, and giving himself shots for pain. He must have just given himself a shot for pain because he was out of it. Theresa call to him," Michael" no answer she felt his pulse on his neck it was strong she called to him again only a little louder. "Michael, Michael." He opened his eyes and said. "Is that you Theresa? I knew you could never stay away, Theresa help me honey, I'm burnt bad and my ribs are broken. Help me."

"Why would I help you all you do is cause pain and sadness to everyone you touch. You murdered my brother, framed my husband, raped my daughter ruined my life! Michael my mother always said you never know what's around that corner and you never know Where Evil Lurks!"

She placed the gun to his head, looked away and pulled the trigger. Bang! Theresa lifted his hand and wrapped it around the gun with his finger on the trigger making sure his finger would leave a print impression, then she quietly left the apartment and exited the building down the back steps locking each door behind her. Now she knew for sure the devil was gone from her life. As she entered her car and drove away the realization of what she had just done hit her like a brick wall. She stopped opened the door, leaned over and vomited up her guts. Never in her wildest dreams did she think it would be this way, so many times she would say I want to kill that son of a bitch.

Slowly she started to compose herself and began to say in her mind.

This was a righteous kill, the evil one deserved to dye anyone who went through what she went through was justified in killing Michael.

# EPILOG.

The next day the limousine drove up to Tom's jet plane. It stopped and the driver got out and opened the door. First Tom got out followed by Lenore and Ashley. They walked to the plane just then Theresa got out with her carryon of money over her shoulder. The beauty of flying on a private jet, was you don't have to worry about security check points. She quietly walked to the plane. As she climbed the stairs at the top she looked back and smiled. Her secret was safe. No one was going to question where did she get all that money. Finally Chaz got out and followed her onto the plane. After talking to Sal, he had taken Theresa's advice. A new life out west close to his daughters was the way to go. Who knows what the future would bring to him and Theresa, he hoped her asking him to come to Henderson was a new beginning

THE END!

www.ingramcontent.com/pod-product-compliance
Lightning Source LLC
Chambersburg PA
CBHW060148050426
42446CB00013B/2731